PLANNING AND DECISION MAKING

**Jon Sutherland and
Diane Canwell**

PITMAN
PUBLISHING

London · Hong Kong · Johannesburg · Melbourne · Singapore · Washington DC

For Joy and Kevin

PITMAN PUBLISHING
128 Long Acre, London WC2E 9AN
Tel: +44 (0)171 447 2000
Fax: +44(0)171 240 5771

A Division of Pearson Professional Limited

First published in Great Britain in 1997

© Pearson Professional Limited 1997

The right of Jon Sutherland and Diane Canwell to be identified
as Authors of this Work has been asserted by them in accordance
with the Copyright, Designs and Patents Act 1988.

ISBN 0 273 62510 1

British Library Cataloguing in Publication Data
A CIP catalogue record for this book can be obtained from the British Library

10 9 8 7 6 5 4 3 2 1

Typeset by M Rules
Printed and bound in Great Britain by Redwood Books Ltd, Trowbridge, Wiltshire

The Publishers' policy is to use paper manufactured from sustainable forests.

◆ Contents

Contents

PART 2 ◆ DECISION MAKING

 # Preface

This book takes both a theoretical and practical approach to the study of planning and decision making. It aims to analyse the nature of organisational planning and decision processes which take into account the fact that organisations often operate within uncertain environments and under constraints.

Organisations adopt very different strategies to tackle planning and decision making and therefore the planning framework within organisations is examined in addition to the decision-making processes themselves. It is also important to recognise the fact that contingency planning plays a vital role in preparing the organisation to meet the 'unexpected'.

Although this book is primarily written for the BTEC HNC/D Core Module: Planning and Decision Making, there is a solid framework for any broader study of the nature of these disciplines.

The book has been written with the intention to avoid technical terms and jargon wherever possible. Obviously some knowledge or understanding of the processes involved in planning and decision making would be an advantage at this level of study, but we have not assumed prior knowledge at any point. Although this book should be seen as taking a broad sweep across the topic area, no doubt the reader will want to refer to some of the theorists mentioned for more in-depth analysis of the subject.

It is hoped that the book will provide the reader with:

◆ the ability to examine the process of organisational planning;
◆ the understanding necessary to analyse the relationship between the various objectives of an organisation;
◆ a framework to facilitate evaluation of organisational functions as an integral part of the planning process;
◆ the ability to identify and recognise the individuals and processes involved in decision making;
◆ an appreciation of the factors which may affect decision making;
◆ the ability to recognise the advantages of different decision-making techniques;
◆ an understanding of the purposes of contingency planning;
◆ the ability to recognise the difference between planned and *ad hoc* contingency planning; and
◆ the ability to understand the processes involved in establishing a clear contingency plan.

We hope that the systematic way in which we have approached the four main sections of the syllabus will enable the reader to access the information that they need easily. The format of the book follows a tried and tested structure which has proved popular with readers in the past.

Finally, it is our hope that you find this book to be a useful and accessible tool in your studies or personal reading.

Jon Sutherland and
Diane Canwell
June 1997

Part 1

THE PLANNING FRAMEWORK

The purpose of this part is to enable the student to:

◆ examine the process of organisational planning;
◆ analyse the relationship between corporate, functional and individual objectives;
◆ evaluate objectives of different business functions within the overall organisational plan.

Corporate objectives and mission statements

 Introduction

Regardless of whether an organisation is industrial, commercial or service oriented, it will have a variety of different objectives. Sometimes these objectives (often specifically stated in writing) may not be borne out by the organisation's actions. Organisations often find themselves in situations which require them radically to reconsider not only their objectives, but their entire purpose. Some of these influences are out of the hands of the organisation. Legal changes, for example, may require an organisation to re-evaluate (possibly overnight) the way in which it either produces or markets a product. Equally, internal pressures, such as financial problems, can cause an organisation to abandon its most important objectives. Also, changes in ownership can vastly affect the way in which the organisation pursues its published objectives.

In most respects, the purpose of any organisation is to be successful. This success is, however, measured in many different ways, which depend on the type of organisation. A good starting point for any organisation is to set guidelines for activity that act as a standard against which it can measure itself. There is always likely to be a major difference between the organisation and how it operates, and the ideal type of organisation to achieve success. It is only when the organisation has clearly set out its goals and objectives that it can identify shortcomings or problems and seek solutions to these.

Many businesses begin with setting out their aims, purposes and objectives in a business plan. This is a formal statement of their goals. However, in reality, the day-to-day achievement of these goals may differ from the business plan. Organisations do not exist in isolation. The environment in which they operate is constantly changing. Therefore, organisations must be flexible. Any environmental change may require corresponding organisational change when old ways of operating are no longer efficient or advisable in the new circumstances.

MISSION (VISION)

PLAN (OBJ)

STRATEGY (LT)

TACTICS (S/T)

HOW ACHIEVE THEM.

OBJECTIVES + TARGETS

A mission statement differs from a business plan as it looks at what the organisation actually stands for. Generally, this is an agreement between managers and employees. These agreed goals are often more valuable than the business plan as they have the common consent of everyone in the organisation. The individuals involved have a shared point of view and perhaps some common ideas of how to achieve them.

Once the organisation has established its goals, it must then find methods of achieving them. These are known as 'strategies' and 'tactics'. Strategies are the main ways to achieve the objectives and tend to be fairly long-term in their approach, e.g. increase turnover by 50 per cent in ten years. Tactics, on the other hand, are more short-term and flexible. These are the individual parts of the main strategy, e.g. in order to increase turnover by 50 per cent in ten years we need to increase our product range and find cheaper suppliers. Thus, strategy answers the question of how the organisation intends to get where it wants to go, and tactics are the means by which it achieves the strategy.

Businesses exist for many different reasons, and perhaps the most common, but not the only one, is profit. Being happy and satisfied is as strong a reason for running an organisation, and this is why many people like to work for themselves. The freedom to make your own choices can also be good compensation for having to work for an organisation that is interested only in profit.

 ## The planning framework

Planning is one of the most important roles in management. It aims to establish the direction in which the organisation is moving, and underpins the leadership and control functions. At its most basic level, planning aims to define the goals and the objectives for future performance. Above all, it identifies the ways in which they will be reached. Planning is, of course, far more complex than this as it aims to set up a formal process with the following objectives:

WHAT TO BE DONE + HOW TO BE ACH'D.

◆ to choose a mission for the organisation;
◆ to choose the overall objectives, both in the short- and long-term;
◆ to create, at departmental and divisional level, the means by which the organisation's mission and objectives may be achieved;
◆ to allocate the appropriate resources to the various objectives, strategies and plans.

There are, obviously, a great many different types of planning, but perhaps the most obvious categories are those of strategic and tactical.

Strategic planning

Strategic planning deals with the organisation's overall objectives and considers things on a more macro level. It is essential to understand that this form of planning is organisation wide and, as we will see, incorporates many of the techniques that are related to identifying the various internal strengths and weaknesses, as well as the threats and opportunities in the external environment. Although we will be looking at some of the following aspects of strategic planning later, it is appropriate to begin by giving them some attention here. We can identify the key aspects of the strategic planning process as addressing the following issues:

i) mission statements

ii) organisational objectives

iii) organisational strategies

iv) resource allocation.

Mission statements

The mission statement will aim to identify the reason for the organisation's existence. It will therefore describe the organisation's activities and operations. It will also define the kinds of products and services that the organisation supplies. It will identify the current and probable future markets, along with the types of customers. Mission statements are designed to help everyone within the organisation focus on their activities and think about their actions in relation to the statement. The statement needs to be clear, unambiguous and realistic, and everyone needs to understand the implications and the direction that is intended.

Organisational objectives and strategies

Objectives need to state both the quantity and quality of the results that are expected. In addition, a series of milestone dates should be set as well as the final date. The strategies adopted help the organisation to establish a range of plans that will assist it in reaching its declared objectives. These need to be clear and unambiguous.

Resource allocation

Once the objectives and strategies have been developed, the organisation can move to allocate the resources that will have to be deployed. Obviously, money is the key resource, but we should not forget the importance of personnel, premises, equipment and land.

Tactical planning

As we will see, the development of tactical plans is crucial if the organisation fully intends to follow through its strategies to successful completion. Key elements of this would be:

◆ developing budgets for each of the separate divisions or departments within the organisation (as well as allocating budgets to the particular projects);

◆ choosing the appropriate ways in which the organisational strategies will be implemented;

◆ agreeing strategies to improve the performance and efficiency of current operations.

As can be seen in Fig 1.1, the nature and scope of tactical and strategic planning are very different. It could be said that there are three outcomes of failing to plan:

1 If an organisation does not plan, then it is unlikely to have a long-term future.
2 The best way to cope with inevitable change is to create it.
3 If the organisation does not know where it is going, then the inevitable will happen: it will fail to get anywhere at all.

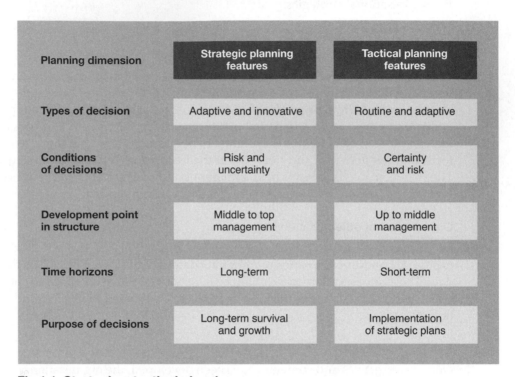

Planning dimension	Strategic planning features	Tactical planning features
Types of decision	Adaptive and innovative	Routine and adaptive
Conditions of decisions	Risk and uncertainty	Certainty and risk
Development point in structure	Middle to top management	Up to middle management
Time horizons	Long-term	Short-term
Purpose of decisions	Long-term survival and growth	Implementation of strategic plans

Fig 1.1 Strategic *v* tactical planning

Corporate objectives and mission statements

Organisations have to manage a number of different objectives at the same time, since this is the only way they can survive in a competitive environment.

The key factors with which an organisation has to contend include the following:

◆ managing change;
◆ maintaining a degree of stability;
◆ minimising any prospect of confusion within the organisation as a result of competing (and simultaneous) factors;
◆ establishing a clear sense of direction.

Managers need to be capable of contending with these demands, particularly as the rate of change accelerates and becomes more complex. Above all, they need to be able to predict and respond to the changes. If the benefits of planning are recognised by the organisation, then it will have a better chance of achieving its objectives. As we will see, objectives vary, but for most organisations the objectives will boil down to profit making.

Stakeholders

A broad distinction can be drawn between social responsibility and organisational efficiency. We can consider here the diverging aims of the various stakeholders of an organisation. A stakeholder is an individual, group or organisation that has a particular interest in the business's performance. The main stakeholders include shareholders, employees, customers, suppliers, the general public and the government. We could also broaden the list to include the providers of finance.

While many of the stakeholders do not have any direct authority in the business, their needs and aims must be addressed. It is in the business's long-term interests to ensure that all stakeholders are considered.

Shareholders

Shareholders and other providers of finance will expect to receive a reasonable financial return for the use of their capital. Given the fact that they have taken a risk in investing in the business, it is the responsibility of the management to protect their investment. Shareholders in particular will have an opportunity to influence the policy of the business. In addition to this, they will be able to question managers about their decision making. The providers of finance may not have the opportunity to exercise day-to-day control over the business, but they may have insisted that certain conditions are met. The vast majority of shares are owned by pension funds or insurance companies. It is worth remembering that this 49 per cent of share ownership in fact belongs to individual investors who have given the pension funds and insurance companies the responsibility of investing their assets. Around 20 per cent of all shares are directly owned by private individuals. In this respect, they are more able to exert direct pressure on the business to ensure that their aims are taken into account than they are through pension funds or insurance companies.

Employees

While businesses may have a legal responsibility towards their employees in terms of the contract of employment, they also have a greater responsibility. Employees quite rightly expect reasonable working conditions, fair treatment, access to training and, above all, reasonable management. The organisation can address these demands by paying attention to job satisfaction, job security and job opportunities.

Customers

Businesses also have a responsibility to address the needs and aims of their customers. Essentially, this includes the following:

◆ to provide reasonable value for money;

◆ to ensure that their products or services are safe and durable;

◆ to provide a good standard of after-sales service;

◆ to deal with queries and complaints in a courteous and prompt manner;

◆ to ensure that there is a regular and reliable supply of products and services as well as spares or replacement parts;

◆ to provide a high standard of information for potential customers;

◆ to make sure that they abide by legislation and voluntary codes of practice in respect of advertising and trade.

Suppliers

The organisation also has a responsibility to take account of the aims of its suppliers and, for that matter, its business associates. This would include the following:

◆ to ensure a fair standard of training is maintained;

◆ to honour the terms and conditions of any contracts signed;

◆ to ensure that accounts or outstanding debts are paid.

The general public

Businesses have a responsibility to address the aims of the community or the general public beyond controls which are contained within legislation and regulations. The organisation needs to address particular concerns such as environmental issues. Typical examples would include a reduction in the amount of packaging used or the use of biodegradable materials. On a broader basis, the siting of buildings and the consequent distribution in and out of those buildings might give cause for concern to the local community. Above all, the public should be assured that the business is not wasting scarce resources.

Government

Organisations must obey the law. There is something of a grey area between legislation and voluntary codes of practice. Organisations might be encouraged not to raise prices, for example, since this would fuel inflation. Equally, organisations are under pressure from the government not to trade with certain countries. Whether the organisation chooses to be influenced by political decisions depends on the importance it attaches to staying on the right side of the government or party in power.

Certain organisations are at the forefront of developments in trade and product design. These organisations are working further ahead of current legislation than is in fact necessary. This shows a degree of social responsibility which is sadly lacking in many organisations' behaviour.

In order to address the different and often conflicting aims of the various stakeholders, the organisation needs carefully to balance its activities and its objectives. It is no longer possible to state simply that profit is the key determining factor of behaviour. Many organisations have successfully incorporated social responsibility towards stakeholders into their profit motive. It is not necessarily the case that adopting a socially responsible attitude means that profit will be reduced.

Mission statements

Many critics suggest that mission statements are little more than public relations exercises. Whether this is true or not, many organisations have developed such statements. These documents detail the aims of the organisation and try to identify a common purpose. Those who support mission statements contend that they focus on specific goals which not only allow employees more readily to understand the objectives of the organisation, but also help customers appreciate its viewpoint. By clearly stating the principal purposes, rather than simply asserting that profit is the main objective, there is a clearer definition which allows many stakeholders to understand the direction and actions of the business.

A mission statement is a general plan which aims to show the direction in which the organisation is moving. Mission statements are often deliberately vague, since it is difficult for them to incorporate possible growth or changes in activities. Equally, mission statements cannot accommodate situations which may arise as a result of a recession. The mission statement may be optimistic and, as actions taken in difficult times may be at variants with the statement, there is a possibility that it may prove very quickly to be out of date.

It is common practice for organisations to try to capture the spirit of their activities in a very short statement. These statements have been differently described as visions, missions or 'what the organisation is about'. The mission statement does not purport to describe in detail the organisation's aims and objectives, which will be developed elsewhere. Above all, mission statements need to be wide in their scope. They should not attempt to quantify the activity or the purpose of the organisation, merely describe it; nor should they attempt to restrict the organisation's possible development in the future.

A typical mission statement would therefore include the following:

i) What type of business is the organisation involved in?
ii) Who is served by the organisation?
iii) What benefits does the organisation offer?
iv) What commitment is there to customers?

As we have already indicated, a basic mission statement may simply be that the organisation intends to be the best and most successful organisation of its type. If there is a desire to develop the statement further, the focus may then be on some of the following:

◆ to be financially strong and consistent;

◆ to be the market leader;

◆ to provide excellent levels of service and good value for money;

◆ to be responsive to customer needs and adaptable to competitors' activities;

◆ to be a fair and committed employer;

◆ to be aware of the organisation's impact on the environment and take steps to ensure that this impact is minimised.

There is no ideal mission statement, not is there a blue print. If an organisation chooses to develop a mission statement, then it should be created in accordance with its expressed aims and objectives. If the mission statement is written at variants with the aims and objectives, then the organisation is probably putting the 'cart before the horse'. In other words, the mission statement should not drive the activities and direction of the organisation's efforts, but should be a statement of current reality.

Role and function of objectives

Although organisations can differ enormously, they do have some common features, which include the following:

1 They often use resources that are in limited supply (such as human resources, money and materials).

2 They provide something (either a product or a service).

3 They normally compete with other organisations.

Each organisation must undertake a wide variety of different tasks or functions to ensure that it operates effectively within its chosen area. Some of these functions include:

◆ *managing employees* – usually through a personnel (or human resources) department;

◆ *selling products or services* – providing customers with the product or service they require;

◆ *distributing the product or service* – ensuring that customers have access to what they need;

◆ *purchasing products or services* – ordering stock for either short-term or long-term needs;

◆ *marketing a product or service* – researching customers' needs and then promoting the product or service;

◆ *keeping financial records* – to monitor the success of the organisation.

An organisation must also ensure that when it needs to make a decision it makes the correct one. This may involve a wide variety of considerations, usually including the use of resources, which may be limited.

Types of organisation

Business organisations do not always have the same purpose. Perhaps the most common is the profit motive, but not all organisations are driven by this goal.

Private sector

Generally, the private sector is made up of organisations that are independent of the government. We can make some simple distinctions between them:

i) Sole traders are organisations which are run or operated by one person.

ii) Partnerships are organisations run by more than one person.

iii) Limited companies are organisations that are owned by shareholders.

iv) Franchises are organisations that have been set up by buying the name and functions of an established organisation.

v) Co-operatives are organisations of groups of people who have joined together to be more efficient and effective.

Public sector

The public sector consists of organisations that are either owned or controlled by the government. The most common forms of public sector organisation are:

i) government departments or the civil service, responsible for running government activities in a specific area (such as the Department of Trade and Industry which assists other businesses);

ii) local government, such as county, metropolitan, district or borough councils, whose task it is to provide services, assist business and promote the area;

iii) public corporations or enterprises, such as the Bank of England, whose task it is to provide services in a particular part of the economy. These are also known as nationalised industries;

iv) QUANGOs (quasi-autonomous non-governmental organisations), which are funded by the government to provide services. Examples of QUANGOs include OFTEL (which monitors the communications industry) and the Arts Council (which provides grants to artists, theatres and film makers);

v) many organisations which were once public enterprises or QUANGOs but have been privatised. These include British Telecom, British Gas, British Airways and the various water companies.

Charities

Charities have a different perspective on business activity to that of many other organisations. Charities have been described as having the following characteristics:

◆ *Non-profit making* – charities are not necessarily in operation to provide a profit, although a modest profit that could be ploughed back into the operation would be useful. After all, the profit motive does not exist as technically charities are not owned by anyone, nor do they have shareholders who require dividend payments.

◆ *Non-loss making* – perhaps this is a slightly better description, but still not quite true. It is obviously advisable for the organisation not to have to dip into its reserves to support its activities. In the recession some organisations found their income diminishing and had no other choice. Even the Church of England has had to dispose of assets.

◆ *Profit-making* – this can be said to be true of many charities these days. They do produce a profit from their merchandising and other fund-raising activities, but the money is not distributed to shareholders or owners. In most cases, the funds are used to support new activities, purchase equipment or expand into new countries, or are simply transferred into a reserve fund for contingencies.

An organisation with 'charitable status' is exempt from many of the legal obligations of a normal organisation. That is not to say that it does not have to comply with such things as health and safety requirements or contracts of employment, but that any profits it makes are not taxable.

In recent times, in addition to the well-known and long-established charities such as Dr Barnardo's, Oxfam and Help the Aged, many schools have adopted this form of organisation.

National organisations

Whether you live in a town or city or in the countryside, there is a network of business organisations to cater for nearly all of your immediate needs and wants. Some may be part of the public sector (such as refuse collection or health care), others will be provided by the private sector (such as supermarkets, newsagents and chemists). Other organisations may not necessarily provide products or services for the local community, but may provide these for the national or international market (such as a mine, a food-processing operation or a government department).

A wide variety of organisations operate on a national basis. In all sectors of the economy we can find examples of businesses that have established themselves in nearly all the major population centres of the UK. In manufacturing terms, food processing tends to be based around the areas which produce the required raw materials. Birds Eye Wall's, for example, is positioned to exploit the availability of fish and vegetables. It is careful to choose its locations since the processing of the freshest possible produce is essential in maintaining its image.

In the service area of the economy, we find banks, building societies, travel agents, betting shops and newsagents creating national networks to cover the population throughout the country.

Multinational organisations

Many organisations have become multinationals or conglomerates, by acquiring businesses, or building up their business, all over the world (*see* Fig 1.2). For some organisations this is a result of the type of business in which they are involved:

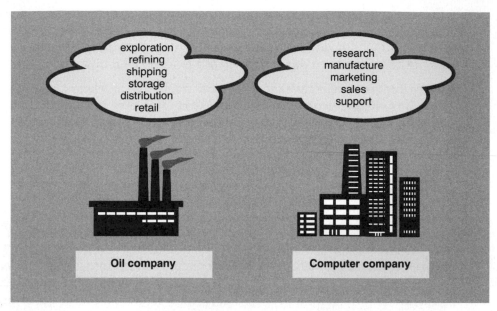

Fig 1.2 Activities of multinationals and conglomerates

◆ Oil companies discover oil in many parts of the world, refine the crude oil, ship it to storage areas and then distribute it, for example via petrol stations (e.g. BP and Shell).

◆ Computer manufacturers market and sell their products worldwide. Although they may research and manufacture in only one or two countries, they must have support, sales and marketing operations worldwide (e.g. IBM and Apple).

◆ Retail organisations have sought alternative markets throughout the world; this is particularly important if their major market has been in recession or decline (e.g. Marks and Spencer).

◆ Franchise organisations, like retail businesses, see expansion abroad as the best course for the future and have encouraged people to set up franchises in areas of the world of which the original organisation has little or no knowledge (e.g. The Body Shop).

◆ Manufacturing organisations need to be able to produce products in the market in which they compete. This may be to overcome import duties or quotas set by the host country, or simply to take advantage of lower wages and set-up costs (e.g. General Motors, Nissan and Ford).

The term 'conglomerate' best describes an organisation that has interests in a variety of different business ventures. An organisation in this position can avoid sudden or gradual downturns in profits for a particular product or in a particular market by distributing its operations and investments around the world.

International organisations can also take advantage of differences in the value of currencies, as well as economic growth or recession in different countries. They have enormous buying power and it is thought by many people that they exert too strong an influence on countries desperate to retain their investments.

These international organisations do suffer from some problems as a result of their size. It is often difficult to maintain any sense of international corporate identity. Modern technology, such as video-conferencing, e-mail and faxes, has gone some way to solving this problem.

Targets

At its most basic level, target setting is a process by which the organisation agrees performance targets. These give the organisation a clear understanding of what to aim for in order to achieve its overall objectives.

It is essential for the management of an organisation to exercise control in order to ensure that targets are met. Information will be available both from within the organisation and outside it to help assess and control the achievement of targets. It is also important to make regular comparative checks on actual performance against planned targets. By doing this, the organisation will be able to assess the impact of any non-controllable factors. It will also be able to take action to rectify controllable effects on performance.

Controlling targets is a complex process, but in effect the basic process is as follows:

i) setting targets which will act as guidelines;

ii) measuring actual performance;

iii) evaluating actual performance against pre-set guidelines;

iv) taking corrective action in order to ensure that the organisation is on the right track.

We should not forget that all targets must be related to the organisation's objectives. The quantifiable targets are merely a part of the objectives.

In trying to assess whether the organisation is capable of reaching the pre-set targets, it is important to note that performance needs to be measurable. This measurement can be made in either quantitative or qualitative terms. As we will see, there may be some difference between the targets which have been set for the short-term and those which have been identified as long-term performance indicators.

Various analytical and measurement techniques can be employed to calculate performance or to set the targets in the first place. We have detailed two such areas below. The first refers to human resources and the second considers financial aspects. Let us investigate these in more detail:

◆ *Human resources* – targets which may be set in human relations terms would normally include productivity and workforce stability. The measurement tools used would normally consist of assessing output, assessing time spent on producing each unit of production or, in relation to workforce stability, labour turnover.

◆ *Financial aspects* – the organisation is obviously very interested in measuring its profitability. It can do this by using ratio analysis. Other financial aspects which could be used as target-setting tools are investigations into costs, cash flow and returns on investments made. All of these are quantifiable. They can be measured by looking at budgets or undertaking some form of financial analysis or audit.

Types of target

Many targets are set in purely monetary terms. This is a natural tendency, since money is comparatively easy to measure and understand. It also allows for direct comparisons to be made between different activities, and means that non-specialists can assess whether the targets have been met. Finally, it is a way in which the organisation can readily compare different corporate or departmental performances.

Any system of target setting will tell managers what they need to accomplish, assuming that they have the necessary authority to make decisions. It will also serve as a means by which managers can compare their results against target, so that they can take appropriate action.

When setting targets it is essential to incorporate the fact that some variables are controllable and others are not. In other words, managers should not be held responsible for not having reached their targets as a result of unforeseen, uncontrollable variables.

As we will see, targets have a definite timescale. Within that timescale, the organisation and the manager responsible should take the opportunity to measure performance frequently. By doing this, they will know what progress is being made. If monitoring is regular then action can be taken in order to put things right before it is too late. This corrective action may allow the target to be achieved despite unforeseen circumstances.

Balancing short- and long-term targets

Organisations will often find themselves in a position where, in order to control short-term targets and objectives, they have affected their long-term targets. On the other hand, if the organisation is preoccupied with long-term targets, short-term ones may be adversely affected. There will always be a conflict between long-term and short-term objectives, often known as the short–long tradeoff. While there is no hard and fast solution to this, there are a number of controlling mechanisms which can be employed in order to make sure that the tradeoff is as balanced as possible:

1   The organisation needs to be aware of possible conflicts between short- and long-term targets.

[handwritten annotation: FOCUSING TOO HEAVILY ON EITHER S/T OR L/T TARGETS/OBJS. IMPAIRS THE OTHER ∴ NEED BALANCE]

2 All managers and other employees who make decisions should be aware of the fact that short-term and long-term targets are sometimes incompatible.

3 The senior management of the organisation needs to minimise the impact that short-term targets will have on the long-term ones. An appraisal of this impact needs to be undertaken before any decisions are made.

4 Senior management should be given as much information as possible together with an assessment of the consequences of different courses of action.

5 Short-term goals need to be realistic. If managers are expected to make unreasonable short-term sacrifices merely in order to reach long-term targets, this could seriously affect their motivation and morale.

6 Managers should be encouraged to review long-term targets regularly in order to ensure that they and the organisation are on the right track.

As we said earlier, performance can be measured either quantitatively or qualitatively. The former is perhaps the easier way of measuring performance since it involves figures such as costs, units produced, delivery times, etc. The latter is in many people's eyes a matter of judgement and as such it is not directly measurable.

Whether the organisation chooses to favour short-term objectives or long-term objectives, it needs to ensure that both accord with the even longer-term objectives or, for that matter, the mission statement of the organisation.

Management by objectives

Management by objectives is essentially a planning aid to assist managers in integrating strategic and tactical planning. It allows them to translate longer-term objectives into workable action plans. There are seven stages or phases of the process, but before management by objectives can be implemented the organisation has to embrace a specific philosophy or management style. The following features are an integral part of this philosophy:

1 The organisation needs to accept the need to establish teams at different levels.

2 The organisation needs to set up an open communication system.

3 Employees need to be convinced that co-operation is the key to both organisational success and employee rewards.

4 The organisation should do its best to eliminate any sense of fear of autocratic managers.

5 The organisation should project a positive and proactive culture at all times.

In addition to this reorganisation, which may be considerable, the organisation needs to establish a number of targets relating to management by objectives in order to ensure that the system works. To begin with, it must appreciate the fact that it has many different objectives. It also needs to understand that there will be occasions when there is risk and uncertainty in setting various objectives. Importantly, it has to prioritise and clarify its objectives. The organisation must also appreciate that there is a definite relationship between team, departmental, individual and organisational objectives. Finally, it needs to deploy its resources, including human resources, to focus on its objectives.

Returning to the seven phases of management by objectives, we can now see how strategic and tactical considerations may be integrated.

Phase 1: the organisational mission

This is the establishment of the mission statement. You will remember that incorporated within this is the organisation's statement of what it is and what it hopes to become. At this phase, the objectives are very broad.

Phase 2: strategic objectives

In this phase the organisation attempts to develop more specific strategic objectives. These should be more quantifiable and a specific timescale should be attached to them.

Phase 3: departmental, team and job objectives

At this stage middle and lower-level managers develop tactical objectives. These should be designed to support the strategic objectives. Remember that the departmental objectives may be relatively straightforward, but each work team and individual needs also to have their own clearly defined objectives. This phase acts as a vital linking stage between strategic planning and tactical planning.

Phase 4: participation

When managers set objectives they will ideally involve subordinates in their formation. After all, it is the individual employee who needs to meet these objectives. It is important for the subordinate and the manager to agree as much as possible. This will lead to higher performance being achieved.

Phase 5: action planning

It is now essential for managers and teams to develop action plans which will carry them towards their objectives. Different organisations involve their employees to a greater or lesser extent at this stage. In order to ensure that the objectives are met, the individual employee is in a far better position to comment on and make amendments to the proposed objectives.

Phase 6: implementation and control

At this point the planning ceases and the day-to-day reality of the work takes paramount importance. While under management by objectives individuals and teams are comparatively free to perform their tasks, it is the role of the manger to ensure that they reach their objectives. There needs to be a delicate balance between trust and control. Individuals are encouraged to discuss problems with their managers, who, for their part, will offer assistance and guidance.

Phase 7: performance reviews

If the system is going to work, it is essential for there to be periodic reviews in order to measure progress and solve problems. There may also be a need to revise objectives. Providing that the review system is fair, all parties can learn a great deal and apply these lessons to future operations. Individuals are encouraged to review and evaluate their own performance. An integral part of performance appraisal is the identification of obstacles or problems which have meant that objectives have not been met. The performance appraisals provide the opportunity for feedback to be given to the manager or the employee, so that the agreed objectives can be assessed. It is, however, very difficult to measure certain types of job, particularly in managerial roles. Performance appraisal may therefore be difficult.

Management by objectives may either be warmly embraced or viewed with a degree of superstition and disbelief. Many organisations refuse to incorporate such a system because they feel that it is often difficult to evaluate. It very much depends on the way in which the system is adopted by the organisation. Some organisations simply use management by objectives to control their employees. Other organisations, who have successfully incorporated the system into their operations, have found that there is too much bureaucracy and time wasted by managers in supervising routine activities. Many managers feel that the system provides a logical flow which allows them to develop personally as well as addressing the needs of their subordinates. Others simply state that this is just another source of information overload in an already overburdened decision-making process.

 ## Types of objectives

Manufacturing objectives

An industrial or manufacturing organisation primarily exists to construct, assemble or otherwise make a product. It is during this process (known as the production process) that an organisation 'adds value' to the raw materials or components with which it began the process, and will eventually produce some form of finished goods. This production process can take many forms, for example:

◆ A car tyre manufacturer uses rubber during the production process to produce car tyres. However, the final selling price of the car tyres is far in excess of the original cost of the rubber. In other words, during the production process the added-value aspect makes the rubber (in its new form as car tyres) more valuable.

◆ A furniture manufacturer constructing various items from wood (or lumber) will similarly put the raw materials through a series of production processes to make tables, chairs, desks, etc. Again, the value of the wood after it has gone through the production process is significantly more than that of the tree from which it came.

Let us now identify some of the key manufacturing objectives.

Method of production

In any industry, there are universally accepted methods of production. However, there are many other factors which determine the organisation's choice of production method (*see* Fig 1.3). These determinants include:

i) available investment;

ii) target customer (perhaps the organisation is producing hand-made products for the more wealthy customer);

iii) availability of skilled labour;

iv) availability of affordable and applicable machinery;

v) availability of raw materials (these raw materials may be completely 'raw' or part processed already);

vi) location (this is particularly true of organisations manufacturing goods in the third world).

Scale of production

The scale of production (in other words, how many products the organisation produces) is an important determinant of the way the organisation operates. Larger-scale production can mean cheaper raw materials and more efficient methods of production. Obviously, the greater the production the more the organisation desires better productivity levels from its employees (this means that the organisation requires them to be more efficient).

Location

Any manufacturing organisation that wishes to do more than survive in a competitive market must take great care in choosing the sites of its factories. Great economies can be made by being close either to the source of raw materials (where the raw materials are grown or mined, for example) or to where the raw materials can be easily accessed (via good transportation links). Equally, the organisation

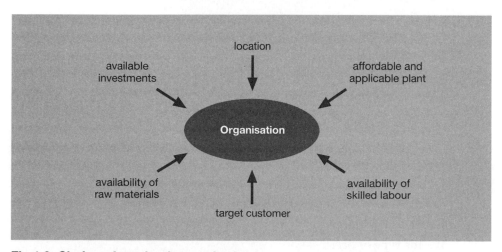

Fig 1.3 Choice of production methods

should be aware that there are avoidable costs which it can save by being close to the market in which it wishes to sell its finished goods.

Service organisations

The commercial or service organisation does not, by definition, actually manufacture goods. Increasingly, however, the boundaries between manufacturing and services are blurred. An organisation which produces computer software will now be involved (either directly or indirectly) in the manufacture of the finished product and be in a position to market the product itself.

Manufacturing organisations have, in the past, been reliant on the commercial or service sector to act as a point of contact between the end-user (customer) and themselves. As competition has grown manufacturers have sought to reduce the distribution chain and deal directly with the customer. This is not always possible, and certainly the commercial or service sector of the economy is without doubt the largest employer in Europe.

Many objectives are common to organisations whether they are manufacturers or service providers. There are, however, some features of a service provider which are not common to a manufacturer. These include:

◆ more direct contact with the customer;

◆ comprehensive after-sales service;

◆ the ability to provide information to customers on demand;

◆ possibly a greater understanding of the market (since the organisation will stock or deal with a variety of different manufacturers' products);

◆ the ability to identify the correct products (both tangible and intangible) to stock, as the organisation understands customers' requirements.

Financial objectives

For many organisations their principal objectives may be financial. The exact mix of financial objectives will depend on a wide variety of circumstances. Essentially, these may include:

a) the nature of the market in which the organisation operates;

b) the period of time during which the organisation has been operating;

c) the requirements of the investors;

d) the availability and awareness of customers;

e) the level of competition;

f) the market share held by the organisation;

g) the size of the organisation;

h) the range of products being produced by the organisation;

i) the type of organisation;

j) the management style employed by the organisation;

k) the stated objectives of the organisation.

Some of the main financial objectives include the following:

Breaking even

This objective can often be used to describe the attitude of a charity or a non-profit-making organisation (e.g. a local authority or government department). Any profits made are simply ploughed back into the organisation to cover running costs and purchase more products in order to continue the cycle. This can be termed 'ticking over', and is another objective often adopted by organisations in times of recession.

Expanding the range of products or services

The more products or services an organisation offers, the more likely that organisation is to survive and succeed. Organisations which only offer a single product or service can often find themselves in great difficulty if demand for what they offer reduces or disappears. There are, however, dangers in offering too wide a range of products or services, as an organisation may not be considered to be the expert or a market leader in any of them. In addition, the organisation is also exposing itself to the risks of several markets failing.

Maximising profits

This is when there is the largest possible difference between how much something has cost to produce and how much you can sell it for. In order to achieve this the organisation needs to know as much as possible about the customer and the market. It needs to know where to get its supplies at the cheapest possible rate, the most economical way of getting the product to the customer, and the maximum price the customer would be prepared to pay for the product.

Maximising sales

On the face of it, this would appear to be similar to maximising profits, but this is not the case. It does not necessarily follow that by achieving high sales you are achieving high profits. There may be only a small profit to be made from each product. It is only when you sell many thousands of units of a product that you make a reasonable profit. This particular objective is most common in the retail trade, when different branches of the same organisation compete with one another to achieve high sales figures. The employees in the branches may even be given considerable cash bonuses to encourage them to sell more.

Providing a return for shareholders and owners

This objective aims to provide a steady and acceptable level of profit to the owners of the organisation. You should understand that here we have made a distinction between owners and shareholders:

◆ shareholders are owners of the business, but may only have a small stake in it and look for profits in the form of dividends from the shares they own;

◆ owners, on the other hand, may be sole traders, partners or major shareholders, who again are looking for income from the organisation related to how much of that organisation they own.

Providing a steady income

In some ways, this is the opposite to sales and profit maximisation. An organisation which states that providing a steady income is its principal objective is saying that it would rather attain realistic goals than overstretch itself. This is perhaps a cautious approach to business, but it is one that is often the most workable. Being able easily to meet sales targets, deliver goods on time and maintain high standards of quality may mean the difference between survival and failure in an uncertain business world. Many of the organisations which grew very quickly in the 1980s overextended themselves in pursuit of short-term profits. We can now see that other companies which plodded along through that time are still trading successfully, having provided themselves with a steady income in good times and bad.

Objectives of charities

There is a bewildering range of different charities which cater for all segments of society and involve themselves in fundraising and the distribution of resources and information. This information increases the public's awareness of an issue or a problem. Objectives of charities include the following:

Raising awareness of an issue

Either through conventional advertising and marketing, or by word of mouth or reputation, various organisations strive to make us aware of the issues which they represent. In this respect, they must compete against all of the other organisations attempting to do the same.

Stimulating action

This can be measured in two main ways. The more obvious one is financial, to encourage the public to send donations or sign covenants to make regular contributions to the organisation. Equally important as this is the goal of convincing the public to make some other kind of response to an issue. This may be in the form of signing a petition or perhaps writing to a minister or government official in support of a particular issue. The call for the banning of live animal exports, for example, has spawned a series of responses from the RSPCA, Compassion in World Farming and other animal-oriented organisations. Each has its own preference in attempting to encourage us to support the issue by direct action in some way.

Providing advice and support

Many charities provide vital support and advice to the public in areas that they feel are neglected by the government. This is particularly true of health concerns (such as AIDS) and children's issues (such as Childline, an organisation set up to help combat abuse and bullying). This support is vital since there are no direct 'official' or government sponsored alternatives.

Distributing resources

Whether this is in the form of cash (such as grants and pensions given to war veterans by the British Legion) or physical resources (such as recreational facilities donated by charities for the old) or the organisation of holiday trips for the underprivileged or orphans (such as those organised by the Variety Club of Great Britain), this is the main way that most of us recognise the activities of a charity.

Market share objectives

Market share is the percentage of sales held by a particular organisation. There are two basic ways in which this can be measured:

◆ the value or revenue generated by the sales;
◆ the volume of units sold.

It is important for an organisation to keep abreast of its market share in relation to its major competitors in order to assess its position in that market. It should be noted that even though an organisation may increase its sales, this may not necessarily mean that it has increased its market share. If the market is growing faster than the organisation's market share is growing, then it is losing pace against its competitors. Short-term increases in sales (and profits) may hide the true situation from the organisation. Among the variety of aspects or objectives related to market share, the following are perhaps the most important.

Being the market leader

A market leader is an organisation that tries to sell more products than all of its rivals, or perhaps all of its rivals combined. There are considerable advantages to being a market leader, since every other organisation's products are compared to yours. Once this status has been achieved, profit maximisation may also follow as you can produce products more cheaply than your rivals because you are producing so many more than they are. A part-way stage of achieving market leadership is to set an achievable level of market share. In other words, the organisation may not directly seek to be the market leader straight away, but will move towards this in stages.

Beating the competition

This objective is similar in a sense to being a market leader, however beating the competition may just relate to achieving higher sales. Measuring this objective in terms of success is difficult, but can usually be assessed by the level of profit or reputation.

Organisational growth

The larger an organisation is, the more likely it is to attract investors and be able to produce products on a vast scale. Being big brings its own particular problems. Keeping track of business activity such as sales, stock and profit requires many extra employees. Should a company grow too quickly and outstrip its ability to keep track of things, it runs the risk of overtrading. It is therefore very important for an organisation to be able to monitor all activities when it is growing quickly.

Customer service

Most organisations now appreciate the importance of an efficient and effective customer service programme. In the past, organisations only paid lip-service to this crucial aspect of their operations. It should not be forgotten that customer service is as vital to an organisation which does not have direct contact with its customers as it is to those that deal with customers on a day-to-day basis. In this respect, when we consider customer service we should not simply focus on the commercial or service sector of the economy. It should also be remembered that both public and private sector organisations are under increasing pressure to provide comprehensive customer service programmes.

Some of the main customer service considerations are as follows:

◆ *Efficiency and responsiveness* – organisations now value the need to be immediately responsive to customers' requirements. This may be achieved in many ways, such as answering the telephone quickly, having sufficient products always in stock and being able to repair products at relatively short notice.

◆ *Sales service* – throughout the organisation's contact with customers, it is vital for the business to do all it can to ensure total satisfaction. Well-trained staff and efficient and effective systems are important to make sure that all has been done to achieve this goal.

◆ *After-sales service* – the organisation's responsibility, as far as the customer is concerned, does not cease when the product or service has been sold. It is an increasingly important feature of organisations that they have enhanced and developed their after-sales service. This may mean having sophisticated systems in place to cope with complaints, queries and returns of damaged or faulty goods.

There are other purposes of organisations that do not neatly fit into the categories above, since they are not necessarily profit related or anything to do with market share:

◆ *freedom* – many people set up a business in order to work for themselves. They prefer the opportunity to make their own decisions and be their own boss, and, of course, take all the profits and risk all the losses.

◆ *survival* – when times are bad and the economy is in recession, a company may simply seek survival. This may be measured by the company's ability to maintain existing staff levels, keep customers and not have to close branches or retail outlets.

Review questions

1 How do organisational goals differ from the content of a business plan?

2 Planning is a formal framework which seeks to identify the means by which the organisation intends to move towards a particular set of goals. What are the key components of a business plan?

3 Explain the purpose of a mission statement and give an example of type of message which would be included in such a statement. To whom is it addressed?

4 Describe the main differences between strategies and tactics.

5 How can organisations cope with the demands which change places upon them, particularly in light of the fact that the pace of change often accelerates beyond the boundaries of the planning process.

6 Describe the main areas of conflict between social responsibility and the need to provide the best return for the shareholders.

7 Is the profit motive the sole reason for the existence of organisations in the private sector?

8 Describe two public sector organisations in terms of their roles and responsibilities.

9 What are the key differences between *non-profit making* and *non-loss making* organisations?

10 Describe, with examples, the differences between multinationals and conglomerates.

11 Describe the key steps which an organisation might take in order to control its targets.

12 Why is target setting so important to organisations in their attempt to control the planning process and the development of the organisation?

13 Why must an organisation be aware of the necessary tradeoff between their long- and short-term goals and targets? Give at least two examples of this tradeoff situation.

14 Outline the seven phases of management by objectives.

15 Describe the three main organisational objectives in terms of customer service.

2

Understanding business functions

It is obvious that the size of the organisation and the nature of its market and environment will determine its mix of functions and activities. As with many considerations, we can only speak in terms of generalisations. In this chapter we will be looking at the role and importance of various departmental or functional areas of the organisation with a view to identifying the relevant aspects that pertain to the planning process.

 ## Marketing

A marketing plan or, to give it its full name, a sales and marketing plan, will assist the management of the business in controlling its activities in a more efficient way. Specifically, this part of the plan will cover the following:

i) focus on the main factors which need to be addressed to remain competitive;

ii) identification and systematic examination of the business's expansion opportunities;

iii) preparation of a series of counter-measures to address potential problems in the future;

iv) setting of identifiable goals and the results which the business hopes to achieve from them;

v) identification of the precise criteria to be met in the achievement of goals and objectives;

vi) description of a series of measurement systems to monitor the progress of achieving goals and objectives;

vii) provision of the necessary information and supporting data which can be used in negotiations with providers of finance.

Drawing up the marketing plan consists of a number of steps which are common regardless of the business's activity or degree of marketing involvement. These are:

1 An assessment of the organisation's potential performance.

2   An assessment of the organisation's historical performance (if applicable).

3   A detailed analysis of the competition's performance.

4   A global investigation of the market potential and any possible opportunities or threats.

5   A clear indication of the main objectives of the owners of the business.

6   The development and proposed realisation of the business's strategic plans.

7   The writing of an action plan which details tactics required to fulfil the strategic aims of the business.

Researching the market

Researching a market which an organisation believes to contain profitable opportunities is a fundamental task on which a marketing plan or, indeed, a business itself can be based. Some initial criteria to consider are:

◆ Is the market growing or it is large already?

◆ Is it supplied by organisations which are either outdated or inefficient?

◆ Is the market a niche which has not been considered by other organisations so far?

◆ Is the market heavily dependent on pricing levels which determine whether a customer buys one product or another?

◆ Is the market supplied by branded products or by products that do not command considerable levels of customer loyalty?

◆ Is the market dominated by a handful of large suppliers or is it supplied by numerous smaller competitors?

Perhaps the first place to start is to determine the market size. This can be measured either by the number of units sold in that market, or the total value of that market in monetary terms.

Estimating the potential of the market is somewhat more difficult, as it is unlikely that everyone within the market is ever likely to buy the product. Focusing on a particular segment of the market may be the best course of action. Although this may not give the business an estimated market potential in terms of sales, it will be in a stronger position to take charge of that market segment and become a market leader.

The market structure itself can be very complex. There are, inevitably, many links in the selling chain before the customer is reached. Even when an organisation sells direct, there may be distributors, agents or dealers through which the product passes before it reaches the retail outlet and then the customer. Knowing how this structure works will enable the organisation to establish, or at least estimate, the potential value of sales. Direct routes can enable the business to fix a selling price as well as to estimate the number of products they may be able to sell. If it knows this, then the business will also know the value of sales, so that forecasting potential demand will be easier. When the organisation has to work through a network of distributors, the selling price needs to be low enough to allow each layer of the distribution chain to earn some income, but still allow the product to reach the customer at a reasonable price.

Distribution networks constantly evolve and a comprehensive research study should be undertaken to help the organisation formulate its own sales plan.

Unless the organisation's product is totally new and innovative, it is inevitable that it will share the market with a number of other businesses. To be able to forecast potential demand, the organisation needs to establish the present market share of those competitors. Knowing this, the organisation will be able to measure how successful its competitors have been. The measurement of market share may be comparatively easy, but achieving a greater market share is not only a longer-term goal, but also significantly more difficult.

You may already have realised that market structure, market size and share of the market never remain the same. Yesterday, today and tomorrow may be totally different in all respects. Trying to look into the future can be assisted by looking at the past and then projecting the lessons learnt into the future. More generally, the economy, legislation and many other external influences may affect these three key considerations. Trying to guess market trends in an environment when there are no external influences would be an easy job. However, this is not reality. Making a realistic forecast of how much the organisation can sell, when it will be able to achieve these sales and how much will have to be spent to achieve them can be a bewildering experience. New businesses, often optimistic of their chances of achieving high sales and market share, are nearly always disappointed.

Setting timescales

Timescales initially set relating to the organisation's objectives should always be doubled. By taking this less optimistic line, the organisation may be able to surprise itself. In any case, ensuring that sufficient cash is available to keep a business going until it reaches the break-even point must be a fundamental consideration. Obviously providers of finance look for a balance between optimism and pessimism with regard to the demand for a product or service. As we have mentioned earlier, looking sufficiently attractive to potential providers of finance is one thing, but achieving your claims is another.

Test trials

It may be a very good idea to carry out some kind of test trial to determine the potential demand for the product or service. If the organisation is intending to set up expensive and complex production facilities or to order in large quantities of raw materials, then the last thing it needs to do is to fail in its initial estimation of demand. Before substantial investment in the organisation is undertaken, it is a good idea for the business to satisfy itself, or, indeed, its lenders, that a demand does exist. Test trials will also help define the sales cycle, which is the length of time between the organisation's first contact with a customer and the receipt of an order from that customer.

Naming products and services

As most businesses offer more than one product or service, separate identification of each product or service is essential. This means assigning a product name or brand name to each. This naming process will also help to identify some of the advantages or benefits which may accrue from the use of the product or service. This is often known as the 'unique selling proposition' (USP), which helps the business to position the product or service in the marketplace. Considerable market research will have already been undertaken to ensure that, at least for the most part, the organisation's perception of the product or service matches that of the customer.

The name of the business can also have considerable implications for success or failure. If the owners of the business want its name to encapsulate emotional or rational feeling about the product, then considerable thought needs to be given to it. The customer needs to associate the name with good feelings and careful thought should be given to ensuring that the name does not cause annoyance or irritation.

Another aspect to consider is whether the business and its main product should share the same name. There is no right or wrong answer to this. However, a new business may not have the resources to create and support two different brand images. In any event, having two different names could prove to be confusing.

When the business has carried out market research, it may have considered the necessity of having a logo or logotype. This means that the company or product name is always shown in the same typeface, colour or shape. The logo should be memorable, slightly unusual and, above all, recognisable. Many small businesses cannot afford the expense of employing a designer to come up with a clever logo. To begin with, any reasonably competent individual who has access to a fairly basic desktop publishing program can create a bewildering range of different logo designs. A professionally produced logo may cost a great deal of money to create in the first place and also to reproduce.

Some of the key points to consider in choosing a name for a product or business include the following:

a) Although the name may not create a positive feeling it should not create a negative one.

b) If the business is going to use an existing word or phrase it is best to try it out first.

c) Brainstorming sessions are useful in the production of a list of names for consideration.

d) The business should try to make sure that the name is not being used by anyone else.

e) The business should be aware that people looking through the *Yellow Pages* or a similar source of information will inevitably contact those at the beginning of the alphabet first.

f) The business should make sure that its name does not mean something that it did not intend it to mean, particularly in a foreign language.

g) The business should aim to avoid the use of complicated words, since customers may have to know how to spell them, particularly if they are writing a cheque.

h) The business should consider using capital letters since these have a tendency to stand out more.

Pricing

In setting a price or deciding on a pricing policy, the business will find that there are a number of factors which will determine where it is in the price range of products generally available. These include the following:

i) Its position in the market.

ii) The price sensitivity of its customers.

iii) The point in its life cycle that the product or service has reached.

iv) How the product compares to the competition.

v) What the price conveys to the customer.

A business may adopt a wide variety of different pricing strategies. Regardless of the strategy, there is one underpinning criterion which a business should consider. It must price its product to appeal to the maximum number of potential customers. It can make bigger profits if it lowers the price, or it can maintain reasonable profits by establishing an average price. If its prices are raised to too high a level, then its profitable business may be the target of competitors who are able to undercut that price.

Even if the business offers a unique product or service and can initially charge quite high prices, there will come a time when it will have to reduce its prices, as its product or service will not remain unique for very long. There is no point in trying to demand high prices when the product or service does not have a technological or competitive advantage.

On the other hand, if the business establishes a policy of low prices it is accepting that its product will only just cover the direct costs and make a small contribution to overheads. Low pricing should thus be considered as a last resort if the business can actually demand a higher price.

In working out its pricing structure the business will, of course, refer to its break-even point. Covering both direct and indirect costs and making a contribution to overheads are vital if the business is to succeed.

A business can justify selling its products or services cheaply if it has spare capacity. In this situation, any sale will contribute to overheads. This should not be a long-term solution. If the organisation is operating in a market where competition is strong, it may be forced to sell its products and services at low prices. In many markets customers will communicate with one another and aim to force their suppliers to reduce their prices. It is very difficult to combat this. Price cutting will trigger off a price war between a business and its competitors and a new business would not be able to sustain this price war for very long.

Clearly, if the business has excess stock or poor-selling lines, then price cutting is a possibility. Before reducing prices, however, the business should consider using an alternative method and/or market to counteract this downturn in sales.

Prices should not necessarily be decided on the basis of cost alone. There has to be sufficient profit margin. If the business has set its prices on the basis of costs, it must remember that these are only forecasts and they can be wrong. The business may discover that, having set a price based on forecast costs, it has not covered all of its overheads. A useful guide to price setting is given below (*see* Fig 2.1):

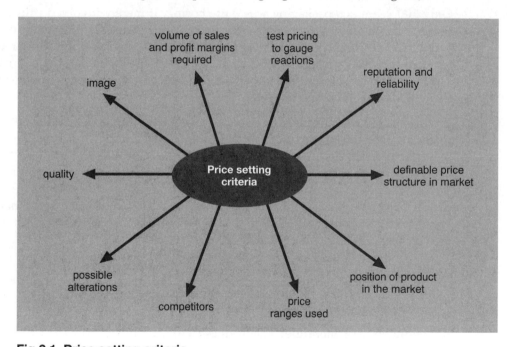

Fig 2.1 Price setting criteria

1 Look at the position which the product or service holds in the market.
2 Has the product achieved a reputation for reliability and does it have a good image?
3 Do the customers perceive the product or service as being of good quality?
4 Are you planning to make alterations to the product or service which will affect its position in the market?
5 How do the competitors rate against your product or service?

6 Is there a definable price structure in the market?

7 Where, within the price range of currently available products and services, is your product or service being pitched?

8 Decide on some particular prices, then estimate the volume of sales, costs and profit margin, as well as levels of profit, for each of these prices.

9 Then choose your price.

10 Finally, test the price chosen in a test market to assess customers' reaction to that price.

Packaging

Packaging is important, since it offers a business the opportunity not only to give information to the customer, but also to reinforce any image or design qualities. Packaging should be an integral part of promotional methods.

Only 100 years ago packaging was quite boring. It merely involved printing the trader's name and product name on a plain bag or carton. In these days of mass production and highly demanding consumer markets, manufacturers have realised that products sell much better if they have identifiable logos, slogans and names. The packaging reinforces the advertising campaigns and assists in point-of-sale merchandising and brand image.

Environmental concerns relating to packaging, particularly in terms of whether the materials used can be recycled, its design and construction, are beginning to oblige manufacturers to produce 'green' packaging. Some retailers in the UK, such as The Body Shop, encourage customers to re-use bottles and containers for repeat purchases. Even supermarkets such as Safeway and Sainsbury's offer re-usable carrier bags and, indeed, it is not unknown for customers to receive a small discount from their shopping bill if they take away their goods in a box left in one of the box disposal bins near the cash registers.

Obviously, if the business is offering a service rather than a product, it may feel that packaging is not of particular concern. This very much depends on where the business draws the line between packaging and sales literature or promotional materials. Is a folder which contains details of the services which a business offers packaging or sales literature? The business will need to give this some thought.

Promotion

Many organisations fail to appreciate the value of regularly contacting local newspapers or trade journals with news stories in the form of press releases focusing on their successes. Contrary to opinion, newspapers and magazines are usually desperately short of news material and will often print an interesting story, particularly if it is accompanied by a photograph. Exposure in the media can generate interest not only within the industry, but also among the general public – something that can often be very difficult to achieve through conventional advertising.

Many organisations develop a rather fixed attitude towards promotional expenditure. Organisations which manufacture fast-moving consumer goods (fmcgs) spend a great deal of their promotional budget on media advertising without really researching the effectiveness of this form of spending.

Research has shown that there is a distinction between 'above-the-line' expenditure (advertising in the media) and 'below-the-line' methods (such as point of sale, catalogues, brochures and leaflets). Above-the-line expenditure tends to relate to long-term effects on sales and below-the-line expenditure can dramatically affect short-term sales. Regardless of the method used, an organisation can try to measure its effectiveness by looking at the following:

i)   catalogues/leaflets:
   ◆ number of enquiries/costs;
   ◆ amount of business/costs.

ii) magazines:
   ◆ number of coupon enquiries/costs;
   ◆ value of business/costs.

iii) samples/merchandising:
   ◆ volume of orders/costs.

iv) exhibitions:
   ◆ number of enquiries/costs;
   ◆ value of follow-up business/costs.

By identifying each particular type of promotional material, an organisation will be able to make an estimate of the most cost-effective method. This cost-effectiveness assessment should always be used in calculating the amount of expenditure that should be allocated to different promotions.

Customers obtain information about products or services in a variety of different ways, including:

◆ paid-for promotional activity;
◆ editorial comment in magazines and newspapers;
◆ on-pack information;
◆ personal contacts and word of mouth.

In order to ensure that any cash spent on promotional activities is used to its best advantage, an organisation should:

a)   understand the type of promotional material required;
b)   set a budget or level of investment in that promotional activity;
c)   ensure that the promotional activity fully supports the organisation's objectives and the product's needs;
d)   set a structure for promotional spending;
e)   be able to measure, monitor and improve the effectiveness of the promotional activity.

Distribution

Organisations should periodically analyse their distribution policy. This enables them to discover whether profitability can be improved by changing the distribution method. Any marketing plan should involve this analysis, which addresses the following considerations:

1 What is the usual frequency of orders?

2 What is the usual size of orders?

3 How many different products are usually involved in each order?

4 What are the overall sales per product?

5 What is the nature of the demand for a product?

6 Are there any seasonal factors involved?

7 Is there a significant and identifiable geographical dimension to demand?

8 What are the costs of distribution at present?

9 How do these costs compare with those of alternative distribution methods?

10 What are the warehouse costs?

11 Can these costs be changed by further investment?

12 How could the order-processing system be improved?

Merchandising

There are various methods of merchandising a product, all of which are aimed at ensuring that the product is displayed in a prominent and attractive manner in the retail outlet. Sales representatives will visit retail outlets and offer merchandising or point-of-sale materials or equipment in the hope that these two criteria are addressed.

A marketing plan should include any suggestions that could be used by the organisation to enhance its merchandising efforts. Simply supplying a customer or retailer with products may not be sufficient to ensure that the products are in fact sold. The last thing that a supplier would want is for a retailer to contact it in a few months' time to complain that the goods have been unsold and wishing to return them. In the hope of avoiding this situation, suppliers must provide a retailer or customer with promotional materials in order to make their products more visible to the end-user. It is natural for a customer who enters a shop in search of a particular product to be drawn to attractive point-of-sale material. Dump-bins, posters, sales literature and shelf stickers may greatly enhance the product's attractiveness.

Some merchandising equipment is supplied to the retailer under certain terms and conditions. Periodically, the sales representative will check to see whether the equipment supplied is being used under the terms and conditions of the agreement. This checking procedure needs to be tempered with a degree of understanding of the retailer's needs as well as the local market situation.

Customers

An organisation's key customers will provide it with a substantial proportion of its sales. When these customers are limited in number, the supplying organisation may feel that it has become somewhat vulnerable. There is a simple equation which states that 80 per cent of a supplier's business is provided by 20 per cent of its customers. The loss of a single customer can therefore mean that a large percentage of sales volume will disappear. Obviously, wider sales coverage will reduce this dependency. There are also other benefits of obtaining wider sales coverage. For example, it will give the organisation a greater understanding of the market in general, as well as of the competition. It is known that small businesses export an average of only 1 per cent of their turnover. Although sales expansion may require greater short-term investment, entering new markets (particularly international ones) can reduce the dependency on current customers and the local market.

Selling

The effectiveness of the organisation's sales effort also needs constant review (*see* Fig 2.2). The points to consider include:

1 How good is the organisation at attracting and identifying new customers?

2 How much preparation is carried out prior to contacting a potential customer?

3 How many sales calls are made per day?

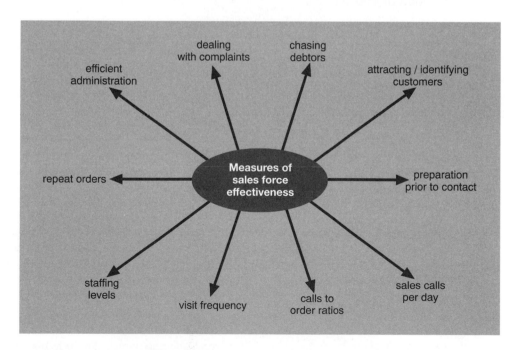

Fig 2.2 Sales force effectiveness

4 How many calls are necessary to secure an order?

5 How often should a customer be visited and how does this relate to the income generated from that customer?

6 Does the organisation need to employ more sales staff?

7 Would there be an extra positive return if the organisation employed more sales staff?

8 Do the sales staff spend time handling repeat orders when they should be contacting new customers?

9 Are the administration systems as streamlined and efficient as possible?

10 How much of the sales force's time is taken up with dealing with complaints and chasing debtors?

Marketing communication methods

Consumer marketing communications encompass:

i)   *aural and visual* – including television, radio and cinema;

ii) *visual* – including billboards, posters, hoardings and sports equipment;

iii) *read* – including newspapers and magazines;

iv) *oral* – including telemarketing and direct sales;

v)   *incidental* – including staff uniforms, advertisements on receipts, stickers and point-of-sale material.

Industrial marketing communications incorporate:

i)   *written publicity* – including bulletins, technical literature and updates;

ii) *display* – including advertising and feature articles;

iii) *in-company* – including presentations and demonstrations to employees and potential customers;

iv) *briefings* – including seminars and demonstrations;

v)   *exhibitions* – including trade fairs and consumer fairs;

vi) *external visits* – including discussions with customers, wholesalers and distributors.

The various forms of marketing communication to be used by the organisation have to be identified at the earliest point possible so that materials and employees required can be prepared. An organisation presenting a business plan with a marketing element would have to identify the viability of the different marketing communication methods and try to establish a budget or priority order for each one.

After-sales

The concept of after-sales service recognises the fact that the organisation's relationship with the customer does not end with placing the product in the carrier bag and taking the money. The organisation will have to make sure that it provides the following:

◆ friendly and supportive advice;

◆ stocks of spare parts;

◆ an efficient maintenance operation.

The above all help to encourage the customer to return to the business and make repeat purchases.

After-sales service can be undertaken by either the manufacturer or the retailer. Depending on the nature of the product or service involved, it may be necessary to have a network of maintenance providers throughout the country who will make home calls or be points of collection for products requiring attention. While many products are covered under guarantees or warranties, the maintenance and repair aspects of the after-sales service are carried out free.

The emergence of the concept of extended warranties and guarantees has greatly increased the need for, and viability of, regional repair centres. Many larger retail chains, such as Dixons, Curry's and Comet, will routinely take back items either within or beyond their guarantee or warranty period for despatch either to their own repair centres or to the manufacturer. This vital service provides considerable peace of mind to the customer who is secure in the knowledge that, should the product be faulty, immediate action will be taken. Sometimes arguments may arise about the nature of any fault found in a product. As a rule, if a product is faulty as a result of inferior parts or poor workmanship, then it is the responsibility of the manufacturer or the retailer to replace the goods.

Many people have commented that the emergence of extended warranties merely underlines the fact that products are considerably less reliable than they were in the past. It has to be said that, in trying to convince a customer to take out an extended warranty, retailers and manufacturers are simply attempting to pass potentially expensive repair costs onto the customer. Since many electrical goods, in particular, become technologically obsolete after three or four years, the extended warranty absolves the retailer or manufacturer of any financial responsibility for faulty goods.

Other important aspects of after-sales service include the following:

◆ in-store advice and information – this service is offered free by the retailer and aims to ensure that the customer is using the product to its best advantage;

◆ care phone lines – these systems have been set up by either retail chains or manufacturers to provide (usually free) advice and support to customers after purchases have been made. They tend to be either 0800 (free*fone*), 0345 (lo-call) or 0891 (premium rate) numbers.

After-sales service systems should be included, at least in outline form, within the marketing plan. Depending on the nature of the product or service, the business may have to cope with either a great number of complaints or queries, or simply the occasional one or two. It is probably not the best use of valuable staff to require the sales force to field complaints and after-sales service enquiries. If the organisation is large enough, then it may need to set up a customer complaints and after-sales service unit or department. Alternatively, this service could be provided by a subcontractor working on the basis of a fee per complaint or repair handled. In either case, the organisation must consider the probable after-sales service implications that could arise from the supply of its products or services.

Timing the various phases of the marketing plan is as important as timing the overall business plan itself. Certain activities must be undertaken before other key activities may be attempted, for instance:

◆ the product needs to be clearly designed;

◆ the product needs to be clearly packaged;

◆ the product needs to be clearly labelled;

◆ the sales force needs to be fully briefed.

All this must happen before the product is ready to be launched on to the market. Another key determining factor in the timing process will be the acquisition and analysis of information gained from market research. Sufficient information must be gathered in order to ascertain the nature, size and growth potential of the market, since these factors will determine the direction in which the sales effort will move.

Context of the marketing plan

While there is no set format for a marketing plan, the following are potential headings or sections:

◆ A sound marketing policy should be based on the ability of an organisation to define what products or services would be required by the customer. This can best be achieved by some form of research.

◆ Basic customer information is absolutely essential for the development of an organisation. Even very routine enquiries may add to the information base.

◆ An evaluation of the profitability of each product should be a key determining factor in establishing future objectives and how they may be achieved.

◆ By investigating the effects of price rises within the market, an organisation will be able to gauge how price sensitive the market may be. The organisation should also consider possible competitive price changes in the future.

◆ By comparing the quality of its own product with both the competition's product(s) and customers' expectations, an organisation will be able to assess the long-term potential of its products.

◆ When considering discounting, an organisation should establish clear and unambiguous guidelines.

◆ Offering credit has important marketing implications and more generally, will affect the availability of working capital.

◆ Evaluating the distribution policy, whether actual or proposed, should be an integral part of the marketing plan.

◆ When considering exports, an organisation must take note of two points – a good distribution network has to be established and potential export sales may offset any changes in the domestic market.

◆ An organisation should continually investigate the performance of all of its products to help it in defining objectives.

◆ Product development should be considered as a key feature of business development.

◆ The costs and benefits of the packaging used by the organisation should be periodically reviewed.

◆ The costs and opportunities of branding should be continually reviewed.

◆ Rather than depend on a small number of customers, an organisation should consider ways in which to extend its customer base.

◆ When developing the business, and in particular when expanding sales, an organisation needs to consider development costs.

◆ The promotion of new products should be explored, together with the costs included in any promotional budget.

◆ The likely returns from, and cost-effectiveness of, the different methods of promotion should be investigated.

◆ Employees who have contact with customers will be expected to have a level of expertise. The training of personnel is an integral part of the marketing mix.

◆ Organisations should review their investment in various outlets to ensure that maximum sales are being achieved in relation to the current environment.

◆ Organisations should consider whether investment is required in customer or after-sales service and these costs should be integrated into the marketing plan.

Normally, the key features of the marketing plan, as part of the overall business plan, can be summarised in perhaps four or five pages, along with appendices containing marketing statistics. The *minimum* areas that a marketing plan should address are as follows:

1 State the size of the market, its history and its potential for growth.
2 Split the market into definable segments and decide which your business is aiming at.
3 Identify your likely customers and establish how many there are and how they buy.
4 Analyse your competition, determine their size and their position in the market.
5 Analyse your customer service and after-sales service requirements.
6 Identify your sales promotion techniques and advertising methods.

7   Determine how your product will be sold (by yourself, retailer, wholesaler, distributor).

8   Determine your sales pitch, which includes an identification of the benefits of your products and services.

9   Determine your pricing policy.

 # Production

Production plans are written to ensure that the resources deployed in the production process will be adequate to meet the potential orders for products and services. It is essential that an organisation ensures it has adequate resources in terms of premises, machinery, raw materials and labour in order to produce the products as and when required. If customers are made to wait, they may become dissatisfied with the organisation and look for their orders to be fulfilled elsewhere.

New product development

New product development and the bright ideas associated with such an endeavour must be tempered with the practicalities of production. While many good ideas appear to be workable on paper, the realities of the situation may mean that the product cannot be produced in a cost-effective and efficient manner.

An organisation has to assess whether it is looking for a new product which its current production process is capable of producing. It would serve no purpose for an organisation to develop an idea for a new product only to discover that the actual production process has to be carried out elsewhere, possibly by subcontractors or business partners. After all, one of the key considerations in developing new products, regardless of their design, is that the organisation should make full use of its production facilities.

The design of new products is often changed gradually as the organisation becomes aware that the actual design presents problems. This process, although not enjoyable for the designer, needs to be considered in terms of efficiency and overall benefit to the business.

Whether the design process is undertaken by the organisation itself or by external organisations, the business must make sure that it carries out feasibility studies. These are undertaken at the earliest possible stage to ensure that resources are not wasted in the development of a new product design when there is no likelihood of that product being produced in a cost-effective way. This screening process needs to be rigorously enforced to make sure that the business does not invest funds in product designs that are impractical and will never come to fruition.

The development of new products can be not only time consuming but expensive. The desire to develop new products should be tempered by an awareness that many small businesses fail as a result of overinvesting in new product development. However, the success of new products is central to the long-term success and growth of the organisation. It should be noted that only a small percentage of new products are ever successful.

It is important for an organisation to plan its new product development using the following steps:

i) Allow an initial screening period in which an investigation is carried out to assess how the product fits in with current products and services.

ii) Investigate whether the new product could be produced using current production methods.

iii) Test the production process.

iv) Fully cost the production process.

v) Carry out necessary market research.

vi) Produce a test batch of new products and test market them.

vii) Assuming that all of the above stages are acceptable, introduce the product into the marketplace.

Costing

Accurate costing in relation to production is essential to ensure that profitability remains at a level which allows the organisation to reach its objectives. Some organisations calculate the costs of production, including the contribution to overheads. Many companies, however, do not have any idea how much it actually costs to produce particular products. Their profits therefore tend to be somewhat erratic and unpredictable.

Control of the production process could be improved by introducing standard costs. These standard costs can be related to either the amount of time it takes to manufacture the product, or the total costs of that particular finished product. Organisations frequently use an efficiency ratio (ER), which is:

$$\text{efficiency ratio} = \frac{\text{standard costing}}{\text{actual costing}}$$

By using this ratio, if an organisation produces a batch of products for £4000 and its standard costing is calculated as £5000, then the production line is working more efficiently than the forecast.

A different ratio to control production processes is known as the capacity ratio (CR). This relates to the current production level and how it compares with maximum potential production. The ratio looks like this:

$$\text{capacity ratio} = \frac{\text{current throughput}}{\text{maximum throughput}}$$

This ratio is used to identify trends in production and parts of the factory which are not paying for themselves.

By applying these ratios and formulae an organisation is able to assess the efficiency of its production process. As a result it may, perhaps, consider whether certain production functions might better be carried out by subcontractors.

Physical resources

The location of its premises is only one of the important questions that an organisation needs to consider. In many cases, the main factors determining the suitability of premises will be their cost and availability. In choosing an ideal location for a business, it is prudent to consider its accessibility in terms of:

◆ markets
◆ raw materials
◆ employees
◆ suppliers
◆ appropriate support services
◆ main utilities.

Another factor is the availability, at least in certain areas of the UK, of government development and resettlement grants.

Depending on the nature of its business, continuity of production may well rely on the use of machinery and other equipment. Machinery may be a key physical resource and the organisation must ensure that it has a reliable supplier of such machinery, together with such back-up support services as are essential to maintain production. With regard to the most efficient running of the machinery, it may be necessary to consider a continuous production process, by which the machinery is run for 24 hours a day, 365 days a year. This will affect the acquisition of other essential resources, such as raw materials and a well-organised labour force (working on a shift basis). In relation to its premises, the organisation must ensure that the building is not only fit for the operating of essential machinery, but also has the necessary licensing, insurance and usage clearance by the local authority.

If an organisation requires large supplies of raw materials, not only must the location of the premises be right, but they must also be suitable for handling these large quantities. Locating the business in an isolated part of the country can mean unnecessary transportation costs which may affect the viability of the business. Although transport and distribution costs have reduced, comparatively speaking, over recent years, it is still a major goal of most organisations to reduce these costs as far as possible. For this reason organisations operating in the same area of business activity, or in a support function to a number of similar organisations, tend to congregate fairly close to one another. This concentration of organisations is known as external economies of scale. Collectively organisations achieve economies of scale by jointly reducing unnecessary costs. In addition, this congregation also ensures that training facilities for staff are available locally. The other major bonus is that smaller support systems, such as servicing contractors and component suppliers, are nearby.

Human resources

Labour costs differ widely from area to area and region to region. Employees in the South East of England, for example, earn some 50 per cent more than those in Northern Ireland and between 15 and 25 per cent more than those in the rest of the UK. If an organisation wishes to ensure that it has an adequate supply of skilled labour, then it may be forced to locate in an area where wage levels are comparatively higher. The mobility of labour has become greater in recent years, but labour is still not as mobile as some employers would wish. Another major reason for locating in a particular area may be to avoid traditional industrial relations problems which are associated with an alternative region. In areas where there have been considerable job losses, employers can, and often do, exploit the situation by calling on the excess labour pool and employing these people at comparatively low wage rates. In terms of an organisation's production plan as a whole, the availability of skilled labour in sufficient numbers is imperative. This ensures that the production process is fully operational at all times and at all levels.

Quality

Although the improvement of quality is a gradual process by which the organisation attempts to make small but constant steps towards perfection, investment in quality is also necessary.

The concept of total quality management (TQM) has begun to be generally accepted as the basis of appropriate practice. Manufacturing processes and all aspects of after-sales service come under the concept of TQM. This approach, Japanese in origin, seeks full quality assurance throughout the organisation. It will hopefully ensure that the organisation addresses the following:

1 Efficiency at every stage of its activities.
2 Making the best use of all available resources.
3 Providing consistency in its production of products and services.
4 Putting a series of quality assurance measures into operation to give feedback on potential quality problems.
5 Paying particular attention to the concept of customer satisfaction.

Timing

If a production run is long, then the start-up costs of that production are lower per unit produced. Longer production runs produce large quantities of stock and consequently affect cash flow. Organisations which have a wide product range may not have the time to maintain single product manufacture. Obviously, if an organisation were to reduce the number of products it produces, then it would be able to improve its production efficiency. However, since longer production runs are more cost-effective, there are timing considerations in ensuring that sufficient stock levels are available for immediate purchase.

Many of these timing considerations may boil down to the use of machinery. An analysis of timing will need to include an analysis of machinery utilisation. In order to make a return on capital employed (in the form of its investment in the machinery), as we said above, an organisation may have to consider round-the-clock production on a seven days a week basis to maximise returns.

Many organisations have been strongly influenced by Japanese manufacturing techniques. They have adopted what is known as a 'just-in-time' (JIT) strategy. Under this philosophy, raw materials arrive at the factory when and where they are required, rather than being held in stock. The timing of these deliveries accords with the needs of the production process. Although JIT strategies may not be necessarily practical or applicable in a small business, an organisation has to ask itself whether there are any ways by which it can ensure that the production process is fed efficiently and at the correct time without having to maintain vast quantities of raw materials or components.

Human resource management

Managing change

The human resource management function is often vital in the implementation of any change initiative. The whole process is very much reliant on the ability of the managers involved.

Certain managerial characteristics are required for a smooth implementation of change. These characteristics can be described as follows:

a) An effective manager manages relationships with employees rather than managing the employees themselves.

b) Management skills, particularly in terms of negotiation, communication, learning ability and goal setting, are essential.

c) An effective manager learns from the experience of management rather than having theoretical knowledge.

d) An effective manager recognises that no two individuals are the same and people cope with stress or change in many different ways.

We shall now address the stages in which the implementation of change takes place. As we have mentioned, the difference between an effective manager and a poor one is their ability to recognise goals and identify methods by which these goals may be attained.

Identifying the goal for change

The first stage in implementing change is to identify the goal itself. The following questions need to be asked at this stage:

◆ What is it we are trying to do?

◆ What is the point of the change?

◆ Who will it affect?

◆ What is in it for the organisation?

◆ What are the short-, medium- and long-term prospects?

◆ What are the constraints involved?

◆ What is the timescale?

◆ Do we have the technology, equipment or machinery?

◆ How will the employees respond?

◆ Who has overall responsibility for the change?

Producing a plan

Individuals set about the process of planning in many different ways. In general, however, we can recognise the following features of the planning process:

i) In relation to the objectives a plan should include what needs to be achieved and by whom.

ii) The plan should also identify the key factors involved.

iii) Above all, the plan should include a list of actions and timings.

Having determined what is to be achieved, the plan should address the following:

1 What will be the changes in working conditions?

2 Will managers have to delegate more?

3 Will there be a change in the location of the work?

4 Will there be a change in the way in which teams work?

5 Are new procedures necessary?

6 Does the organisation have to be restructured?

7 What are the training requirements?

8 What new skills will need to be learnt?

9 How will they be acquired?

10 What will be the format of the training?

11 Will there be changes in communications procedures?

12 Will the change make communication more difficult?

13 Does the organisational structure support the new conditions?

14 Does someone need to be appointed to oversee the new changes?

15 How will individual employees be affected?

16 How will groups in general be affected?

17 Who precisely will be affected?

18 Who will not be affected?

19 Who, therefore, needs to be informed?

20 What information has to be relayed?

21 Who needs to be consulted?

22 When should they be consulted?

23 How will the changes be presented?

24 What are the likely reactions or resistance to the change?

25 What are the anticipated reactions?

26 Who will present the greatest resistance?

27 What is the estimated cost of the change?

28 What is the timetable for introducing the change?

29 Should milestones be identified?

30 What steps need to be achieved?

31 How will the changes be measured and monitored?

32 Who will measure and monitor the changes?

33 When will the changes be measured and monitored?

Once the effects of the changes have been thought through in detail, the following need to be addressed:

◆ The more complicated the change, the more there is a need for schedules to be drawn up.

◆ Assuming that there are limited resources, how realistic is the timetable?

◆ What will be the net effect on the day-to-day running of the organisation while the changes are being undertaken?

Setting milestones

As we have mentioned in previous sections, the establishment of milestones, or means by which the progress of the change can be assessed, is essential. Certain targets or objectives must be readily identifiable in order to assess not only the progress of the change but its current impact on the organisation. When we consider significant structural changes relating to an organisation's premises, it is fairly easy to recognise and establish these targets. However, when we are considering less tangible changes in working conditions, we must, perhaps, turn our attention to either the reactions of the employees or their gradual acceptance of the changes. To this extent, measurement or acceptance that the target has been reached may be rather problematic. Regular meetings and subsequent feedback from employees are essential in ensuring that changes are being made in the smoothest and most beneficial manner.

Monitoring and evaluation

Normally, when changes are implemented, a specific individual will be responsible for monitoring and evaluation. Indeed, this individual's time and effort may be solely directed at the implementation of the change. Unfortunately, this is not always the case, and monitoring and evaluation will have to be undertaken by an individual in addition to their normal day-to-day duties. If this happens, the individual may find it difficult to fulfil both roles effectively.

If the organisation does not think through clearly how it will ensure that the change remains on schedule, then delays may be inevitable. In more formal situations, the organisation may require that certain documentation is completed and feedback given at the identified milestones.

If, as is generally the case, things do not go according to plan, the organisation and the individual responsible for the implementation may find themselves in a difficult situation. If the production process has been significantly affected by the change(s), but much of the change is not completed, then this may have an impact on the organisation's viability and profitability.

A pragmatic view needs to be taken when setting the targets and establishing the timetable. It would be foolish to rely on the change being completed according to the pre-planned timetable. In this respect the organisation must have a contingency plan in order to address the problems that may occur if the change is behind schedule.

A rigorous review of progress is essential as the organisation must have the opportunity to reset targets and timetables, as well as investigating the ramifications of the delay.

Training

With any change in working conditions there may be a need to train, retrain or refresh individuals' understanding and knowledge. Factored into the overall implementation plan should be a rolling programme of training. Obviously, depending on the nature of the change in working conditions, more or less training will be involved. In the field of health and safety, particularly relating to new legislation, significant amounts of training may be required. If, for example, individuals are required to wear protective clothing or maintain equipment, then this may have a significant impact on the productivity for a short period.

If new equipment or machinery has been installed to be used in the manufacturing process, significant retraining may again have to be undertaken. It is often the case that the suppliers of new equipment include in the cost a basic training programme for all operators or users of the machinery.

Change champions

An individual may be identified as the 'driving force' behind the change, i.e. its 'champion'. This individual will have been prepared in advance and should know about the nature of the changes and any significant impact that may occur. Ideally, this individual should be a good communicator. In monitoring the implementation of the change it may be necessary for this individual to come into conflict with those who are instituting or affected by the change.

Resistance to change

Resistance to change can be identified as the change nears completion. In the earlier stages of implementation resistance may be greater, but through careful communication the individual responsible for monitoring the change may be able to allay fears and dispel myths.

Relaying information is essential throughout the whole process of change. Organisations should call regular meetings, particularly with those most affected by the change. These feedback opportunities should not be ignored, as employees may have good ideas or suggestions to overcome problems and aid development and implementation.

Finance and purchasing

As we have seen, the resource requirements of a business plan can be categorised as human, physical and financial. One of the main functions of a business plan may be the precise identification of the resources needed to ensure that not only production but general business activity is maintained.

Organisations are concerned with ensuring that they gain economies of scale at the earliest possible opportunity. For example, a production plan which makes up part of the overall business plan will be concerned with the batching of orders so that production runs are long enough to ensure economies of scale. This particular technique can have its drawbacks, however, since it may cause delays in the fulfilment of customer orders. If this is likely to happen, then customers should be kept informed of the status of their orders at all times.

Resources can be deployed to ensure that quality is maintained at all levels of the production process and the service supplied. It is not sufficient for an organisation just to supply the products or services required by its customers. Much more is demanded, for example better sales and customer service, more user-friendly product design, etc. Human and physical resources can be considered in the following ways:

◆ *Physical resources* – suppliers will be expected to deliver raw materials and part-finished materials of an acceptable quality.

◆ *Human resources* – the workforce should be instilled with the notion of quality. Special training in quality and customer service may also be required. It may be dangerous for an organisation to ignore these features, as it is certain that its competitors will be paying close attention to them.

◆ *Financial resources* – frank and honest contact must be maintained with the providers of finance. All potential problems regarding cash flow or profitability must be discussed at every stage. If there are shareholders they will demand to know the true state of affairs within the organisation. It may be necessary for them to make additional share capital available to finance short-term cash-flow problems, or indeed long-term investments.

Forecasts and analysis

At this stage in assessing resource requirements, the sales, production and administrative conclusions need to be passed on to a financial expert for further analysis. This expert will attempt to make some projections relating to the following:

i) cash-flow forecasts (usually on a month-by-month basis);

ii) profit and loss assessments (on a month-by-month basis);

iii) balance sheet calculations (on an annual basis).

All of these forecasts are strongly interrelated. In planning terms, it is important that the organisation compares forecasts with what has happened in the past.

The financial projections will be able to provide an indication of the following:

◆ the underlying profitability as suggested in the forecasts;

◆ the organisation's probable future finance requirements.

This analysis will inevitably throw up a number of issues that may require reassessment. Typically, these would include some of the following:

a) Are there some products which are not performing particularly well and should be dropped so that resources can be channelled into new products?

b) Are wage levels too high?

c) Are sales per employee indicating that the organisation is overstaffed?

d) How does the organisation's discount and credit structure assist or impair profitability?

Financial data and forecasts form the basis of an organisation's ability to raise finance, negotiate the purchase or acquisition of premises and order raw materials. If an organisation is foolish enough to make an inaccurate forecast, then the inevitable outcome may be that insufficient funds are available. Also, if an organisation fails to meet its projected forecasts, then it may be difficult or impossible for it to acquire further funding. A provider of finance would not look kindly on an organisation which returns to ask for more money because its forecasting has proved to be inaccurate.

An organisation must attempt to make an estimate of the following:

◆ sales

◆ costs

◆ cash balances.

Over-optimistic sales figures, coupled with low cost figures, will throw a forecast into disarray. An organisation starting out for the first time does not want to have to cope with financial problems created as a result of poor or ill-conceived financial forecasts.

Cash-flow forecasts

A cash-flow forecast, in its simplest terms, is a record of cash received by the organisation and an indication of when cash will need to be paid out. Within a business plan it is common to make a cash-flow forecast that extends for two or three years. Providers of finance may require an organisation to extend that forecast for up to five years.

It is worth remembering that the business needs to make realistic assumptions about cash received and cash paid out. The main purpose of the cash-flow forecast is to show an organisation when it needs cash so that the provider of finance knows its funding requirements.

An organisation may choose to detail its financial data and forecasts using different time periods: weekly, monthly or yearly. Certainly, for cash-flow forecasts, it is the monthly period that is most important. Totals will have to be calculated for cash received and cash outgoing for each month. It is probable that certain assumptions will have to be made, particularly in the case of forecasts relating to months in the far future.

Profit and loss accounts

A profit and loss account is also usually formulated on a month-by-month basis. An organisation needs to calculate the total income derived from invoices received during that month and the costs of any outgoings during the same period. This will give a balance per month which indicates the profit or loss in that month.

Balance sheets

Balance sheets, on the other hand, tend to be drawn up on a yearly basis, working from information derived from actual cash flow and profit and loss. Remember that a balance sheet only shows what an organisation owes and what it owns at a particular time on a particular day. A projected balance sheet will similarly show an estimate of what the organisation will owe and own on a particular day in the future.

A start-up balance sheet, can only contain items of income and expenditure of which an organisation is already aware. It is advisable for a new business to use the services of an accountant to help produce a balance sheet at this stage. A new business is likely to be on a fairly small scale to begin with: if an organisation does not require a great deal of finance its provider of finance may not ask it to supply a start-up balance sheet. However, it is important to note that the key headings that need to be considered are the following:

1 *Fixed assets* – which include all equipment received, even if this has not yet been paid for.

2 *Current assets* – which include cash in hand, debtors and stock.

3 *Capital* – which the owners have put into the organisation to start the business.

4 *Liabilities* – which include overdraft, any tax or VAT payable and creditors.

A profit forecast should be made in order to establish the level of profit which the organisation hopes to produce at the end of a specified period. Taken together, the projected profit and loss and balance sheet should indicate whether the business will be in a position to break-even or show a small profit. From these two information sources it will be possible to calculate the expected return on capital employed.

Financial control

By constructing a monthly profit and loss account and a monthly balance sheet, an organisation will be able to monitor its adherence to its business plan. This control mechanism should be able to identify any causes for concern and allow the organisation to react in time. The normal procedure is for an organisation to create a cash-flow forecast which includes budgeted figures for various items. Then, as the actual figures become available, the organisation can compare these with the budget. Similarly, it will be able to compare actual output with production targets and actual sales with projected sales.

A business plan will also need to explain how financial data and forecasts will be reviewed. Simply put, the business has to establish the following:

i) who will carry out the review;

ii) how often reviews will take place;

iii) what authority the reviewer will have to institute changes;

iv) what records will be kept;

v) what the distribution procedure for information will be;

vi) what restrictions there are on the distribution procedure.

Review questions

1 Outline the key aspects of a sales and marketing plan.

2 Describe the main research areas necessary to support the compilation of a sales and marketing plan.

3 How could an organisation assess market size and potential?

4 How can test trials help to define the sales cycle?

5 Why is choosing the name for a brand of such crucial concern?

6 Describe the main approaches which may be adopted in the creation of a workable pricing policy.

7 Describe, with examples, the main differences between above- and below-the-line marketing activities.

8 Outline the key steps which an organisation will have to take in order to ensure that they have a coherent customer service provision.

9 To what extent should distribution policy and provision be a concern of the marketing function? Give an example of how this can be integrated into the overall marketing plan.

10 What is the purpose of a production plan?

11 Outline the main stages in the development of a new product idea.

12 How can the control of the production process be facilitated by the introduction of standard costing?

13 What is the purpose of the capacity ratio?

14 In which part of the UK do employers enjoy the lowest labour costs? Suggest some possible reasons to explain this.

15 Describe the basic purpose of TQM.

16 What is JIT, and why has it been embraced so enthusiastically by UK manufacturers?

17 What are the main stages of dealing with change in terms of human resource management?

18 What are *milestones* in the context of planning and why are they so important?

19 Why are organisations keen to establish economies of scale at the earliest possible opportunity? How might economies of scale improve the overall effectiveness of the organisation?

20 Outline the three main ways in which financial forecasting can be achieved as an integral part of the planning process.

3

Public sector organisations

Despite large-scale privatisation, there still exist numerous organisations which provide a public service in some form (*see* Fig 3.1). Primarily, these include:

◆ central government departments;

◆ local authorities;

◆ quangos (organisations appointed by the government to provide certain services);

◆ directly or indirectly funded organisations (such as hospitals and colleges);

◆ specialist organisations (such as those set up to advise businesses and direct certain government initiatives).

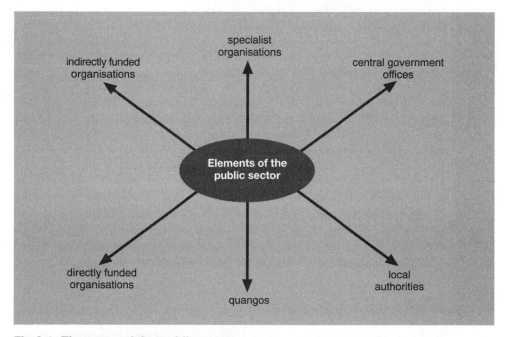

Fig 3.1 Elements of the public sector

In the past many public services were that in name only: they did provide a service, but they were not necessarily accountable or responsive to public needs. Recent UK government legislation requires them to be accessible, responsive and efficient.

Some of the key public service considerations include:

1 *Providing benefits and grants* – organisations such as the DSS (Department of Social Security) or councils are responsible for providing a range of benefits and grants, to the unemployed or students, for example.

2 *Providing advice and guidance* – councils and central government, through a range of different suborganisations, provide a vast range of support services to industries and individuals. These services include business advice and guidance through the Department of Trade and Industry, and more local support for business via Chambers of Commerce. Individuals can obtain useful advice on demand through the Citizens' Advice Bureaux that exist in nearly all towns and cities.

3 *Collection and monitoring* – the Inland Revenue not only collects income tax and other forms of taxation based on profits from business, but also provides useful business advice on matters such as financial control and monitoring. Customs and excise, which is responsible for the collection and monitoring of VAT (value added tax), provides useful guidelines for the collection, payment and monitoring of this 'sales tax'.

4 *Data collection* – many central government departments routinely collect data which is of great use to businesses. Data are readily available on employment trends, family expenditure, growth or decline of markets and export information.

 ## Privatisation

In the UK a massive privatisation programme has attempted to bring the public sector into private hands and make it more accountable to the public. Whether or not this has proved to be the case, customers' charters have certainly moved newly privatised companies in this direction.

The gradual movement towards accountability in organisations that are still in public hands, leading to 'promises', 'charters' and other agreements, is seen by many as a precursor to privatisation. By highlighting the deficiencies in public sector provision, the public are encouraged to support further privatisation. Even deregulation can be seen as part of this, with the public sector openly competing and sometimes collaborating with the private sector.

 ## Business organisations

Business organisations such as the CBI, trade associations, employers' associations and Chambers of Commerce are, perhaps, the most enduring and powerful advisory group. Many of the larger organisations use professional lobbyists or have specific departments whose role it is to liaise with the various government departments, agencies and other organisations. These activities are designed to make sure that the organisation's point of view is held in high regard by the government. In some cases, such as the debate on the banning of tobacco advertising, the businesses find themselves directly opposed to government policies.

Not only do these business organisations attempt to influence and advise the UK government, but they find themselves increasingly involved in attempts to influence the EU.

Confederation of British Industry

The Confederation of British Industry (CBI) represents thousands of companies that employ literally millions of people. The members of the organisation are drawn from all the different sections of the economy and from large and small businesses. The organisation promotes the interests of the business community in general. It has regular contacts with both UK and European politicians. It has been working closely with the UK government on environmental policies, for example. To this end, it has set up a policy unit (*see* Fig 3.2) which aims to:

i) provide information;

ii) offer contacts with MPs;

iii) offer advice to MPs;

iv) monitor developments in legislation;

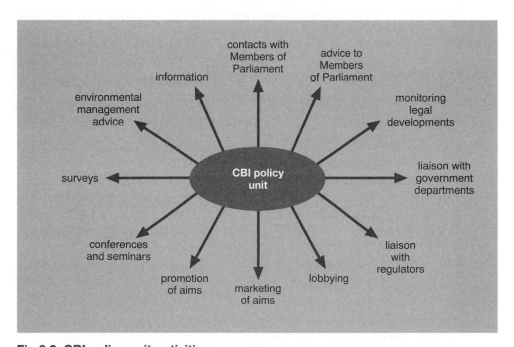

Fig 3.2 CBI policy unit activities

v)   liaise with government departments;

vi)   liaise with enforcement agencies;

vii)   lobby the government;

viii) produce promotional materials;

ix)   organise conferences and seminars;

x)   conduct surveys;

xi)   help members to develop good environmental management practices.

Office of Fair Trading

The Office of Fair Trading (OFT) issues guidelines to help business in the following areas:

◆ what consumer and competition law requires of businesses;

◆ the procedures any business must follow and what happens if it fails to follow them;

◆ the information that the OFT needs from businesses to pursue its statutory duties.

The OFT is committed to observe the Code of Practice on Access to Government Information. It is well aware of the sensitiveness of the information that it receives from businesses. Its target time for responding to requests for information (under the Open Government Code) is just 20 days.

The OFT is keen to keep in touch with the views of businesses, consumer organisations and enforcement bodies. To this end:

a)   it maintains contact with the business community through trade associations;

b)   it liaises with consumer organisations;

c)   it liaises with Trading Standards Departments;

d)   it consults businesses when changes in the law are being considered;

e)   it holds public hearings;

f)   it undertakes customer surveys.

The OFT is committed to being courteous and helpful at all times, responding to complaints quickly and fairly. It tries to keep the costs low by making its operations as efficient as possible.

Director General of Fair Trading

The Director General of the OFT has a number of key enforcement powers, as follows:

Consumer credit

Under the Consumer Credit Act 1974:

◆ administration of the licensing system;

◆ adjudication in cases regarding the issuing, renewal, variation, suspension and relocation of businesses;

◆ resolving disputes about credit reference agencies;

◆ superintending the working and enforcement of the Act.

Estate agents

Under the Estate Agents Act 1979:

◆ issuing prohibition orders;

◆ issuing orders against estate agents guilty of misconduct;

◆ superintending the working and enforcement of the regulations.

Restrictive practices

Under the Restrictive Trade Practices Act 1976:

◆ to compile and maintain a public register of restrictive trading agreements;

◆ to refer agreements liable to be registered to the Restrictive Practices Court.

Mergers

Under the Fair Trading Act 1973:

◆ to be aware of any merger that may have to be referred to the Monopolies and Mergers Commission;

◆ to recommend to the Secretary of State for Trade and Industry the action that may need to be taken in relation to such a merger.

Monopolies and anti-competitive practices

Under the Fair Trading Act 1973 and the Competition Act 1980:

◆ to review commercial activities with a view to detecting monopoly situations and anti-competitive practices;

◆ to investigate monopoly power and anti-competitive practices and realise remedies by obtaining assurances and undertakings.

Trading practices

Under the Fair Trading Act 1973:

◆ to review commercial activities with a view to identifying practices that may affect the interests of the consumer;

◆ to seek assurances from trades where practices are detrimental to consumers or break the law. In extreme cases the matter will be referred to the courts.

Advertisements

The Director General of Fair Trading has powers under the Control of Misleading Advertisement Regulations 1988. He has the power to step in if the public interest requires that advertisements complained about need to be stopped by a court injunction. The bulk of the complaints are handled by the following organisations:

◆ Trading Standards (or Consumer Protection) Departments, who enforce the Trade Descriptions Act and other consumer laws.

◆ The ASA which administers the British Code of Advertising Practice and the British Code of Sales Promotion Practice in conjunction with the Code of Advertising Practice Committee.

In addition, there are a number of other organisations, such as the Department of Health, which have responsibilities imposed by legislation, for example by the Medicines Act.

 ## Advertising Standards Authority

The Advertising Standards Authority (ASA) is an independent self-regulatory body responsible for supervising the content of non-broadcast advertisements in the UK.

It is estimated that some 25 million advertisements are published annually in the UK. The ASA spot-checks thousands of them (and indeed sales promotions) as part of a rigorous monitoring programme.

The ASA also advises thousands of advertisers, agencies and publishers on how to avoid misleading or offensive advertisements that may lead to complaints being made. The aim is avoidance, since complaints are not only costly but may involve adverse publicity and criticism of the industry.

The ASA operates on a levy charged on all advertisements. This levy, only 0.1 per cent of the advertisement's cost, is collected on the ASA's behalf by the Advertising Standards Board of Finance. This separation helps to ensure that the ASA maintains its independence.

The ASA has the power to investigate any complaint and compare the advertisement to the Code of Advertising Practice. The ASA rarely tells the advertiser to stop the advertisement immediately, as the advertiser is given time to tell their side of the story.

If the advertisement is found to be unacceptable under the rules of the Code, then the advertiser will be told to 'pull' the advertisement or amend it. Failure to do so will entail the advertiser being suspended, or they may suffer the withdrawal of privileges and the publishers of magazines and newspapers may be advised not to take their advertising.

Further refusal may entail the advertiser being referred to the OFT for refusing to abide by the Code. Under the Control of Misleading Advertisements Regulations 1988 the organisation can be restrained from using the advertisement ever again.

The ASA covers all advertisements in the following areas of the media and marketing activities:

i)   newspapers

ii)   magazines

iii)   posters

iv)   direct marketing

v)   sales promotions

vi)   cinema

vii)   videocassettes

viii) Ceefax.

Advertisements on ITV, Channel 4 and cable are covered by the Independent Television Commission and the Cable Authority respectively. Radio is regulated by the Radio Authority. Claims made on packets and labels are the preserve of Trading Standards or Environmental Health Officers.

In conclusion, the ASA deals with only what is written or shown in an advertisement or a promotion. Complaints must be made in writing to the ASA with as much detail about the advertisement as possible (preferably a copy of the advertisement should be enclosed).

Consumer protection

There are a number of public sector organisations charged with the responsibility of defending and legislating in favour of consumer rights. These organisations, primarily funded directly by the government (or, in some cases, via other means, such as local Trading Standards Department), cover all aspects of the area of consumer protection and legislation.

There are some key aspects to assist in the identification of these organisations:

a)   some of the organisations are part of major central government departments;

b)   some of the organisations operate on behalf of central government departments: these are often known as QUANGOs;

c)   some of the organisations are financed by central government but are fairly independent of it;

d)   some organisations are independent apart from a reliance for some or all of their funding from central government;

e)   some organisations are part of the local government structure and receive finance from the local authority.

These organisations tend to be either charities or limited companies, relying on membership fees or other forms of funding in order to continue their activities. Maintaining their independence is not only vital to the organisation in terms of giving it freedom to do as it wishes, but also for the consumer, for without freedom of action these organisations could never support or promote the rights and needs of the public.

All pressure groups in this area are committed to making information available to the consumer. Many of them have campaign units whose job it is to take up the recommendations for change and improvement revealed by the research. Campaigning in this way costs a great deal of money, so pressure groups do sell their merchandise, charge membership fees and accept donations, if appropriate.

Although some of the following examples are drawn from the private sector, we have highlighted organisations that are either recent entrants into the private sector, or where the complaints and accountability considerations are still controlled by a public sector organisation.

Citizens' Advice Bureaux

The Citizens' Advice Bureaux (CAB) are funded by the local authorities. They have a particular interest in the following:

◆ social security (pensions, benefits, national insurance);

◆ employment rights (unfair dismissal and tribunal procedures).

Consumer issues can usually be dealt with by telephone. For the most part the CAB will be able to help the enquirer access the information needed to pursue a grievance or problem. There are over 1000 CAB outlets throughout England and Wales, which are staffed by volunteers and paid employees. They offer impartial, free and confidential advice.

The National Association of Citizens' Advice Bureaux (NACAB) covers England, Wales and Northern Ireland. This organisation monitors the type of complaints that the local bureaux handle. In some areas the CABs are known as Consumer Advice Centres.

Consumers' Association

The Consumers' Association (CA) offers an ideal example of how the investigatory and lobbying process works. It came into existence to try to balance the power between sellers and buyers. Founded in 1957, it provides an independent guidance service to the consumer. The CA methodically tests and investigates goods and services available to the consumer. It publishes comparative reports which look at the following aspects of goods and services:

◆ performance

◆ quality

◆ value.

This information is published in *Which?* magazine.

In order to maintain its independence, the CA states the following:

i)   it only serves the interests of the consumer;

ii)   it does not accept money from the government, trade or industry;

iii)   it carries no advertising in its magazines;

iv)   it never accepts free samples, holidays or meals;

v)   it does not allow its findings or recommendations to be used by trade or industry to promote products or services;

vi)   it is not politically motivated;

vii)   it does not allow practising businesspeople to sit on its governing council.

Typical of the many organisations involved in investigatory or lobbying activities, the CA is often involved in several campaigns at a time. Among those that would interest groups in the consumer protection area would be:

◆ safety standards;

◆ labelling;

◆ anti-competitive activities (monopolies etc.);

◆ pollution;

◆ improving the availability of information;

◆ simplifying contracts;

◆ simplifying activities such as house buying.

By gaining publicity for the issue in question, the CA can at least make people begin to talk about the problem. Using contacts to ensure that the consumer's viewpoint is heard and considered is the next step, and one that can only be taken because of the organisation's many years of activity in the area.

Members of the CA's council, management, staff and ordinary members represent consumers on statutory and public bodies. They also make a valuable contribution to such organisations as the British Standards Institution.

Unfair contracts

Consumer groups have recently started a new campaign against insurance policies and other contracts that use fine print to deny policyholders payments or impose unfair penalties. The Consumers' Association and the National Consumer Council (see below) have encouraged consumers to send examples of unfair contracts to the Office of Fair Trading. The OFT's response was that investors do not need to have bought a product to be eligible to complain. All they need to show is that the contract was unfair.

Under existing UK law, there is some protection under the Unfair Contract Terms Act 1977, although the insurance companies have been exempt. New legislation will ensure that the UK complies with European directives which cover contracts for all (or most) goods and services.

Timeshare contracts are due to be covered under the new law, as are mortgages and package holidays. This will have a massive impact on the excessive cancellation penalties demanded by package holiday operators. It is in the area of travel insurance that the bulk of the complaints have been made regarding contracts.

New European directives give the OFT the power to take legal action against organisations which issue contracts considered to be unfair. In order to monitor this, a special unit has been set up, but both the CA and the NCC feel that it may not have sufficient resources. To this end, the NCC supports the notion that consumer groups ought to be able to challenge contracts on behalf of individuals.

There have been some cases of sentences running up to 130 words in some insurance policies. One particular example, using a 37-word sentence with no punctuation, defined money as: *'current legal tender cheques money orders postal orders current postage stamps (not being part of a collection) national insurance stamps savings stamps or certificates premium bonds travellers cheques travel tickets luncheon vouchers gift tokens and phone cards'*.

National Consumer Council

The National Consumer Council (NCC) was set up by the government in 1975 to represent the wishes of the consumer to the following:

◆ the government
◆ the utilities
◆ the public services
◆ the business community.

As well as its lobbying and pressure group activities, the NCC also carries out extensive research and publishes its findings and recommendations. It is the council's duty to insist that the interests of all consumers are taken into account. Its major priority is in consumer education and development of a network of information and advice centres nationwide. The NCC has no statutory powers and does not deal with individual consumer complaints. It is fully funded by the government but is an independent organisation. There are similar councils set up for Scotland, Wales and Northern Ireland.

Recent NCC campaigns

In 1996, Britain's biggest water company, Thames Water, cut its investment programme by £350 million. What annoyed consumer organisations was that it will not be passing on these savings to its seven million customers. This comes at a time when there is growing public anger about the huge rises in water company's profits and directors' salaries. These appear to be funded by massive rises in charges since privatisation. Thames Water's bills, for example, have risen by 50 per cent above inflation to an average of £162 per household since privatisation. At the same time, the salary of the current chairman, Sir Robert Clarke, has risen 154 per cent from £41 000 to a staggering £104 000 per year. The utility regulator, OFWAT, supports the NCC's feeling that the reduction in investment should be passed on to the customer in either improved services or lower bills. The NCC states that there is a very strong case for reducing bills if big savings are being made. In response to these statements, the Thames Customer Service Committee replied: 'The customer is financing the company's investment. If the investment is reduced, the customer should benefit.'

In 1996, in response to telephone regulator OFTEL's proposals that British Telecom (BT) should be allowed to charge customers as much as it likes for line rentals, the NCC stated that it was deeply concerned and would watch BT's response very carefully. Some three million customers, or one in five, take advantage of BT's Low User Scheme, and it is suggested that these will be protected by guarantees that charges will not rise above inflation. Despite the fact that the UK's telecommunications services are the most open in the world, with over 190 companies, BT still controls 85 per cent of all telecommunications traffic. Mercury Communications has managed to gain a quarter of international telephone traffic, but has only recruited 750 000 domestic users. These proposed changes will probably accelerate the move from BT to its rivals.

 ## Ombudsmen

Ombudsmen were set up to investigate complaints about government departments or public sector organisations. They cover the following:

◆ poor service
◆ bad administration
◆ abuses of power.

There are a number of ombudsmen operating in both the public and private sectors. In order to use the relevant ombudsman you must first have approached the organisation about which you wish to complain in writing. This gives them the opportunity to sort the problem out. The ombudsmen can be seen as a cheaper (free) alternative to taking the matter to court. In any case, they tend to act more quickly than the courts.

Ombudsmen have different amounts of power to make sure that the organisation complies with the proposed resolution of the complaint. Sometimes the ombudsmen can demand compensation from the organisation on behalf of the complainant.

The main features of the ombudsman scheme are:

i) they operate independently;
ii) they investigate complaints;
iii) they decide whether there has been unreasonable delay, neglect, inefficiency or some other failure;
iv) the complainant has the right to continue the complaint into court if they are unhappy with the ombudsman's findings;

v) they can make recommendations about improved procedures and services for the future.

In 1995 the insurance ombudsman received 2027 complaints about life policies and endowments, compared with around 1000 complaints about both motor insurance and household insurance. He found against life insurance companies in 42 per cent of cases, compared with 33 per cent in the case of motor insurance and 31 per cent in household insurance. Valuations were a major cause of complaint when cars were written off. The ombudsman maintains that the valuation should reflect the market value of the car: not its second-hand value, but its replacement value.

Valuations were also a problem area when it came to household insurance – particularly with jewellery theft claims. Insurers frequently knock down claims, arguing that there is insufficient proof of value.

Travel insurance is another area increasingly seen as a problem black spot. Complaints frequently arise because travellers buy policies without knowing the exclusions, and in 1995 travel insurance companies lost half the claims they were contesting.

 ## Trading Standards Departments

The safety provisions of the Consumer Protection Act 1987 allow local authority Trading Standards Officers the following rights in respect of the safety of goods:

a) to make test purchases to check on the safety of the goods;

b) to enter and search premises to obtain information (in certain cases);

c) to issue suspension notices which prohibit suppliers from selling goods which are believed to break the safety legislation;

d) to apply to the magistrates' court for an order which allows them to seize and destroy such goods.

Local Trading Standards Departments check the following on behalf of the consumer:

i) that products meet safety requirements (with labels, warnings and instructions);

ii) that the composition of food meets the legal standards (accurate food labels which are not misleading);

iii) that the weighing and measuring equipment used by traders is accurate;

iv) that the quality marking on food and other products is accurate;

v) that price claims and descriptions are not misleading;

vi) that credit and hire agreements meet legal requirements,

They do this by:

◆ advising manufacturers, retailers and service providers on how to comply with the various laws;

◆ inspecting goods at all stages of the production and distribution chain;

◆ monitoring advertisements, catalogues and brochures;

◆ taking food samples for analysis;

◆ investigating complaints made by the public and other businesses;

◆ seizing dangerous and illegal goods to stop them from being sold;

◆ prosecuting businesses if trading standards advice has been ignored.

In order to contact Trading Standards Officers, the consumer may either ring, write a letter or call in personally. In special circumstances, Trading Standards Officers will visit you at home (if you are disabled or housebound, for example).

Regulators

When various publicly owned industries were sold to private individuals there was a very real fear that the overriding concerns of these organisations would be purely profit based. Given the fact that the majority of these industries are monopolies (they are the only organisation to offer this service in a particular area), they had to be controlled and watched.

Whatever your view about privatisation, the old state monopolies became private ones, at least initially, especially in the case of British Gas, British Telecom and the electricity companies.

Regulators were put in place to oversee their operations. Again, there are differing views about the effectiveness of these regulators. Many people feel that the consumer is not sufficiently protected. The organisations have seen huge profit rises, for example, even during the recession.

The key regulatory bodies are:

1 Office of Electricity (OFFER), set up in 1990 to regulate the prices of regional electricity companies.
2 Office of Gas Supply (OFGAS), set up in 1986 to regulate gas supplies to domestic users.
3 Office of Telecommunications (OFTEL), set up in 1984 to regulate BT, including line rentals, calls, licences and equipment,
4 Office of Water (OFWAT), set up in 1989 to regulate the supply of water and sewerage, as well as price increases.

OFWAT

OFWAT is responsible for making sure that the water industry provides customers with a good quality and efficient service at a fair price (*see* Fig 3.3). It is independent of the industry itself and headed by a Director General. If an individual has a complaint about any of the following, then the matter should be taken up with the company in the first place to give it an opportunity to put things right:

- billing errors
- methods of payment
- new connections
- interruptions to supply
- water quality
- meter installation
- debt and disconnection
- liability for repair
- flooding from sewers
- leakage from pipes
- low water pressure.

All of the water companies have procedures for handling customer complaints. This is laid out in their Code of Practice for Customers. If the company fails to reply to the complaint within ten days, then the customer may be entitled to compensation under the Guaranteed Standards Scheme. If the company has not resolved the complaint to the satisfaction of the customer, then one of the ten regional Customer Service Committees (CSCs) will investigate the problem. If the complaint is found to be justified, then the company will be required to take appropriate action.

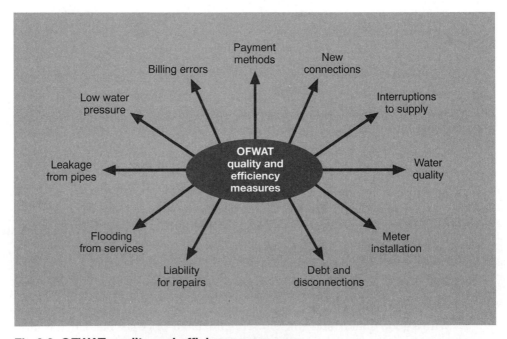

Fig 3.3 OFWAT quality and efficiency measures

OFGAS

According to the annual report from OFGAS, complaints and queries about British Gas rose by more than a quarter in 1996 to 2318 incidents. Disconnections rose to 16 393 from 16 088, reversing the trend of previous years. OFGAS blamed British Gas's restructuring for the surge of unrest. Prices and discounts for direct debit customers were most to blame. OFGAS decided that British Gas was entitled to offer the discounts, provided that customers were offered prices in line with the company's costs. British Gas has promised to introduce these lower charges in 1997. Philip Hame, field officer with the Gas Consumers' Council, said that the rise in complaints showed that many customers felt the discount scheme for monthly direct debit customers was unfair. The OFGAS report shows that the North Thames region had the highest number of complaints, followed by South Eastern and North Western. The Northern and Scottish regions registered the smallest number of complaints. The company has already been warned by the government that its Charter Mark is under review because of concern about slipping standards.

 ## Citizens' Charter

The Citizens' Charter (CC) covers the following types of institution or organisation:

◆ schools
◆ hospitals
◆ council housing
◆ police services
◆ courts
◆ prisons
◆ postal services
◆ tax offices
◆ benefit offices
◆ job centres
◆ railways
◆ roads
◆ central government
◆ local government
◆ gas
◆ electricity
◆ water
◆ telecommunications.

The principal aim of the Citizens' Charter is to improve public services across the board. Through it consumers should get a better deal along with better choice. One of the key aspects of this is to increase the amount of competition. This, it is hoped, will mean that the consumer will get better value for money.

The main purpose of the Citizens' Charter is best summed up by the principles published back in 1992. These laid out the following:

1 *Standards* – to set, monitor and publish clear standards of service that the public should expect. To publish actual performance for comparison against the standards.

2 *Information and openness* – to ensure that full, accurate information is readily available in a way which all the public can understand. This information should show how public services are run, what they cost, how they perform and who is in charge of them.

3 *Choice and consultation* – to ensure that courteous and helpful service is given by all public servants. They should always wear badges so that individuals can be identified. All services should be available on an equal basis and be run so that the public can have maximum access.

4 *Putting things right* – if things do go wrong, then the public service should apologise and give a full explanation, along with a quick and effective remedy. There should also be a well-publicised complaints procedure that is subject to independent review from time to time.

5 *Value for money* – to ensure that the public receives efficient and economical delivery of public services within the resources available. All services' performance should be measured against published standards.

The Citizens' Charter aims to set standards and publish them. In this way the consumer will have access to more information about services and have remedies if the standards are not met. Let us have a look at some of the principal improvements that have been suggested.

Health

Patients now have a guaranteed maximum waiting time of two years for admission into hospital. Now nine out of ten patients are admitted within a year. The waiting period is down to 18 months for three main treatments (hips, knees and cataracts).

Education

Parents now have more and better information about decisions made regarding their children. All parents receive a written report on their children at least once a year. Performance tables are now produced to cover the following:

i) examination results;

ii) truancy rates;

iii) national curriculum test results;

iv) information about school leavers;

v) summaries of the independent reports.

Rail travel

Rail companies have to publish details on the punctuality and reliability of each line. The charter also introduced two compensation schemes which give compensation if performance is below, or the number of delays are above, the published levels.

Council services

Local councils are now obliged to tell their residents how they are performing. The Audit Commission publishes tables showing how the different councils compare.

Housing

The Housing and Urban Development Bill aims to introduce competition into local authority housing management. Tenants, for example, now have the right to have their houses repaired quickly and efficiently.

Roads

Road and highway authorities have a legal duty to tell the public why they are digging up the roads. They are also meant to control the times when roadworks are in operation to avoid traffic chaos. As far as the motorways are concerned, new laws allow developers to build more service stations to improve choice and competition on most stretches of motorway.

Despite the intentions of the Citizens' Charter, many people still think that they are receiving a poor deal from many public services. It is true that there have been some improvements:

◆ hospital waiting lists are down;
◆ parents receive a school report;
◆ court delays have been cut;
◆ benefit payments have been speeded up;
◆ driving tests can now be booked by telephone and paid for by credit card;
◆ the waiting time has been reduced from 13 to 5 weeks for a driving test.

Despite all of that, the cash refund side of the Citizens' Charter has all but failed. With the exceptions of OFTEL and OFGAS cutting the phone and gas bills, the Charter appears to have had little effect on the rail companies, for example. Despite refund payments of around £10–£15 million per year, they have been incredibly slow in making these payments. The problem is that the Passengers' Charter states that 90 per cent of the trains should arrive within five minutes of the published time. In fact, some routes can only achieve around 66 per cent on time. With season ticket holders entitled to a 5 per cent rebate for late trains, and another 5 per cent if the train is cancelled, there is a real problem. Putting the rights of the public aside, the rail companies have asked the government to lower the targets!

As another example, the amount paid to phone users who had cause to complain to BT has risen to some £16 million. This is about £43 000 per day, but the fact is that the public cannot get anyone else except BT to mend their telephones. How else can an acceptable level of service be guaranteed? The Charter does assume that BT will do its best, otherwise it will have to pay for not getting it right.

Rebates occur in the private sector, of course. One of the most famous is that offered by Domino's, a pizza delivery service. Its pledge of '30 minutes or free' gives the customer confidence as well as being able to create a sense of responsibility from the employees. National Breakdown offers to pay £10 if its car or rescue service takes more than one hour to arrive. Rover will give you your money back if you are unhappy with one of its new cars. The bookseller, Books *etc.*, will refund the cost of the book you have purchased if you do not like the story.

In other public sector areas, such as local government, new initiatives also offer protection. Edinburgh District Council will refund £30 for enquiries about planning permission, building warrants or completion certificates if the request is not dealt with after one week. Its sports facilities will give the public a free booking as compensation if they find that their court or pitch is double booked. In the long term, protection such as this may well extend to theatres, cinemas and concert halls when the performance is late or the acoustics are poor.

Returning to BT, typical protection schemes that provide compensation for the customer are:

i) if a faulty line is not mended by midnight the next day;

ii) if an appointment is missed;

iii) if a customer is disconnected from the service by mistake.

Payment is usually credited to the next bill or, if requested, can be made by cheque, with a covering letter.

Complaining under the Citizens' Charter

A booklet called *The Citizens' Charter Complaints Taskforce – Effective Complaining Systems* lays down the basic principles and checklists to be used. The complaints system needs to be:

◆ accessible;

◆ easy to understand;

◆ effective in its response;

◆ independently reviewed.

Complaints should be seen as a positive feedback method that can provide valuable information about weaknesses. They allow the organisation to take action and improve standards of service. The principles of the complaints system are that it should:

a) be accessible and well publicised;

b) be simple to understand and use;

c) be handled speedily with well-established limits for action;

d) keep the complainant well informed;

e) ensure a full and fair investigation;

f) respect the complainant's desire for confidentiality (if applicable);

g) address all of the points raised and provide an effective response and appropriate redress;

h) provide information to the management of the service so that it can be improved.

It also lays down a number of thoughts in the form of a checklist. These could well be used in other areas and for other organisations:

1 Is there ready access to the complaints procedure?

2 How effectively is the complaint handled?

3 What are the outcomes of the complaint?

Review questions

1 Outline the main purposes of public sector organisations.

2 How might charters be seen as a precursor to privatisation?

3 What is the purpose of the Confederation of British Industry?

4 What are the main functions of the Office of Fair Trading?

5 Outline the main enforcement powers held by the Director General of the Office of Fair Trading.

6 What is the purpose of the Advertising Standards Authority?

7 What is the status and purpose of the Consumers' Association?

8 The National Consumer Council fulfils a number of different functions, whom does it serve?

9 How could OFWAT seek to control the activities of the utilities under its jurisdiction?

10 To what extent do you feel that OFTEL has been unable to control the activities of BT. Give reasons for your answer.

11 What is the role of an ombudsman? Give examples of these in practice.

12 What role is fulfilled by the Trading Standards Office?

13 What is the role of Customer Service Committees (CSCs)?

14 What is the difference between a Charter Mark and a Citizens' Charter?

15 State the dates of the establishment of OFFER, OFGAS, OFWAT and OFTEL.

Setting up a new business

When individuals or groups of individuals consider starting to run a business, they have a series of basic choices. Essentially, these relate to the nature of the business and whether to start a new business or buy an existing one. We intend to look at these basic choices in turn, starting with the nature of the business.

 ## What kind of business?

The nature of the business depends on the business sector into which it falls. These business sectors are the following:

1 *Primary sector* – which covers all industries involved in the extraction and basic production of raw materials. It should be remembered that this also includes most forms of agriculture and fishing.

2 *Secondary sector* – which covers all industries involved in the processing of raw materials in some way. In other words, these businesses turn raw materials into finished goods or components.

3 *Tertiary sector* – which relates mainly to service industries. These businesses do not involve themselves directly in the processing of materials. This sector, therefore, includes tourism, transportation and financial services.

The choice of a business will largely depend on two main criteria:

◆ the knowledge and experience of the individuals embarking on the business activity;

◆ the potential demand for the products or services they wish to offer.

Whether one wishes to establish a new business or to buy an existing one, there are a number of risks and costs involved. We shall begin by looking at starting a new business from scratch.

Starting from scratch

Inherent in the decisions and circumstances relating to the establishment of a new business are the following risks and costs:

i) There are potentially high financial risks involved.

ii) Market research should be extensive.

iii) As the business will be unknown in the market place, time will be needed for it to establish itself.

iv) Any mistakes made in the first few months may prove disastrous.

v) Careful consideration should be given to the location of the business.

vi) The new business must make sure that it makes an impact very quickly so that its cashflow is not adversely affected by poor performance in the first few weeks or months.

Purchasing an existing business

If the idea is to purchase an existing business with a track record, perhaps the first consideration is whether it is currently doing well or badly. There are several other considerations to be taken into account:

a) Although the business may be established and there are all the benefits of the infrastructure being in place, this may mean that, comparatively speaking, it will be more expensive.

b) The new business may be expected to pay for 'goodwill', that is, the value placed on the trading name and existing trading relations with customers.

c) Although the business is up and running, this may not necessarily mean that the new organisation will know what to do with it.

d) The new organisation will have to make a careful investigation into the assets and liabilities of the business. It may be simply buying someone else's problem.

e) Constant monitoring is essential, since the new organisation cannot rely on what the previous owner claimed about the strengths and weaknesses of the business.

Expanding an existing business

Somewhat different from purchasing an existing business is buying into an organisation which needs to expand or diversify. Although strictly speaking this is not setting up a new business, this could be a way of gaining the advantages of an existing business, while at the same time having the advantages of setting up your own one. If an existing business person is interested in taking on a new partner, or a small limited company is looking to take on another shareholder, then the injection of new cash may be exactly what both sides are looking for.

Expanding an existing business has some risks attached to it from the point of view of the person joining the business. These include:

i) they may not be as independent as they would like to be;

ii) they should consider why, if the existing business structure was sound, profits acceptable and management in control of the situation, the organisation needs a new investor;

iii) they should also consider why the business has waited until this point to expand or diversify;

iv) although diversification is a good idea, since it spreads the risk across different business enterprises, it does stretch available resources too. Is this a good idea?

Franchises

The last business opportunity to consider is the purchase of a franchise. A successful business may offer its name, operational procedures, products or services to interested parties under a franchising agreement. Inevitably, there are some risks:

a) While it is easier to obtain a loan to buy a franchise than some other businesses, the franchisor may require quite high 'set-up' fees.

b) Franchises are considered to be a comparatively low risk but they may only offer fairly low returns. The franchisor will also require a percentage of all of the profits made.

c) Franchises are usually restricted to a very tight geographical area, so it must be remembered that the franchisee will not be allowed to operate outside of their specified territory.

 # Which product or service?

The foundation of any business is firmly rooted in the nature of the products or services which it offers. Coming up with the right idea can often be very difficult. When an individual first considers starting a new business, they will have to determine what products to sell or what service to offer. A good way of approaching these questions is to consider the following:

1 Is the business related to assembling things? Examples could include the production of toys, clothes, jewellery or lampshades.

2 Is the business related to arts and crafts? Examples could include drawing, photography, picture framing, pottery, design work or candle making.

3 Is the business related to fashion and beauty? Examples could include hairdressing, knitting, beauty therapy, aromatherapy, massage or dressmaking.

4 Is the business related to home-based activities? Examples could include catering, childminding, growing produce, taking in lodgers or curtain making.

5 Is the business related to office services? Examples could include bookkeeping, wordprocessing, desktop publishing, printing or typesetting.

6 Is the business related to writing? Examples could include translating, copy editing, indexing or proofreading.

Perhaps your proposed business does not fall into any of the above categories. After all, there are many other forms of occupation. You could consider some of the following:

i) acting as an agent for a mail order, party plan or telesales organisation;

ii) teaching or tutoring;

iii) repairing things such as clocks or bicycles;

iv) building work, including decorating and gardening;

v) removals and doing odd jobs.

In relation to the supply of products or services, the business may also have to look into the distribution aspects and see whether it can identify cost-effective methods of bringing products and services to potential customers.

A great deal of basic information can be found by referring to statistical information provided by the government or agencies working on behalf of the government. Equally, much information may be gleaned by careful analysis of competitors. Also, trends in customer spending can provide useful data on which to base the criteria needed to establish objectives related to the supply of products or services.

 ## Legislation

Businesses are required to ensure that they have complied with various legal guidelines. The following is a checklist of the legal aspects that a business should consider as an essential part of its business plan:

1 What are the current planning consents or authorised uses of the business premises to be used by the organisation?

2 Do the premises meet Health and Safety At Work Act (HASAW) regulations?

3 Do the premises meet fire regulations and do they have a current fire safety certificate?

4 Do the products conform to the Weights and Measures Act?

5 Do the products conform to the requirements of the Trading Standards Office?

6 Do the products conform to the Environmental Health Office requirements?

7 Is there a possibility that the business may breach any environmental protection laws?

8 Do any aspects of the marketing or advertising effort breach the Trades Descriptions Act?

9 Do any aspects of the marketing or advertising effort breach the Consumer Credit Act?

Employees

Particular attention should be paid to providing a contract of employment for all those who work for 16 hours per week or more and adhering to the laws relating to discrimination.

Employer's liability insurance covers a business against claims that may be made by employees who have suffered injury in the course of their duties. The term 'employee' is a broad one in this respect and covers all of those individuals who are under contract in some way to the business.

Employees should be 16 years of age in order to be legally in full-time employment. There are some restrictions on the number of working hours for the under-16s in part-time employment.

Recently the retirement age has been changed to 65 years for all. Formerly the retirement age was 60 for women and 65 for men. Individuals may, of course, work beyond their normal retirement age, but if they do so there are implications with regard to their pension rights.

Health and safety

Health and safety at work has become an increasingly complex area. In effect, a business should ensure that it complies with the Health and Safety At Work Act 1974 in the following respects:

i)   providing safe machinery and equipment;

ii)   ensuring that regular maintenance is undertaken;

iii) ensuring that all operating procedures for machinery and equipment are carefully monitored;

iv)   ensuring that safe methods of handling potentially dangerous or hazardous materials are adhered to;

v)   ensuring that employees receive sufficient training in safety matters;

vi)   ensuring that employees are well supervised at all times;

vii) providing healthy and safe working conditions;

viii) ensuring that access to and exit from the premises are safe, unblocked and clearly marked;

ix)   ensuring that any visitors to the premises encounter a safe environment.

The environment

Customers are becoming increasingly aware of environmental issues and consequently certain businesses will cite environmental considerations as key objectives. Specific environmental policies which may be adopted include:

◆ the use of environmentally friendly products and processes;

◆ the careful disposal of all waste;

◆ the use of energy-efficient heating systems;

◆ the use of biodegradable packaging materials.

The Environmental Protection Act 1990, and its implications for UK businesses, has been further supported by a number of EU Directives. These attempt to ensure that businesses take full account of their social and environmental responsibilities at all times. These laws, coupled with considerable consumer pressure, have caused businesses to re-evaluate many of the costs of production. There is no doubt that certain products or services have become more expensive as a result of more stringent environmental protection. However, these costs are far outweighed by the positive impacts which both businesses and the country as a whole enjoy.

When considering environmental concerns, a business will attempt to examine the following aspects of its activities:

1 Do any of its activities involve any environmental risk?
2 Do any of its processes involve any environmental risk?
3 Does it use any materials which are environmentally suspect?
4 Do its products have a detrimental impact on the environment?
5 What type of waste does it produce?
6 What level of waste does it produce?
7 Can it implement cost-effective ways of eliminating pollution?
8 If it establishes environmental policies, will this make the organisation more efficient?
9 Is there a real public or consumer demand for environmentally sound products in this area?
10 What environmental protection legislation is in the pipeline?
11 Does it have systems and procedures in place to make sure that it adheres to existing and expected legislation?
12 Can it improve its corporate image by implementing environmental policies?
13 What are the implications to its owners, shareholders, investors and providers of finance if it implements environmental policies?

If an organisation decides to implement a comprehensive environmental policy, then this should form an essential part of the business plan (*see* Fig 4.1). Commonly, an environmental policy will take the form of a statement which will include the following:

i) the business's commitment to make environmental concerns a central part of all planning activities;
ii) an undertaking that a series of processes will be put in place to identify possible environmental threats;
iii) an assurance that the policy is fully endorsed by both senior management and the board of directors;
iv) a commitment that these policies will be communicated to all employees;
v) a commitment to seek assistance and guidance from external agencies as a matter of priority when required.

One of the problems relating to environmental protection is the constant development of new production processes which are not covered under existing environmental protection legislation. Initially, governments and authorities rely on the social responsibility of organisations to carry out their activities in the spirit of

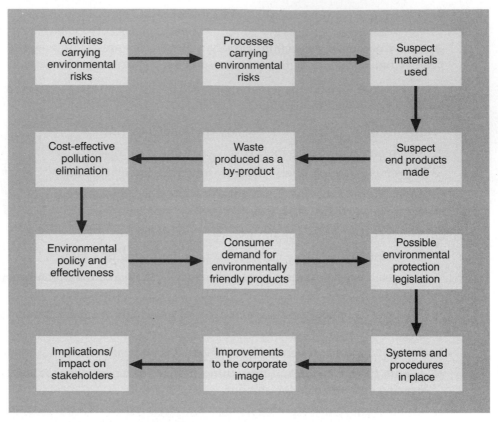

Fig 4.1 Environmental impact factors and business decisions

environmental protection and existing legislation. It is inevitable that the development of legislation lags behind the development of industrial processes.

Products

There are some key considerations and obligations in relation to the products which a business supplies. Essentially, the legislation states the following:

◆ a product must comply with its description;

◆ a product must be capable of performing to the levels claimed by the manufacturer;

◆ faulty products should be replaced or a refund made to the customer without exception;

◆ products should meet all existing safety standards;

◆ an organisation faces prosecution if it is found to be selling unsafe products.

 # Insurance

Insurance is often seen as an incredibly boring issue, but unfortunately it is not a subject that can be avoided by the business. Sorting out insurance should be one of the high priority jobs for anyone starting a new business. If they fail to obtain the correct insurance this could lead to failure of the business itself.

Insurance falls into two main categories:

◆ insurance required by law;

◆ insurance which is desirable to cover possible risks or accidents.

Obtaining insurance at the right price and covering the right risks can be tricky. The Association of British Insurers, the British Insurance and Investment Brokers Association and the Life Assurance Association can all offer the business useful advice in obtaining the right insurance at the right price.

Asset insurance

Asset insurance attempts to ensure that the business is protected against loss or damage to stock, equipment or processes as a result of various uncontrollable factors. Essentially, there are four different types of asset insurance.

Damage and loss insurance

This covers the premises and contents of the premises from fire. The term 'fire' used in insurance in fact covers floods, lightning, explosions, earthquakes, storms, riots and vandalism.

Theft insurance

This covers the theft of all removable assets, including computers, machinery, office equipment, money and stock. An organisation must ensure that its insurance provides cover for loss both on and off the premises. Additionally, it must be careful to ensure that the insured value is for the replacement value of items and not the current value. This is known as 'new for old'.

Interruption of business activity insurance

This may automatically come into operation if the business has suffered damage as a result of a disaster under the fire cover. This insurance also covers the business against loss of business while the premises or vital equipment are being replaced or repaired. The cover will also ensure that the business is protected against an interruption in production as a result of loss of the power supply.

All-risks insurance

Under this type of insurance the business is covered for damage, loss or destruction of items anywhere within the UK. This insurance will compensate the business at full replacement value.

Liability insurance

A business must make sure that it is fully covered against injury to a member of the public as a direct or indirect result of any occurrence or event related to the business. This insurance also covers loss or damage to the customer's property.

Related to this is the need for the business to obtain employers' liability insurance. It is the responsibility of the employer to compensate an employee who is injured or becomes ill as a result of working for the business. This is particularly true in cases when the business has been judged as being negligent. This cover should amount to at least £2 million. The certificate of insurance should be displayed in the business premises and be accessible to all employees.

As an extension of public liability insurance, a business needs to insure against claims arising from the use of its products or services. If a customer has suffered injury, loss or damage as a result of faulty products or services, the business will be able to refer this claim to its product liability insurance. This insurance also covers any legal costs that may be incurred against claims that are made under consumer protection legislation. Recent damages in courts have been as high as £1 million. It is, therefore, absolutely essential that the organisation protects itself against this potentially crippling burden.

Business plans

Business plans, particularly in the case of small businesses, cover all of the aspects of that business (*see* Fig 4.2). They aim to establish operating objectives that can be measured in a meaningful way. For new businesses in particular, a business plan is essential as it is the means by which they attempt to attract finance.

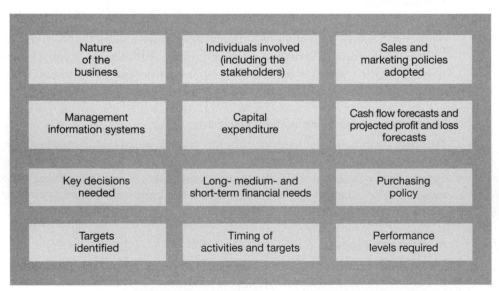

Fig 4.2 Key elements of a business plan

As we will see in the final section of this chapter, the business plan can be 'all things to all people', but in essence the key purposes of the business plan may be some, or all, of the following:

i) establishing the nature of the business;

ii) identifying the individuals involved in the business;

iii) identifying the marketing policy;

iv) identifying the sales policy and approach;

v) setting out cash-flow forecasts;

vi) presenting projected profit and loss forecasts;

vii) detailing any proposed capital expenditure;

viii) outlining the purchasing policy;

ix) detailing long-, medium- and short-term financial needs;

x) establishing management information systems;

xi) pinpointing the key decisions that will have to be made;

xii) establishing targets in terms of timing and performance.

The business plan will seek to identify the organisation's financial situation. The specific financial items that will be covered are:

a) the financial resources that are currently available;

b) the financial resources needed;

c) the cost of production;

d) the prices of products and services;

e) the organisation's ability to repay loans.

Having covered these elements, the organisation should be able to identify what finances will be required to ensure that it runs in an efficient and productive manner.

In seeking to obtain additional finance, perhaps to expand or diversify into a new area of activity, an existing organisation has to operate from existing sets of information, particularly forecasts and financial statements, as opposed to the projected profit and loss accounts and balance sheets which would be used in the case of a new business.

A bank manager or other individual who is asked to provide the business with finance will obviously want to know the true state of the proposed business. Some businesses adopt the strategy of creating two plans. These, in essence, are:

1 *an outsider's plan* – which is fairly conservative with regard to projected sales and costs. It will stress the unlikelihood of the business failing and will be used primarily to raise finance. The figures included in this form of plan should be more realistic than optimistic since any experienced financial provider will be able to interpret the figures easily. The figures must be achievable and not misleading. After all, if you mislead the lenders you will end up misleading yourself.

2   *the internal plan* – this plan is for the personal use of the owner(s) of the business. In this plan higher targets will be set, but they must still be within the realms of probability. The figures should not be too low as they will fail to encourage the owner to strive for higher levels of achievement.

 ## Acquiring finance

Once the business plan has been completed and any necessary cash-flow and profit forecasts have been made, the next step is to acquire the finance. It should be remembered that banks are not necessarily the first port of call. One should think about the amount of finance required before making any moves.

Even if the projected financial requirements have been worked out as carefully as possible, things may not go as well as planned. If the need arises to go back to a lender after only a short period and ask for additional financial assistance, this may not instil confidence in the person or the business.

On the other side of the coin, the borrower should not ask for finance greatly in excess of what they feel is actually needed. To take on the burden of additional loan repayments when the initial loan is sitting in the bank idle is to cause unnecessary pressure on the business in the crucial early period.

It is advisable to be pessimistic, but at the same time to be positive and sensible in all financial requirements. Surprisingly, it is easier to find larger sums of money than smaller amounts. Lenders are not particularly interested in advancing many small sums when they could more easily monitor larger sums loaned to fewer borrowers. Equally, there are more investors willing to risk their money on businesses which have some form of track record than there are prepared to back new businesses which have yet to prove themselves. One of the preconditions for obtaining a loan, regardless of the age of the business, is that the management is sound and that the market is buoyant.

If you are starting up a new business you will need money for the following:

◆ *one-off expenses* – which include spending on premises, equipment, furniture, professional and legal advice and marketing;

◆ *working capital* – which is necessary to bridge the gap between the payment for raw materials or stock and the point at which your customers pay you.

There are a wide variety of different sources of finance, for example bank loans, owners' funds and the shareholders, which, not surprisingly, set a range of different criteria and conditions that the business must meet before they will agree to give financial support.

The profit motive

Making a profit is, perhaps, the most obvious of all business objectives, and yet, not all organisations will consider this to be the most important consideration. Perhaps simply surviving in a highly competitive world is just as important.

Making a profit has obvious benefits for the owners of the business: the more apparent ones are being successful in their chosen career and obtaining wealth. The employees of the business will benefit too, as they will probably receive better pay and conditions of employment. If the need to make a profit is too powerful and things get out of control, however, this can have detrimental effects on the business and how it is run. The business may cut corners and risk breaching legislative guidelines, particularly those relating to employees or the environment.

Being profitable, as you will no doubt be aware, brings additional benefits for the running of the business. These include:

i)   economies of scale – being able to buy materials more cheaply and producing units at a lower unit cost;

ii) being able to buy environmentally friendly materials;

iii) being able to use environmentally friendly production processes;

iv) being able to obtain the best staff for the job.

The profit forecast should show the level of profit that the business is confident of producing over a set period. There are three ways of increasing profits or, at least, maintaining them at an acceptable level:

i)   cutting costs

ii) increasing prices

iii) selling more.

Some organisations do not consider that the maximisation of profits is an essential measure of success. The importance of the profit motive very much depends on the stage that the business has reached. In the early stages of a business's life it is unreasonable to assume that profit maximisation is a key consideration. Bearing this in mind, it is wise for a business to state on its business plan that profits will be modest, particularly in the first few years. If it claims that profits will be exceptionally high, this will inevitably lead providers of finance to question not only the judgement of the business managers, but also their figurework.

Break-even point

Breaking even means covering costs. For most businesses this is the key factor which will signal their survival or failure. Any organisation considering making a loan to a business will at least insist that in the medium term it must break even. Profits may, of course, take a little longer to happen.

The target to aim for is ensuring that the business stays afloat. This is known as the break-even point, where sales are large enough to cover the overheads of the business. Breaking even may seem fairly straightforward, but as a business attempts to reach the level of sales required to reach the break-even point, it will have to overcome many financial pitfalls.

Using a break-even chart often gives a false impression in relation to the setting of a particular sales target. The break-even point has the unfortunate habit of moving without telling you! As sales increase, unforeseen expenses may be incurred. However, the longer the business remains afloat, the more chance it has of exceeding the break-even point and moving into profit.

It is essential that when calculating the break-even point an organisation considers the following:

◆ projection of sales income

◆ cost of sales

◆ gross profit

◆ net profit.

Further information on calculating break even is given later in this book.

We have mentioned the problems, but what about the solution to achieving the break-even point? The first thing to realise is that a business cannot hope to break even at all times. It may be necessary, at least temporarily, to obtain additional finance to see the business over a sticky patch. If the business is unable to obtain more funds, then certain steps may have to be taken to control expenditure:

◆ controlling debtors

◆ negotiating with creditors

◆ reducing stock levels.

Operating at a loss

There are certain circumstances in which organisations may operate at a loss. They may receive funds from other sources to ensure their survival. The government, for example, subsidises organisations which operate in designated redevelopment or assistance areas. It also offers assistance to organisations developing new technological equipment.

A business which is part of a larger organisation, such as a conglomerate or multinational, may receive subsidies while developing a particular market or product. The parent company in effect subsidises the running of the business during the expensive start-up period.

Returning to the role of government, we can identify many hundreds of organisations which do not operate on a profitable or break-even basis. Working on a fixed budget, they are expected to provide a service on behalf of the government. Typically, QUANGOs, other government bodies and, to some extent, local authorities operate on a subsidy basis. Local authorities, in particular, have their own means of raising income in the form of rents, rates and other charges. However, a large proportion of their financial commitments are provided by the government in the form of a grant or subsidy.

The EU also subsidises many different forms of organisations. The Common Agricultural Policy (CAP) provides subsidies designed to support farmers and agricultural businesses, particularly in parts of the EU where traditional forms of production are unable to compete with the more technologically advanced equipment and machinery used by the wealthier members of the EU.

 ## Assessing the market

In order to assess your own sales accurately, it is necessary to try to make some kind of judgement about your share of the market. In other words, you will need to have information about your competitors' businesses and their products. This will enable you to position your product and set pricing levels. Many small businesses operate in a market where there are many suppliers and no one individual business has more than about 5 per cent of market share.

Measuring a business's market share is relatively easy. Attempting to wrest market share from competitors may be much more difficult. Ensuring that the business has a good reputation and has consistent quality throughout its operations and activities can help in obtaining a higher market share.

In order for a business to assess its competitors (*see* Fig 4.3), the following should be considered:

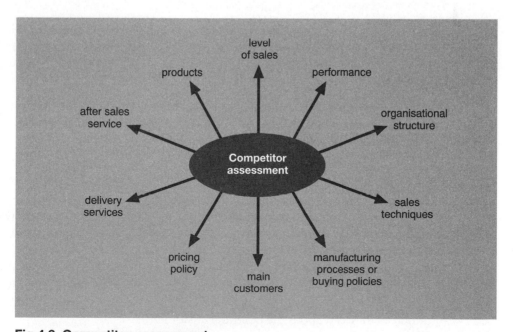

Fig 4.3 Competitor assessment

1 What are the competitive products?

2 How many do they sell?

3 How have they performed in the past few years?

4 What is the organisational structure of competitors?

5 What are their sales techniques?

6 Do they manufacture the products?

7 How do they manufacture the products?

8 Who are their main customers?

9 What is their pricing policy?

10 What is their delivery service like?

11 How good is their after-sales service?

For a business to be in a dominant position in any market it is necessary for it to have a 25 per cent market share. An organisation in this position is said to have a monopoly. Monopolies are unusual, and it is far more likely that you will find several businesses sharing or dominating a market. This is known as an oligopoly.

The market size is the key factor in determining potential demand. You can measure the potential demand for the product in strictly monetary terms or by the number of units that can be sold. It is important to try to estimate the market potential which is, of course, somewhat different from the market size. Potential refers to the probable growth or contraction of the market. If the business has obtained an overall figure for the market itself, then it needs to concentrate on a particular market segment that it is feasible for it to supply.

Market research

When trying to acquire new customers it is probably a good idea to start out by doing some market research. A business could use any of the following methods to establish the size of the potential customer base:

a) Using a 'raw' list of names to act as a blanket mailing list. This method has its disadvantages, since the mailing list will probably be too long to allow follow-up and direct sales techniques.

b) Following leads from a list of individuals who have approached the business either as a result of mailing or advertisements. These individuals may have asked for additional information or sales literature.

c) Making use of referrals by existing customers. This is particularly valuable, as satisfied customers are probably the business's best advertising and public relations asset.

d) Establishing the name of the decision maker within an organisation that is a potential customer and making sure that this person is the one that receives information about the business. In addition, the business should find out as much as they can about the potential customer.

Whatever method a business uses, it is important that it does the following:

◆ keeps records about all potential customers;

◆ devises a follow-up strategy;

◆ ensures that any potential customers receive regular information updates.

Trying to establish the exact size and nature of the potential customer base is very difficult. Without having established this, however, it is almost impossible to make any kind of meaningful financial forecasts.

Knowing which market the product or service is being aimed at will help the business in obtaining statistics and other numerical data. The first step in collating these statistics and data is to identify the target group itself by finding out the following:

1 Is the target market a consumer one or an individual or professional one?

2 Does age, sex, family size or marital status form the basis of the target group?

3 Does the product or service rely on the local area alone?

4 Is social class important?

5 Is frequency of purchasing behaviour important?

6 Is the target market characterised by such factors as the wish to appear fashionable or to set trends?

7 Is the target market influenced by the price of the product or service?

8 Where does the target market currently purchase its products or services?

9 How big are the businesses who might be your industrial or professional customers?

10 Does the target market require fast and frequent deliveries?

11 Does the target market require a high level of after-sales service?

For a business to understand its customer base and to attempt to allocate some numerical value in terms of either numbers or income from that group, it must acquire the above data. One way is to use suppliers, asking them to provide an analysis of potential customers and to investigate the nature of the products and services they desire.

 ## Customer relationships

Even when a customer places an order with an organisation, this should not be seen as the end of the transaction. Any business worthy of the name should aim to build up a long-term relationship with its customers. Just hoping that repeat business will happen does not mean that real orders or profits will result. Customers will not return to a business if it does not ensure that they are kept happy throughout the entire sales process and beyond. Simple steps can be taken to ensure that a customer remains loyal to a business:

i) Stay in constant contact with the customers.

ii) Inform customers about special offers and deals.

iii) Make sure that deliveries are made on time.

iv) Inform customers if the products are likely to arrive late.

v) Give prompt attention to complaints and other criticisms.

Many organisations rely on a handful of large customers, a situation in which there is perhaps a tendency for the organisation to have its eggs in too few baskets. It is therefore essential not only that these important customers remain loyal, but that steps are taken to ensure that there is an ongoing process for acquiring new customers.

Having a good working relationship with existing customers can mean that they will recommend the business to new customers. They may also be willing to give vital early sales leads if one of their colleagues or associates is considering purchasing a particular product or service. In other words, they act as a referee for the business. Because of this, it is vital that good records are maintained about existing customers so that the business can give them the impression at all times that they are valued and important.

Turnover

Turnover may be a specific objective of the business. The organisation needs to set a particular level of sales in terms of units sold that will enable it to establish a basic level of business activity. The ideal situation is to have in operation a production process that requires equipment or machinery to be running at full capacity. Perhaps the organisation can achieve the volume of sales required by supplying other businesses with part-finished goods. In this way, the supporting organisation helps to ensure that volume of sales and production levels are maintained at all times.

Setting the likely volume of sales is a procedure that needs to be addressed with considerable caution. When a business states initial volume levels in its business plan, the potential provider of finance is likely to expect it to give assurance that such levels are possible. Again, as with many other things, caution may be the best approach. In this respect, it is probably better to set the volume of sales at a slightly lower level than actually expected. This will have a twofold impact. First, it will appear to the provider of finance that the business is actually doing better than was expected. Second, the difference between the projected and actual volume of sales may serve as a motivating factor for both the business and employees.

As an alternative to achieving sales *volume*, we can consider sales *value*. This means than an organisation is concerned with the total revenue accrued from its sales. This objective is relevant to both low unit value and high unit value products. Such value will be particularly important to organisations which have high capital expenditure and, as a result, require high revenue in order to service existing loans.

The maintenance of high sales value, or turnover, is essential to ensure that the business maintains its competitive edge, as any reduction in turnover may result in a loss of working capital. In some cases, even though these are extreme, an organisation could lose its liquidity and will have to reduce its costs elsewhere. This might mean a reduction in its workforce.

Another way of achieving high sales value is to increase the profit margin per unit. This is a tricky technique, since it may mean that the business's products or services lose their competitive edge in terms of price. Again, setting a likely turnover should be approached with considerable caution as it may be a deciding factor in whether potential investors agree to continue their relationship with the business at the end of the loan period.

Resources

Human resources

Central issues in the business plan are the co-ordination and organisation of the resources that are currently available or those that are required. Planning human resources involves considering not only the skills of the owners or managers, but the skills of others. These others may include individuals directly employed by the business, or specialists who are 'bought in' for specific projects or advice. Specifically, we should consider the following:

◆ the nature and availability of experienced management;

◆ the nature and experience of employees;

◆ the employee support systems that will be required.

In order to maximise the effectiveness of a business in the early stage of its development, it is essential to deploy human resources well. The short-term considerations include the skills required in the following areas:

a) management

b) administration

c) marketing

d) selling

e) accounts

f) production

g) research and development.

It does not necessarily follow that all of these specialists must be supplied by directly employed staff. An organisation may choose to buy in assistance in some of these areas. These could include the following:

i) directors who assist only by providing finance;

ii) self-employed individuals contracted to carry out specialist functions;

iii) individuals employed via employment agencies on a temporary basis;

iv) younger or inexperienced employees employed with the intention of training and developing them in specific roles.

In long-term planning of human resources an organisation will have to consider the following:

◆ maintenance and improvement of output;

◆ maintenance and expansion of productivity;

◆ maximisation of profit;

◆ ensuring job satisfaction;

◆ maximising the relationship between labour costs and productivity.

Relating these human resource needs to the business plan should include the following:

i) assessing the precise staff requirements of the organisation;

ii) ensuring the availability and implementation of staff training programmes;

iii) maintaining good industrial relations;

iv) providing staff welfare facilities;

v) providing competitive wage levels;

vi) establishing mutually acceptable conditions of employment;

vii) adhering to health and safety, employment law and other legal requirements relating to employees.

Physical resources

Planning physical resources will involve consideration of the following requirements:

◆ premises

◆ machinery and equipment

◆ stock

◆ materials (raw, part-finished and finished).

The first major consideration in terms of physical resources is the premises. There are a number of legal implications which relate to the nature and use of the premises.

Planning

All premises have a usage designation which is monitored by the local authority. Particular buildings will be considered unsuitable for certain business activities. It should also be remembered that a business operating from home may render the premises liable for payment of business rates.

Licences

To trade legally certain businesses may require a licence. The following types of business will require a trading licence which will be monitored by the local authority:

◆ restaurants, cafés and bars;

◆ food processing and manufacture;

◆ mobile food outlets;

◆ retailers of alcohol;

◆ retailers of tobacco;

◆ nursing homes;

◆ children's nurseries;

◆ scrap-metal dealers.

Leases, covenants and restrictions

The lease on business premises may restrict the business activities allowed. It is also worth considering the length of lease and the possibility of renewing it, before investing considerable sums of money on improvement of the building. The lease should be available for renewal under agreeable terms and, above all, affordable ones. With regard to covenants and other restrictions, there may be certain by-laws relating to the building. These may not only restrict the type of business activity allowed, but also relate to any potential development of the site.

Environmental matters

The location of the premises and the availability of services capable of handling waste and other emissions may make the premises unsuitable. Environmental legislation, for example, does not allow certain business activities to take place in residential areas.

Fixed assets

The other major physical consideration relates to fixed assets such as machinery, equipment, materials and vehicles. Specifically, an organisation must consider the following:

1 What machinery, equipment and vehicles should be obtained immediately?

2 Should they be bought or leased?

3 Which suppliers offer the most acceptable terms of purchase?

Financial resources

Planning the financial resources involves consideration of the following factors:

◆ capital available from the owners of the business;

◆ sources of finance needed.

The following need to be taken into account:

i) the financial resources required for the purchase and maintenance of fixed assets;

ii) the amount of working capital required;

iii) how fixed assets will be financed;

iv) how working capital will be obtained;

v) who will provide the finance.

Time resources

Planning the time resources involves undertaking the following tasks:

a) accurately charting when all other resources will be required;

b) co-ordinating all other resources;

c) constructing a timeframe within which all other resources will be needed.

Applying a timeframe to all of the various resources required to start the business is essential to ensure that the correct resources are available at the right time. The level and complexity of planning needed can be very difficult for new business-people and they will require the assistance of qualified specialists to enable them to plan the time considerations effectively. Typically, an organisation will use two main techniques for time planning – critical path analysis and Gantt charts. We shall look at these in some detail.

Critical path analysis (CPA)

This method relies on the identification of all of the component actions and the minimum time required for each main project. The analysis takes the form of a series of arrows, against which are marked the activities and the time required to carry out each activity. Each arrow will come from and go to a node (which is, in effect, an event, *see* Fig 4.4). By tracing actions along a series of arrows and events, a business planner is able to identify the maximum time required to carry out particular projects. In addition, activities which take the longest time to complete are identified as critical activities. These will tend to be drawn on the diagram as a thick line. By carefully analysing the completed chart, the planner should be able to identify particular 'bottlenecks' and predict potential future problems.

Gantt charts

An alternative method of illustrating the processes and activities in the planning schedule is to create a Gantt chart. This consists of a number of activities listed against numbered weeks. The activities are cross-referenced against the weeks in which the activity is intended to begin and end. The process is continued down the list of activities, with the later activities, which rely on the completion of earlier activities, beginning in the week after the previous activity has been completed (*see* Fig 4.5). Again, it is necessary to identify critical activities which have major implications for the beginning of other activities.

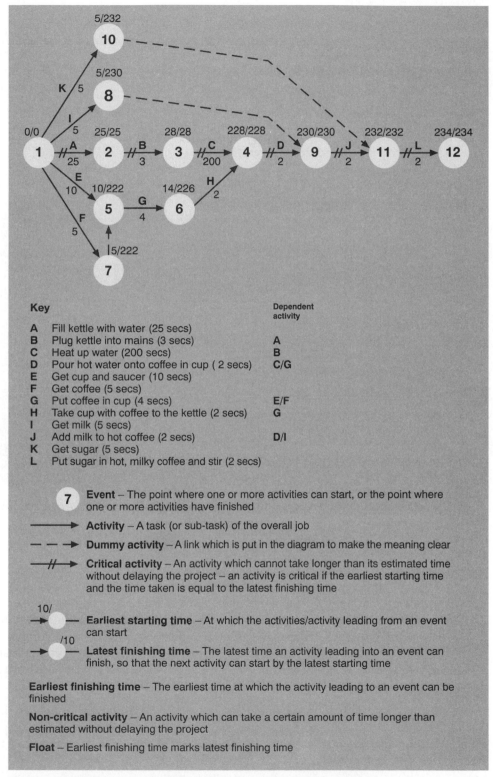

Key

		Dependent activity
A	Fill kettle with water (25 secs)	
B	Plug kettle into mains (3 secs)	A
C	Heat up water (200 secs)	B
D	Pour hot water onto coffee in cup (2 secs)	C/G
E	Get cup and saucer (10 secs)	
F	Get coffee (5 secs)	
G	Put coffee in cup (4 secs)	E/F
H	Take cup with coffee to the kettle (2 secs)	G
I	Get milk (5 secs)	
J	Add milk to hot coffee (2 secs)	D/I
K	Get sugar (5 secs)	
L	Put sugar in hot, milky coffee and stir (2 secs)	

7 **Event** – The point where one or more activities can start, or the point where one or more activities have finished

⟶ **Activity** – A task (or sub-task) of the overall job

– – ⟶ **Dummy activity** – A link which is put in the diagram to make the meaning clear

–//⟶ **Critical activity** – An activity which cannot take longer than its estimated time without delaying the project – an activity is critical if the earliest starting time and the time taken is equal to the latest finishing time

10/ ⟶ **Earliest starting time** – At which the activities/activity leading from an event can start

/10 ⟶ **Latest finishing time** – The latest time an activity leading into an event can finish, so that the next activity can start by the latest starting time

Earliest finishing time – The earliest time at which the activity leading to an event can be finished

Non-critical activity – An activity which can take a certain amount of time longer than estimated without delaying the project

Float – Earliest finishing time marks latest finishing time

Fig 4.4 Making a cup of coffee using the critical path method

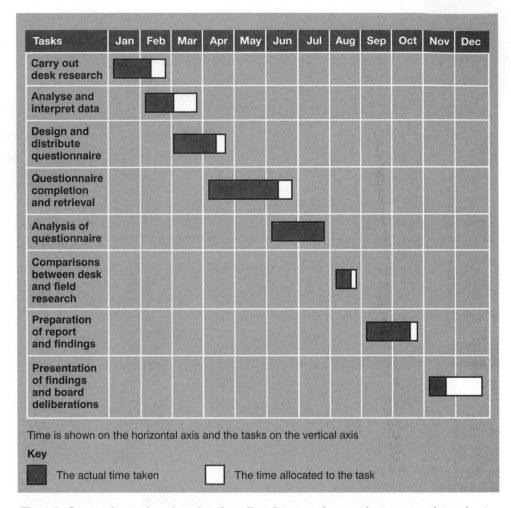

Fig 4.5 Gantt chart showing the time line for a major market research project

◆ External assistance

No business, whatever its size, can realistically expect to be able to form a full business plan by itself. It will inevitably require the assistance of specialists to formulate particular aspects of the plan. In some cases, some of the skills needed may be available within the organisation, but may not yet have been identified. In other cases, different organisations will be able to offer support and assistance with procedural or legal matters. Alternatively, an organisation may require the assistance of specifically qualified individuals to undertake monitoring and development tasks on its behalf.

Some individuals or departments from within the organisation itself will have been identified as being the primary source of assistance for particular aspects of the business plan (*see* Fig 4.6). Specifically, an organisation would expect the following assistance from each key department:

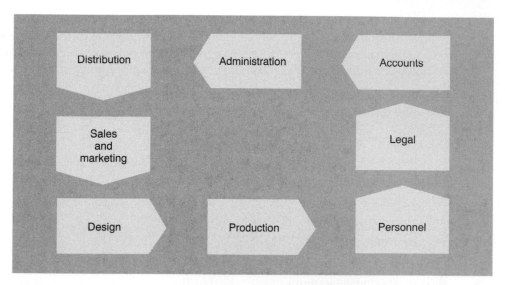

Fig 4.6 Inter-departmental integration and co-operation

◆ *Accounts* – individuals carrying out accounts functions should be able to identify and construct all necessary profit and loss accounts and balance sheets. They should also be able to give a clear indication of the cost implications of the implementation of particular business plans.

◆ *Legal* – the company secretary should be abreast of all current legislation relevant to business activity and should be able to advise the organisation whether new business activities will involve compliance with additional legislation.

◆ *Personnel* – the personnel department or personnel manager should be able to identify any additional human resource requirements of any planned business activities.

◆ *Production* – the production manager will be able to advise about the feasibility of new production requirements. He or she will be able to identify possible suppliers of materials and equipment required to carry out new functions.

◆ *Design* – designers in their research and development role will probably have been consulted at an early stage to assess the viability of new products. They will be able to identify any cost implications in consultation with the production manager.

◆ *Sales and marketing* – the sales and marketing department or managers will have a clear idea of whether potential new business projects will meet the needs and approval of proposed customers. They will be able to offer advice in the formulation of the marketing plan, which as we have seen is an integral part of the overall business plan.

◆ *Distribution* – there may be distribution considerations, particularly if the organisation is proposing to produce and provide new products or services different from those previously offered. The distribution manager may have to consider alternative distribution and transportation methods in order to ensure prompt and safe delivery of the proposed new products.

◆ *Administration* – the administration at various levels of the organisation will be able to provide a key support function in the formulation of the business plan whether simply in the presentation of the business plan, or when there are additional considerations that relate directly to the main administration functions.

Examples of other external organisations or individuals who may be called in to assist the formulation of a business plan include:

i)   financial advisers

ii) insurance specialists

iii) tax consultants

iv) solicitors

v)   architects and surveyors

vi) design specialists

vii) management consultants

viii) marketing consultants

ix) small business advisers

x)   local authority small business initiatives advisers

xi) advisers from specific industries

xii) co-operatives advisers.

These individuals or organisations will be employed only if it is strictly cost effective to do so and if there are positive benefits for the employing organisation. These benefits may relate to the specialist knowledge they possess or to the additional advisory skills they can provide.

It is normal for banks and other providers of financial assistance to be able to advise on the employment of particular specialist organisations or individuals, or, in fact, to have their own advisers available.

Writing the business plan

In writing a business plan, the business should remember that it includes its long-term objectives, estimates and forecasts in a written format. Note that, no matter how detailed the business plan may be, it is not written in stone. Every forecast or estimate made may be subject to change, particularly in the light of the experience the organisation will gain once it is up and running. The estimates and forecasts should be a 'best guess', based on the information the business currently possesses. By writing all this information down managers are better able to clarify in their own minds the nature of the business and to identify many of the potential weaknesses of their ideas.

The initial plan needs to be well thought through and logical. The business must devote sufficient time and resources to organising it. This can be done by preparing an action plan which identifies what the business will have to do in the preparation of the business plan in order to present it to a potential provider of finance or other interested parties.

So what should the actual business plan contain? Essentially, we can identify the main headings for consideration as:

1 A brief summary of the business plan, which highlights:
   - the nature of the business;
   - the potential market;
   - the forecast profit figures;
   - the finance required;
   - the financial returns for investors or lenders.

2 A brief history, which includes:
   - when the business was established;
   - an indication of past performance;
   - an indication of future performance.

3 The management, which includes:
   - the owners' past employment;
   - the owners' qualifications;
   - the owners' business record;
   - the owners' past achievements;
   - details of employees;
   - weaknesses identified and solutions proposed.

4 The product or service, which includes:
   - a non-technical description of the products or services offered;
   - an indication of the unique nature of the product or service offered;
   - a survey of the competition;
   - a description of how products or services will be developed in the future;
   - a statement of patents, trademarks and registered marks applied for.

5 The marketing angle, which includes:
   - the size of the market and its potential for growth;
   - an analysis of the market by sector;
   - an identification of the likely customers;
   - an investigation into the competitors and their likely responses;
   - the promotion and advertising proposed;
   - a description of the salespeople and their sales pitch;
   - the pricing policy.

6 Operational considerations, which include:
  – the location and premises;
  – an identification of potential suppliers;
  – the manufacturing requirements;
  – equipment and machinery required.

7 The financial analysis, which includes:
  – monthly profit and loss forecasts;
  – profit forecasts for at least three years;
  – cash-flow forecasts for at least two years;
  – forecast balance sheet for at least two years;
  – the last three years' audited accounts (if applicable);
  – assumptions made in the preparation of the forecasts;
  – a risk assessment, which could alter the figures.

8 The future prospects, which include:
  – what the short-, medium- and long-term objectives are;
  – finance needed, when and why;
  – prospects for investors or lenders.

Central to the formulation of a business plan is the need to be sure that the plan is workable. We can use this word 'sure' to compare the proposals with a real workable plan. Ask the following questions:

S – is the business **s**oundly based?

U – does the business **u**nderstand what it is actually doing?

R – is the plan **r**ealistic and credible?

E – is the **e**xpertise available?

As you will now realise, a good business plan aims to cover all of the potential opportunities and threats that may face the business. In addition to this, the business plan aims to set out, clearly and logically, the processes by which the necessary implementation of policy will be undertaken. To recap, the main aspects of the complete business plan will address the following:

a) the establishment of a business idea that incorporates an assessment of the viability of that idea;

b) market research in order to determine the level of competition and the expected reaction (and profile) of the potential customer;

c) the review of the existing business location or the identification of a potential site that incorporates a good infrastructure and is close to the raw materials/components/market;

d) the attempt to secure finance in order to pay for the launch of the new business or the launch of a new initiative: this is essential as the business needs to have sufficient liquidity and cash for emergencies;

e) a realistic cash-flow projection so that the organisation and its financiers can monitor whether the financial performance will meet the obligations;

f) the acquisition of sufficient legal or professional advice in order to make sure that the business does not make a mistake or miss an opportunity through lack of understanding;

g) identification of the key personnel who will be involved, which will help the business recognise whether it has a skills shortage;

h) monitoring systems which can handle the operations of the business and alert the managers/owners to potential problems before these get out of hand.

Theoretically, if the business follows these essential considerations, then there is every chance that the business plan will work. Some of the major problems that can be associated with business plans are the following:

1 Some business plans are ill conceived and over-optimistic.

2 Some business plans appear to be well thought through but lack depth and true understanding.

3 Some business plans ignore essential considerations such as the effects of change in government policy or the level of competition.

4 Some business plans appear to be fine in practice, but the business lacks the expertise to ensure that they are put into effect.

5 Some business plans are overcomplex and as a result only the individuals who constructed them understand what is meant by the terms and the objectives.

6 Some business plans are too rigid and have no flexibility to deal with the changing business environment.

7 Some business plans do not have sufficiently detailed back-up or contingency plans attached so that alternative sources of action can be implemented with the minimum disruption to the organisation.

8 Some business plans assume too much and certain conclusions or assumptions are undermined if a different set of circumstances occur.

Essentially, a good business plan does not have to be immensely detailed. It does not have to cover all of the possible eventualities. It must, however, be relevant, workable and, above all, flexible.

Review questions

1 Describe the nature of the three sectors of the economy. Provide examples of each of these.

2 Explain the factors which a potential buyer would be advised to consider before purchasing an existing business.

3 Briefly outline the relationship between a franchise holder and a franchisee.

4 Describe the public opinion and laws that influence an organisation in terms of its external environment.

5 Outline the key considerations which should form the basis of a comprehensive environmental policy.

6 Describe the main types of basic insurance that should be obtained by a business.

7 Why are financial resources such an important consideration in the formulation of a business plan?

8 Outline the main differences between an internal plan and an outsider's plan.

9 Why might it be wise to be pessimistic as well as being positive and sensible in establishing financial forecasts prior to seeking sources of finance?

10 Explain the purpose of the break-even point. How can this be used by an organisation.

11 What are the basic functions of the Common Agricultural Policy?

12 What is an oligopoly? Give at least one example of this.

13 How can turnover be measured?

14 What are the differences between sales value and sales volume?

15 List at least five items which should be included in the long-term planning of an organisation.

16 Describe the purpose of critical path analysis.

17 What is a Gantt chart and how can it be used for planning purposes?

18 List the main operational considerations which should be included in a business plan.

19 What is SURE and how might this help the business planner to make sure that all eventualities and considerations have been covered?

20 Describe four reasons why a business plan might fail.

5

Analysis tools

SWOT analysis

A SWOT analysis provides a summary of the strengths, weaknesses, opportunities and threats of an organisation. This is a critical list drawn out of a strategic audit: the strengths and weaknesses address the internal state of the organisation and the opportunities and threats consider the external environment (principally, the operations of competitors).

Obviously, it would be pointless to list all of the features of an organisation. It is the critical success factors that are important when considering strengths and weaknesses. The strengths and the weaknesses will be relative ones, they are unlikely to be absolute. In this respect, a list of strengths and weaknesses that is too long is considered to be rather unfocused and indiscriminate.

SWOT analysis (*see* Fig 5.1) is undertaken as an integral part of the preparation for planning. If the analysis is thorough, then the recommendations arising out of it will be valuable. At corporate level, the SWOT analysis is useful in building up the framework or whole picture so that meaningful evaluations may be made by managers. As you will have realised, the strengths and weaknesses will be drawn from an internal audit or appraisal, whereas the opportunities and threats derive from an external appraisal.

Internal appraisal

The internal appraisal seeks to identify shortcomings in the organisation's skills and resources, and at the same time to highlight the strength areas that the organisation can exploit. The main point here is that the strengths and weaknesses analysis will help shape the organisation's approach to the external environment. The analysis is carried out both quantitatively and qualitatively, focusing on the strengths and weaknesses that need attention.

The full internal appraisal needs to address the following areas:

1 The past accounts of the organisation, incorporating ratio analysis. This is facilitated by meaningful comparisons with similar organisations in the same type of

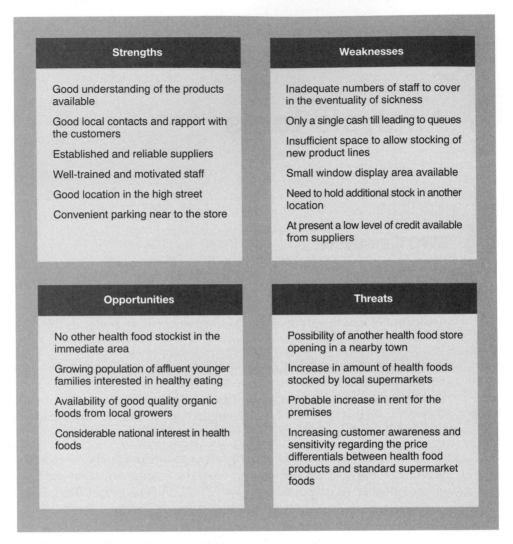

Fig 5.1 SWOT analysis for a health food retail outlet

market. This information will provide much of the hard data that is needed to justify some of the qualitative material.

2 Study of the organisation's products, their position in the market and the organisation's product/market mix.

3 Study of the financial structure of the organisation, which may reveal the need, or surfeit, of money for investment and diversification.

4 Investigation into the cost structure of the organisation to identify fixed costs and variable costs. The organisation will then be able to see whether these are tied to high production in order to cover fixed costs, or whether they are more flexible.

5 Analysis of the managerial ability within the organisation.

Specific areas of the organisation will also need to be investigated, particularly the following:

i) *Marketing* – success rates of new products; success rates of advertising campaigns; an analysis of the market share and market size; study of the portfolio of business units in the different markets; evaluation of the sales force and its performance; the level of quality relating to the servicing of customers and customer care strategies.

ii) *Products and services* – sales by area, market, product groups and outlets; margins and contributions for each product; product quality; product portfolio; price elasticity of demand for products and price sensitivity.

iii) *Distribution* – delivery standards; lead times (against competitors etc.); warehouse and fleet capacity, and geographical availability of products.

iv) *Research and development* – where new products and services will fit into the marketing plan; expenditure on new products and services in relation to available assets; evaluation of new products and services against currently available ones; analysis of schedules in relation to current progress.

v) *Finance* – availability of short-, medium- and long-term cash; analysis of cash flow; investigation into return on capital invested; analysis of ratios to identify strengths and weaknesses of returns and overall financial performance.

vi) *Production* – analysis of capacity, age, value and suitability of existing plant and machinery; valuation of all assets; investigation into the nature, purpose, leases, book value and area of all premises and land; identification of output capacity in relation to economies of scale and minimisation of unit production costs.

vii) *Management and employees* – age profile; skills and attitudes audit; investigation into industrial relations history; employee morale and labour turnover; availability of training; utilisation of manpower; and strengths and weaknesses of the management team.

viii) *Organisational structure* – investigation into how it relates to the functional needs of the organisation; analysis of the viability of profit and cost centres; analysis of management styles and leadership philosophies; evaluation of communication and information systems.

ix) *Stocks and stores of products* – investigation into sources and security of supply; inventory of items stocked; calculation of turnover periods; assessment of storage capacity; identification of depreciation or obsolescence of stocked items; analysis of wastage and pilferage rates.

External appraisal

Following the internal appraisal, the organisation can turn its attention to the external environment. The opportunities and threats could take the following form:

◆ the specific opportunities that present themselves in the environment in which the organisation operates;

◆ a full evaluation of the profit-making potential of the organisation;

◆ the capacity of the organisation to exploit the opportunities as they arise;

◆ the capacity of competitors to exploit similar opportunities;

◆ the organisation's ability to perform (to date) in areas of opportunity;

◆ the threats to the organisation in the environment in which it operates;

◆ the competitors' position in relation to these threats and an analysis of likely actions;

◆ the organisation's capacity to resist potential and actual threats;

◆ the corrective actions that may have to be taken to account for these threats;

◆ the organisation's use of contingency planning and policy.

Obviously, the opportunities and threats will come from a number of different areas. These would include the following:

1 *Economic opportunities and threats* – including unemployment levels, wage and salary levels, growth or decline of major suppliers and competitors, overall demand for products and services, international trade levels and trends, recessions, exchange rate, and level of import controls in markets.

2 *Government-inspired opportunities and threats* – including legislative changes, tax incentives, environmental concerns, investment grants, public expenditure trends, political change at home and abroad and investment prospects in the light of probable government policy.

3 *Technological opportunities and threats* – including the organisation's relative position in the exploitation of technology, new products and services arising out of new technology, cheaper or more efficient production systems and improved distribution, communication and information systems.

4 *Social opportunities and threats* – including changing social attitudes, social issues (such as environmental concerns), the changing role of women, demographic changes, changes in the population structure and unemployment, and consumer spending power.

As can be seen from Fig 5.2, the organisation needs to consider the potential competitors' strategy, especially in export markets. In many countries where import controls have receded, home markets are under considerable threat from overseas organisations that have been operating in more competitive markets and are consequently leaner and more efficient. It is also prudent to consider the fact that the comparative strengths of the suppliers and the customers will have an affect on the organisation. Remember that all organisations operate in the real world and not in a vacuum.

Evaluating strategies

Once the internal and external audits have been brought together, the organisation is now in position to evaluate current and alternative strategies. At this point corrective strategies can be formulated or contingency plans enacted.

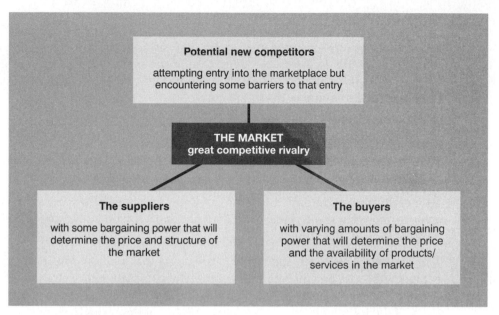

Fig 5.2 The three-ring circus

The information is displayed in the form of a cross, which represents a matrix of the strengths, weaknesses, opportunities and threats (*see* Fig 5.1 on p. 102). It is worth restating the fact that the opportunities and threats are independent of the organisation as they are created by the external environment.

The matrix itself can be used as a guide for the formulation of strategy. In essence, there are two main strategic options:

i)   a *matching* approach that aims to link the strengths of the organisation with the opportunities in the market. In this way, the organisation can assess whether its strengths are useful to them (it can exploit a market opportunity) or whether the opportunities in the market are false hopes (as it does not have the strengths to exploit them).

ii) a *conversion* approach that requires the organisation to come up with viable strategies that could convert its weaknesses into strengths in order to take advantage of the opportunities. At the same time, there is a chance that the organisation can convert some of the threats into opportunities which can be exploited by its strengths (it is worth remembering that a weakness or a threat may be shared by all of the organisations operating in a market, in which case the winner will be the first that is able to adapt).

SWOT analysis is quite useful in suggesting the direction in which the organisation should move, but for more specific strategic help, the organisation needs to consider some more analytical approaches, such as gap analysis, forecasting and trend analyses.

Gap analysis

Individuals who are engaged in strategic analysis need to try to develop strategies that can meet the declared objectives. One of the many ways of doing this is by using gap analysis. Before we explain the nature and the techniques involved, there is a need to examine the following:

◆ Does the organisation have a clear idea of the achievements it wishes to make over a specified period of time?

◆ Does the organisation have a clear idea of the achievements that it would expect if it did nothing new?

Essentially, that is the gap: the difference between what the organisation hopes to achieve and what it will achieve if it does nothing. Obviously, the key is to close the gap as much as possible.

The difference between the target profits and the forecast profits needs to be bridged. This can be achieved with a variety of complementary strategies that aim to make their own contribution to filling the gap. Typically, these would include some of the following:

a) *market penetration strategies* (to force a way into a market and take a larger share);

b) *market development strategies* (to seek out and exploit new markets);

c) *product development strategies* (to identify and develop new products and versions of existing products that can be sold into new and old markets);

d) *diversification strategies* (that enable the organisation to target potential markets and exploit them with existing or new products).

This technique can be modified to suit any particular gap or set of circumstances. In other words, once some estimates have been made on how the gap can be filled, the organisation can set about instituting the necessary policies to achieve this aim. Broadly speaking, as can be seen in Fig 5.3, gap analysis fits into the overall strategic planning process after the main analytical tasks have been undertaken, but prior to the formulation of the long-term plan.

It is fairly clear that the success or failure of both SWOT and gap analysis will be determined by their applicability to the organisation. At the very least, the organisation must be able to recognise some of the successes and failures that are highlighted by these analyses. At the end of the day, any analysis is only useful if it brings about positive action; without action these techniques are simply another time-consuming exercise that diverts attention away from the day-to-day business of the organisation.

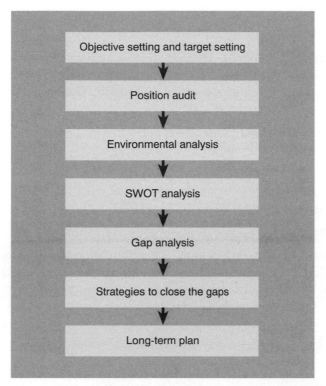

Fig 5.3 The strategic planning process

 Funds-flow analysis

To be feasible a plan should not encounter any insurmountable problems or resistance. In addition to this, the plan has to have a degree of support from both within and outside the organisation. There is also, of course, the matter of the plan being financially viable, with the probability of it making some reasonable performance in terms of returns to the organisation.

Many plans fail on account of the availability or the quality of resources; others may fail as a result of the lack of appropriate supporting technology. Bad timing can be another significant concern and will either hamper the plan or bring about its abrupt end. For those plans made in isolation from the external environment in which the organisation operates, the ever-present threat of competitor activity and comparative strength may mean that the plan becomes inappropriate, is cut short or proves to be a disastrous move in retrospect.

As we have already mentioned, the availability of suitable resources is the key to ensuring that the plan has a chance of success. There has to be the finance available, not just at the inception of the plan, but throughout its life. It will demand continued and consistent support. Even in situations when the planning, as part of an overall strategy, appears to be making good financial returns for the organisation, there is the danger that other events may cause there to be a shortfall in the available funds to continue the financial support of the plan. In these cases, no matter how well the plan is performing, it will fail.

In relation to the availability of finance, it is therefore essential that the organisation carries out a funds-flow analysis to ascertain whether there is likely to be a situation in the future that will put the funding of the plan in jeopardy. This would entail the following:

1 Identification of the timing of the capital expenditures and other costs for the plan.
2 Identification of the size of the capital expenditures and other costs related to the plan.
3 Identification of the timing of the revenues generated.
4 Identification of the size of the revenues that will be generated.

These calculations cannot be made in isolation. The organisation needs to extend its funds-flow analysis to incorporate all other expenditure and revenue related to other operations and strategies that are in existence during the period that the plan is in effect. If this funds-flow analysis is accurate, then the organisation will be able to identify potential funds-flow problems that may occur in the future and take steps to counteract them.

 # Planning cycles

It makes sense to draw up a timetable or control schedule which outlines the tasks, responsibilities and targets which will ensure that the desired progress of the business is maintained. Doing this will also help the business to identify potential bottlenecks and to decide on completion dates, which can often be a great source of motivation.

Forecasts

Forecasts, budgets and projections for the business plan can, of course, be in any kind of format. During the planning exercise, the plan should be tailored to the needs of the individuals running the business. It is crucial that, having settled on the forecasts and timetable, a systematic method is identified which ensures success. The organisation will already have a set of objectives. These can form the basis of the planning exercise. In this respect, it is logical that the development of the plan, and any calculations which may be needed to create this plan, relate to the fulfilment of the objectives.

Each business will have a different approach to the timescale of the plan. Some individuals consider a five-year forecast to provide a foundation for continuity. However, looking too far into the future can lead to a series of meaningless calculations that will prove to be unworkable and useless in the future. Practically speaking, a one-year detailed plan, together with indications of the proposed plan for the next two years, will give any new business the necessary clarity of direction and purpose.

A forward plan, in essence, only gives an indication of the development of the business and, at best, this should only be an outline and not written in stone.

The overall plan is made up of a number of segments which may include the following:

◆ production schedules

◆ marketing and selling forecasts

◆ distribution implications

◆ financial information which refers to the successful reaching of a break-even position.

The combination of all of these considerations produces the overall forecast and gives vital information about the resource requirements of the business. It is very important that all of these considerations are discussed, as the plan needs to be developed from a variety of different directions. Likely sales levels, for example, provide the business with information on the probable volume of customers as well as that relating to projected sales and various production requirements.

Sales forecasts

The setting of preliminary sales targets will give the business some idea of its production and supply needs. Matching production with sales can be a little difficult, but it is essential that a new business tries to calculate its production needs accurately. Being able to fulfil orders on time may mean the difference between success and failure.

In a similar way, if the business builds up too high a stock level at too early a stage in its life, this can be both damaging and expensive. The main purpose behind setting these preliminary sales targets is to try to determine the quantity of products which have to be either produced or assembled in a set period. It also gives the business information about the quantity of raw materials or components that it will have to buy in order to fulfil these needs.

For many businesses the sales forecast is the most important aspect of their business plan. There are a number of forecasting models which may be adopted and which would prove to be of great value in the development of forward plans. The business needs to consider, in addition to its detailed analysis of the first year, the probable sales levels in future years. In other words, it needs to establish what it plans to do in at least the first three years. This is essential, as its activities in the first year will determine its activities and success in future years. New businesses, which do not have the benefit of being able to analyse their present customers, must attempt to make a detailed forecast which links sales to major customers with the following:

i) probable pricing levels

ii) discounts offered

iii) credit to be provided

iv) products which will sell to each target segment of the market.

In attempting to estimate the benefits and cost of each proposed sales and marketing action, a business can begin by considering the resource allocations in both the short- and the long-term. A similar model to that used for the calculation of production costs and their implications can be used for this purpose.

Distribution policy

The distribution policy of the business is very much related to its production, marketing and selling activities. The choice of distribution method may, of course, depend on the type of product or service, but, inevitably, there may be a wide variety of different distribution methods available. These need to be assessed in terms of their effectiveness and appropriateness. The business needs to have a clear understanding of what it requires from its distribution network. Perhaps more fundamentally, it needs to consider whether its distribution will be carried out as an internal function or provided by an external organisation. Specific requirements may include the following:

◆ speed of distribution
◆ efficiency of distribution
◆ safety of products during distribution.

Many organisations rely on specialist distribution companies to ensure that their products reach customers in a fast and reliable manner. Some of the benefits which may accrue from using an external organisation far outweigh possible savings which the organisation might enjoy by providing the service itself. These specialist distribution networks offer not only a higher degree of flexibility and responsiveness, but often a more reliable form of security, (particularly in terms of insurance etc.) than any small business could hope to provide.

Review questions

1 What is SWOT analysis?

2 State some of the sources of information used in SWOT analysis.

3 What is internal appraisal and what sort of information could be gleaned from such an exercise?

4 State some of the aspects of marketing which should be addressed in a SWOT analysis.

5 How might an investigation into the organisational structure be a useful part of the SWOT analysis?

6 Explain at least three economic opportunities and threats which could face a manufacturing organisation.

7 How might the existing operators in a marketplace seek to bar entry to newcomers?

8 What is 'conversion' in the SWOT analysis context?

9 What is Gap analysis?

10 How might an organisation go about attempting to bridge the gap between projected sales and actual sales?

11 Outline at least three different reasons for the failure of a long-term plan.

12 What is fund-flow analysis and why is this important?

13 What is a planning cycle?

14 Why is it very difficult for an organisation to match production levels with the actual level of demand?

15 Describe how a break-even graph is constructed and detail the sources of data which must be included.

Part 2

DECISION MAKING

This section aims to enable students to:

◆ examine and explain the process of decision making by individuals in organisations;

◆ identify and evaluate organisational factors which affect decision making;

◆ select and use decision-making techniques.

The decision-making process

When a manager chooses to use the available resources in a particular manner, a decision has been made. Deploying materials, manpower, finances and machinery is a constant task for managers, as are reflection and appraisal. Having a series of choices, where alternatives have to be weighed up, is the precondition of decision making. If the manager does not have a choice of alternatives, then this is not a choice at all and, therefore, not a decision.

There are many cases when many of the possible choices are not in fact feasible. This is also true of situations when the manager has a series of choices, but experience and past decisions lead to a particular course of action. Real decision making has to have a sense of uncertainty about it: the manager does not really know exactly what to do in a particular set of circumstances. In other words, there is a degree of risk involved, and the manager could be making the wrong decision.

There are a number of preconditions that we have alluded to already, many of which are recurrent themes that will form the basis of the decision-making process. These themes or fundamentals are:

◆ There is a difference between the desired objectives and outcomes (or performance), and the current status or situation. This means that the organisation has identified a gap between targets and performance: although the situation may not be serious, there is some cause for concern. The situation needs attention and some sort of decision needs to be made to rectify the problem.

◆ The decision makers within the organisation are aware of the problem. Once it has been brought to the attention of the decision makers, steps can be taken to rationalise the problem and begin to present alternatives and solutions.

◆ The decision makers are able and willing to make a decision to help solve the problem. This infers that the managers in question are motivated enough to take responsibility for the risks that are involved in making or, for that matter, not making a decision. There is always the possibility of a small problem that is ignored or left unsolved becoming a major problem in the future.

◆ The decision makers have the resources available to make an impact and bring about a positive outcome to the problem.

For the majority of managers, these preconditions are subliminal: in other words, they do not recognise them and simply initiate a decision process. Their assessment of the conditions is often so quick that they have internalised the preconditions and have made a rational decision within the confines of their areas of responsibility before they have realised they are doing so.

 # The process of decision making

It may seem obvious to state that no single decision-making technique or model will solve all of the different types of situations and decisions that will have to be made in the course of a manager's day, week or month. We can, however, identify three major types of decision. These will be referred to as 'organisational decisions' throughout the remainder of this part of the book. Although we will be enlarging on them later, they are:

i)   routine decisions

ii) adaptive decisions

iii) innovative decisions.

A *routine* decision would be dealing with a customer's complaint, following the procedures laid down by the organisation, but having to make a particular judgement to suit the circumstances. An *adaptive* decision would include situations of having to reorganise the workforce to cater for extended manning hours, which would involve negotiations and decisions being made on the basis of the needs of the organisation and the wishes of the employees. An *innovative* decision would include having to decide on a particular research and development project among several different and competing possibilities.

In essence, we are now able to identify the nature of the problem and consequently the decision. Routine decisions are often known and well defined by common practice and procedures. Adaptive decisions tend to have a series of alternatives attached to them, increasing the complexity of the problem. Innovative decisions tend to be far more ambiguous, with no preconceived sets of solutions attached to them, making them far more risky and potentially contentious. All of the solutions in the latter case are untried and the decision maker may not know for some considerable time whether the decisions that have been made are the right ones.

Routine decisions

Standard operating procedures and regulations provide a vital base set of conditions for many routine decisions. However, all of these predetermined procedures may throw up a situation that appears to be routine but, in effect, needs an adaptive or innovative touch. All procedures and automatic reactions are subject to change, so organisations need to be adaptive and open to the possibility of having created the wrong type of procedure that does not suit every situation. To this end, 'kneejerk' reactions based on previous practice may not be sufficient to deal with all situations that may occur. By blindly following historical precedents, and not tackling the situation in an adaptive manner, an organisation may also miss an opportunity.

Adaptive decisions

Situations that offer alternatives, particularly in unusual sets of conditions, require the decision maker to approach the problem in a truly adaptive manner. An initial misinterpretation of the situation may have drastic consequences and, as a result, the manager needs to be able to consider a range of alternatives at each stage of the decision-making process. This means that the manager needs to have a degree of insight into the problem and be able to diagnose the potential outcomes of various courses of action. Although the majority of managers need to have this skill, areas that involve technology and advanced production techniques are the most common background requiring this ability.

This adaptive approach is the keystone to notions of continuous improvement, or *kaizen*, which involves gradual improvements prompted by the shopfloor. The Japanese have been given the credit for coming up with this approach, but all organisations strive for it as a matter of course. Each and every organisation will attempt to improve, year on year, the quality of its products and services in terms of production, delivery, distribution and after-sales service, and many other criteria. By making small, but significant, improvements that build on each other over a period, the profitability of the organisation should improve. This means that in an organisational culture that encourages *kaizen*, managers must be able to make adaptive decisions.

Innovative decisions

Once a problem has been identified and diagnosed, it may be categorised as a situation that requires an innovative approach. At the very least, the problem needs to be categorised and defined, which will facilitate the decision maker in framing the response and solution to the problem. In most circumstances, innovative decisions are made against a backdrop of information scarcity. The very nature of the problem that needs such an approach means that the decision maker has never encountered the problem before. To this end, the manager may not be in possession of all of the information needed to make an informed decision. A part of the whole problem may emerge before the rest of it: in other words, the appearance of the problem may not be in a logical order. Or an apparent solution could be seriously undermined by the discovery of a deeper and more important layer of the situation at a later date.

Innovative decision making should be seen as part of an evolutionary process that is affected by a number of different considerations. Obviously, these would include such matters as the relative power of the interest groups within the organisation, the availability of relevant information and the priorities that are placed on the resolution of the various problems.

Decisions can only be made in the light of the information that is available to the manager. This presupposes that the information is sufficient in terms of quantity and quality. The other key consideration is that the decision needs to take into account the fact that there will always be a degree of uncertainty, which is what separates the routine decisions (where there is a high level of certainty) and other forms of decision. Adaptive decisions have a degree of uncertainty about them, while innovative decisions have a far higher level of risk and uncertainty attached to them.

Probability

External forces, or other influences within the organisation that are beyond the control of the decision maker, will obviously have an impact on the risk factors related to decisions. Certainly in larger organisations, a systematic assessment of the external risk factors will be undertaken by particular individuals whose job it is to predict the probable consequences of potential and actual changes in the business environment.

Without doubt, managers would prefer to make decisions based on probability. This may be either subjective (in the sense that this is a hunch on behalf of the decision maker, or a 'best guess') or objective (requiring the ability to stand aside from the decision and weigh up all of the possibilities). In situations where the decision maker has a degree of certainty in what they are proposing, the results of each of the alternatives can be more clearly understood and their outcomes predicted. Obviously, the decision maker will choose the option that has the best possible outcome. The problem is that the higher up the levels of management the decision maker is, the less certain that individual will be regarding the outcomes: line managers (lower down the scale of management) will be in a better position to predict the outcomes and will be faced with a higher level of certainty.

Probability can help if the decision maker is able to calculate the possibility of an outcome actually occurring. Personal judgements and beliefs will largely determine the nature of the subjective probability. This approach is based on character traits, experience, familiarity with similar situations and a host of other individual characteristics. Objective probability rests on the decision maker's ability to predict the likely outcome based on the facts and figures that are available. This is where good documentation and recording of information will pay dividends, allowing the decision maker to recognise and extrapolate the relevant information.

Whether the decision maker uses subjective or objective probabilities, it is virtually impossible to be able to predict the exact outcomes each and every time. Many decisions, even with the availability of data and previous experience, are based purely on intuition.

Decision making within the planning process

The decision-making process is usually triggered by either searching for a better way to achieve the objectives of the organisation, or by the search to find better objectives that more closely accord with the organisation's current direction. Obviously, any manager will be a decision maker at a particular level commensurate with their level of management within the organisation. They will all have to plan, organise, lead and control to some extent. As we have already mentioned, objectives are vital for the organisation and its employees to understand where it is going. The planning process itself will be primarily concerned with the adaptations and innovations that are necessary in identifying and revising the various objectives. The process is also crucial to allow the organisation to find better ways to achieve the objective that it has set itself.

Whether the objectives are targets, goals, standards, deadlines, quotas or ends, they will all have specific results or outcomes attached to them. We can identify two main types of objectives that will have an integral decision-making process:

1 *Operational objectives* – these are quantifiable objectives that state exactly what has to be achieved, by whom, within a specified timescale.

2 *General objectives* – these are broad, directional objectives that are designed to show managers the way in which they should be moving over a period of time.

General objectives could include a number of definite outcomes, which include: improving the quality of the management or the products and services, getting the most out of the investments that the organisation has made, to be financially sound, to be well known for innovation or to be environmentally friendly. Some of these general objectives are so broad and 'woolly' that almost any approach would be acceptable. The interpretation of the objectives will be largely personal to the individual decision maker.

The majority of organisations will have a range of objectives, some of which will be more important than others. At this point we can identify the hierarchy of objectives and how this works in practice:

i)   Most objectives are interlinked, which means that the organisation will have to be moving towards successful completion of the outcomes at various rates of speed and coherence. Some objectives may be stalled by other objectives being less developed and achievable.

ii) By formally linking the objectives, the organisation is often reliant on the lower-level objectives (under the control of junior managers) succeeding in order to ensure that the more general objectives are reached.

iii) In order to ensure that these lower-level objectives are achieved, it is essential that the lower the level, the more detailed the objectives become.

iv) Decisions made at any point in the hierarchy of objectives will directly affect the success or failure of the other objectives (both integral, implied and implicit) at all other levels of the hierarchy.

v) If higher-level managers set objectives that are at variance with the objectives being fulfilled elsewhere in the organisation, there will be a series of damaging conflicts as time and resources are wasted attempting to cater for both differing sets of objectives.

Stakeholder theory

Stakeholder theory overlays another series of complications on the achievement of objectives and the nature of decision making within the organisation. Naturally, the demands of the various stakeholders will differ, imposing conflicting objectives on the decision makers. The more powerful the stakeholder, the greater the influence they will have in shaping the objectives and determining the nature of the decision making. The comparative strength of shareholders, directors, departmental managers and other interested parties will mean that there will be a range of differing views on the achievement of objectives and ultimately how these objectives affect the decision-making process. In some cases, the strength and opinions of certain stakeholders will put particular options out of bounds and the decision makers need to be made aware of this before they can attempt to implement processes to achieve the objectives. In situations where the external stakeholder influence is strong, the choices open to internal decision makers may be limited, since the demands and constraints that the stakeholders place on the organisation may adversely affect the decision makers' ability to achieve the declared objectives. Primarily, these powerful external stakeholders would include institutional investors (such as unit trust managers and major pension investment managers) and the government (through legislative control and policy).

Decision-making models

Various management theorists have attempted to put forward a number of different decision-making models that aim to describe the decision-making process. Before we investigate the nature of decision making at the various levels of the organisation, it is appropriate to look at the three main decision-making models. It is important to realise that models are, in effect, theoretical: they do not refer to specific methods of decision making, but do help us to understand that objectives are the common thread that ties all of the models together.

Rational model

Logical decision making is often referred to as a *rational* model. By this it is meant that the focus is on the achievement of the objectives (the means by which the objective is achieved) and not the objective itself. In other words, there is a defined process by which all objectives are achieved, particularly with reference to the fact that risk is minimised and all stages are closely controlled. As we can see from Fig 6.1, there are clearly defined stages to the decision-making process, some of which are not relevant if the decision maker is involved in making a routine decision. In many respects this model is a standard operating procedure or set of guidelines that are applicable to most decision-making processes. The system is

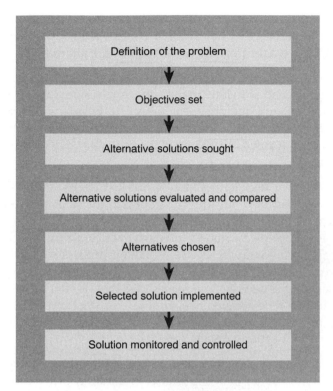

Fig 6.1 The rational decision-making model

also very useful when decision makers are involved in more complex decisions that may be adaptive or innovative.

The first stage of this process presumes that the decision makers are aware of the need to address a particular problem. In addition to this, they also need to be conversant with the causes of the problem and the background behind its occurrence. Part of the definition of the problem also entails identification of not only the external and internal pressures and influences that have brought this problem about, but also those that will have to be considered during the decision-making process. It is also at this stage that decision makers need to recognise problems from occurrences that appear as a result of another problem. In other words, the decision makers need to distinguish symptoms from causes. If decision makers are unable to complete any of these vital diagnostic tasks, then it will be inevitable that they cannot solve the problem correctly or in an efficient manner.

At the second stage, which involves the setting of objectives, the decision makers have already defined the problem and are ready to propose solutions to it. This can be a very difficult task since there will be a number of different alternatives that can be put forward, particularly in cases when there is a high level of uncertainty about the approach needed.

Assuming that the objective has been set, the decision makers now turn their attention to the tricky problem of identifying all of the relevant alternatives to achieve that objective. This may be the longest and most involved process, and often means that the decision makers need to carry out research, consult with other people and engage in creative thinking to come up with a series of viable alternatives.

Comparisons and evaluations of the various alternatives form the next step. Many of these techniques will be dealt with later in the book, but it is important to stress that the focus here should be on quantifiable results. This begins with a rational assessment of the alternatives in an objective manner, often measuring them in purely financial terms, so a detailed calculation of the probable costs of each of the alternatives is essential.

It is important to realise that decision making is not just deciding on the final choice of action. The steps outlined already, in addition to the steps which follow this part of the process, are each of equal importance. There is a great danger in focusing on the chosen alternative solution too early, which will mean that the majority of individuals involved in the decision-making process will only have access to one or, at best, a limited selection of alternative courses of action. This is, without doubt, the stage of the decision-making process that has the greatest level of uncertainty attached to it. The decision makers should expect and welcome the complexities that are inherent in careful selection of the alternatives and not be too swift to rule any of them out without detailed analysis.

As we will see later, when we consider the question of contingency planning, there is a need to have a 'second' choice of action available should it prove difficult to implement the first choice. A solution that appears to be the correct one, on paper and from previous experience, may prove to be too problematic to implement over a period.

Corrective action may have to be undertaken if the selected solution appears not to be working very well. Continuous monitoring and evaluation constitute one way in which the problems that are associated with the chosen course of action can be dealt with at the earliest opportunity. This may mean that the whole situation needs to be re-evaluated and redefined, entailing a restart of the whole decision-making process.

Bounded rationality model

Dealing with adaptive and innovative problems means that a totally different approach has to be considered. Using the *bounded rationality* model, a closer link can be made between the ways in which decisions are made in relation to the different types of individuals that are involved in the decision-making process. This model allows us to look at why certain individuals are more, or less, likely to choose a particular alternative, how far they will go in their search for a range of different alternatives, and how the availability of information regarding the problem and the wishes of the external stakeholders can affect the outcomes.

The choice of a particular alternative may have more to do with what is acceptable to the majority of interested parties than with the ideal solution. Objectives that are linked to this form of approach are often known as *satisficing* objectives: they are challenging and correct, but not too difficult to achieve. Choosing an adequate solution is all too common, and is particularly true of situations that involve a limited investigation into the background information that would be required in order to make a truly objective decision. Bearing in mind that all forms of research and consultation take time and cost a great deal of money, it is inevitable that in certain cases decision makers are bound to try to take short cuts. It is often the case that the search for an acceptable alternative ceases when one has been found: there is no need for the search to continue, incurring more costs and time.

Even when a full investigation into the alternatives has been undertaken, but particularly when the process has been short-circuited, there is a possibility that the information and data have been misunderstood. By making snap decisions, based on acceptable and logical conclusions, the decision makers would hope that they have chosen the correct solution. Whatever the process undertaken, they are faced with the prospect of having, inadvertently, introduced a degree of bias into the process.

It is fairly common to think that certain outcomes are inevitable based on past experience; it is even more common for individuals to think that these outcomes are numerous and inescapable. An individual's preconceived ideas about the probable outcomes of a particular situation are often difficult to work around. Some may actively search for collaborative data to support their own preconceptions, others may interpret the information that is available in a particular way so that it reinforces their preconceptions. In this way, statistical, 'hard' evidence may have less weight than personal experience. It is common for direct, personal views to be considered as more important than abstract facts and figures. This may prove to be doubly problematic if it is coupled with the adoption of information with a limited degree of quality as being representative of the possible outcomes in a given set of circumstances. Alternatively, the decision makers may base their opinions on the principle that 'lightning never strikes the same place twice'. This means they will contend that a poor outcome in the past, based on similar factors, will not occur again. As often as not, it will.

Political model

Returning to the topic of stakeholders, there is another decision-making model that attempts to incorporate the relative power of the various interest groups that may influence the organisation. In this model, known as the *political* model, the various power blocs will try to define the problem in accordance with their own viewpoints on the situation. In addition to this, they will attempt to influence the course of the decision making in order to ensure that their own particular needs and aspirations are furthered. Naturally, this leads to considerable conflict: each of the stakeholding groups will vie for control and outcome of the decision-making process. At the end, the winners will be the ones that have the greater level of relative power. In some cases this conflict is clear cut: one of the stakeholding groups has overwhelming power and can influence the organisation at all levels. In the majority of cases, however, there has to be a degree of compromise, before which a series of debates will ensue in order to establish the relative strength of the various power bases.

Stakeholders tend to take a very black-and-white approach to many of the decisions that are made by an organisation. Shareholders, for example, may take the view that a rise in employees' salaries will mean that their dividends are reduced. This may be a short-sighted viewpoint, as the increased salaries may trigger a higher rate of productivity and performance, leading to higher profits and larger dividends.

The role of stakeholders within the organisation is a difficult one. For example, they may choose to withhold information that could lead the organisation to decide on a course of action that is at variance with their own goals. This means that there will be a distortion of the decision-making process, perhaps leading to the wrong decision being made. As an alternative to withholding information, the data may be offered out of context or in an unfavourable light. These problems are at considerable variance with the more open-minded approach of the rational model.

We will, of course, be looking at more complex decision-making models and techniques later in this book, but we now turn our attention to the decision-making process at the various levels of the organisation.

 ## Decision making at strategic levels

For many larger organisations, decision making and planning at the strategic level are very complex issues. Before we investigate some of the means by which decision making can be undertaken at this level, it is worth looking at the relative complexity of the issue in relation to the diversity of the organisation's operations. Obviously, the more diversification, the more complex the issue. We can identify the key elements in Fig 6.2.

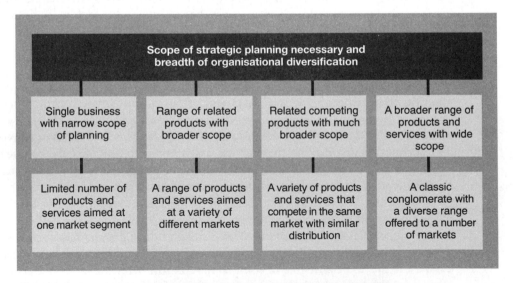

Fig 6.2 Organisational diversification and planning complexity

Diversification

One of the ways in which the larger organisations can handle the complexities of a widely diversified business is to establish a series of strategic business units, (SBUs), subdivisions of the main organisation. The management of the SBU are responsible for all the strategic planning related to their business, but it has to be cleared by the main board or headquarters. It is this part of the strategic planning function that will pass judgement on the SBU, deciding whether to maintain their commitment to the SBU or make adjustments to their investment in some way.

At corporate level, the organisation will attempt to frame and control all of the activities of the business. This is particularly complex if we consider that the higher the level of diversification, the more detailed and fragmented the decision-making process is likely to be. As we will see later, the decision making process at the functional and operational levels is determined by the strategy that is framed at the strategic level. If this level of decision making is confused, contradictory or difficult to implement, then the operational and functional side of the organisation will suffer.

The degree of diversification will depend on a number of factors, which are firmly rooted at corporate level and influence the way in which the organisation operates and reacts to all internal and external opportunities and threats. Essentially, we need to consider the level of integration within the organisation or the way in which the organisation has diversified over a number of years.

Integration refers to the degree to which the company's growth strategy involves either a forwards movement towards the consumer of the product or service, or a backwards movement towards the suppliers. This is also known as *vertical integration*. This policy may be achieved by acquisition or some form of joint venture. As an alternative to this, the organisation may consider *horizontal integration* through the acquisition of a competitor.

As we mentioned earlier, diversification could be considered as one way in which the organisation's strategic objectives may be achieved. *Concentric* diversification or *related* diversification concerns new activities that have a definable link with current operations. This enables the organisation to take full advantage of compatible skills, processes and distribution networks. At corporate level the growth strategy may be more effective if *conglomerate* diversification is considered. This, in effect, means that the acquiring organisation takes over control of an existing venture or starts one from scratch. There may well be no definable similarities between the new operation and the original organisation. This is also sometimes known as *lateral* diversification or integration.

At various stages in this chapter we will be referring to strategic business units, and it is at this level that many of the more tangible effects of strategic decision making will be felt. Once the main board has decided on a particular strategic course of action, decisions will filter down the organisation and superimpose themselves on the operations of the SBUs. This means that an SBU involved in a particular area of activity will be more or less affected by the broad sweep of strategic decision making. The board will be very interested in the effects and contributions that will be made by the SBU to the overall operations of the organisation. It will be able to measure in quantifiable terms the net contributions and costs associated with each SBU. In this way the overall effectiveness and resource allocation can be established at board level, once it is fully conversant with the probable impact on the SBUs. It may appear from the point of view of the SBU that the board is taking strategic decisions without reference to the peculiarities of the SBU's own situation or market. However, a board which is fully in tune with the probable outcomes of each of its strategic decisions will be able to take account of the probable impact and project some kind of meaningful assessment.

As we will see later, at the functional or operational level various guidelines will be established in order to control marketing, human resources, manufacturing, engineering, finance, and research and development. We should consider this as a very similar set of circumstances to that of the SBUs. Each functional area will be expected to make a contribution to the overall objectives of the organisation and establish its own functional-level strategies with detailed plans. In a truly integrated and responsive organisation, regardless of its size and complexity, there should be no real definable difference between the corporate-level strategy and the functional level strategies or the strategies related to SBUs. This is a set of circumstances that can only be achieved if there is considerable communication between the various parts of the organisation, as well as a degree of experience at each level.

Strategic planning

The strategic planning process, as we have seen in the first part of the book, relates to the gradual development of a fully integrated system capable of taking into account all of the strengths and weaknesses of the organisation, as well as the potential opportunities and threats in the marketplace. The development of a mission statement or core objectives can be achieved relatively simply. However, converting these broad statements into definable areas capable of being addressed in a logical manner can prove to be a great difficulty. At some point before the mission statement and core objectives are established, there needs to be an assessment of all of the forces which can contribute towards a threat or an opportunity, both internally and in the external environment. Not only this, the establishment of these statements needs to take into account the political forces and stakeholder objectives within and outside the organisation. To some degree the organisation may have to amend, or completely change, its mission statement in order to incorporate these wishes. In this respect we are really considering SWOT analysis, coupled with the demands of the various stakeholders. To be truly effective, strategic planning and decision making needs to incorporate a careful diagnosis of all these forces. The relative strength of these forces at particular points in time may also be variable. At the very least, the organisation needs to be aware of their comparative strength and make an assessment of their ability to affect the company itself.

Competitors

Within this process the organisation will pay particular attention to any rival organisations operating in the same marketplace. Paramount among the considerations are fluctuations in price, marketing activities, availability or introduction of new products and services, and the relative strength and quality of customer service. Not only this, the organisation needs to consider the number of potential competitors, as well as the relative health of the market itself. In markets which face intense competition, the organisation may be more concerned with the key players in that marketplace rather than the more numerous 'under-studies'. In any event, all organisations should have as much awareness as possible of each other's activities.

There is always the ever-present threat of new competitors entering the marketplace. Even in an apparently stable market, where market shares are firmly established and only fluctuate by a few percentage points each year, there may be room for a new competitor to change the balance of power. If we consider the apparent strength of Coca-Cola in the global soft-drinks market, we can see that in certain geographical areas it has lost considerable market share. In the UK, for example, Virgin Cola and, more importantly, the emergence of quality 'own-brand' colas, have meant that Coca-Cola's market share has been reduced, while it is still the undoubted market leader. New strategies have been developed by the Coca-Cola corporation in order to combat these new competitors and regain its full share of the market.

It is, perhaps, the more traditional organisations which have relied on the perceived quality of their brands and not their price competitiveness that have suffered the most from the emergence of new competitors. Organisations which do not embrace new technology or more modern working practices cannot hope to compete or survive in the long term in the face of new, leaner and more technologically forward competitors. Traditional companies who relied on favourable economies of scale and reduced capital investment have found that they have been usurped in the short term, requiring them to make considerable investments and repositioning of their brands.

Customers

Within the strategic decision-making process, the consumer is often a neglected consideration. With the widespread availability of most products, it is the customer who has a greater degree of bargaining power, and they can play one organisation off against another in order to obtain a better deal. Most organisations would prefer not to get into a price war with their competitors; they would much rather compete on a non-price basis. Major organisations have decided to introduce expensive and extensive customer loyalty programmes which positively discriminate in favour of their regular customers. Customer loyalty cards or similar bonus schemes have, of course, been in operation for a number of years. However, in areas such as fuel and food shopping, competitors have been quick to develop copy-cat schemes rather than resorting to price cutting. Obviously, the more organisations there are competing in a single market, the less strength each one has to manipulate and control that marketplace. As a result, the relative strength of the customer has increased.

Suppliers

Strategic planners would be fool-hardy to ignore the power of suppliers, who have the ability to raise prices and affect the quality of the goods and services provided to the purchasing organisation. Since they are one step away from the consumer, they have far less to fear in terms of adverse reaction to changes. However, as we have seen, integration and diversification can put paid to this apparent problem. Where there are a small number of suppliers selling to a large number of buyers, each supplier's relative strength will be high. The suppliers will know that it is difficult for the purchasing organisation to obtain supplies elsewhere and can manipulate the supply itself. Where there are a large number of suppliers, their relative strength in relation to the purchaser is weak. This is also a very good reason for the introduction of customer loyalty schemes in crowded marketplaces.

Assessing strengths and weaknesses

We have identified the process by which the organisation can assess its internal strengths and weaknesses in the first part of this book. Essentially, the core competencies within the organisation need to be identified. It is human nature for the organisation to be able to identify its strengths rather than its weaknesses: after all, an acceptance of weaknesses implies that there are deficiencies and, consequently, individual managers and employees feel under threat. The unwillingness to acknowledge weaknesses until they are too advanced to be corrected is often a key determining factor in the failure of organisations.

There are a number of different ways in which the strengths and the weaknesses of the organisation can be assessed and then dealt with. In all cases this involves a systematic (and objective) look at the organisation and its operations.

The framework in Fig 6.3 offers a way in which the organisation can begin to prioritise the problems that it may uncover as a result of SWOT analysis. The majority of the classifications and actions require some comparisons to be made against competition.

Turning to the areas of the organisation that can be assessed in this way, we will need to look systematically at various quantifiable areas (*see* Fig 6.4 overleaf), which must include the following:

i) the organisational structure and administrative functions;

ii) the financial health and position of the organisation;

iii) the production methods and allied features;

iv) the marketing successes and failures;

v) the technology used by the organisation.

As we will see when we look at functional and operational decision making, this process will involve the participation of key employees at all levels of the organisation. The specific problems outlined by the line managers at the sharp end of operations will be very different from those that have a more strategic perspective

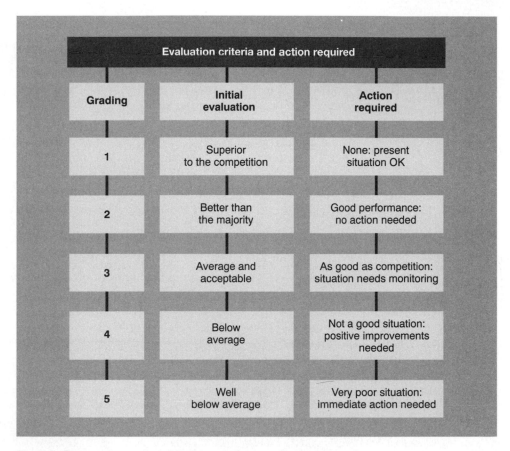

Fig 6.3 Strengths and weaknesses diagnostic framework

on the business. Specific manufacturing considerations will be identified by the production managers, while the board and other senior executives will have more of a fix on the external environment and will consider the impact of legislation and other considerations. Taken together, these two approaches can be seen as complementary and valuable to the clear identification of the strengths and weaknesses of the organisation and the external threats and opportunities.

Implementing strategy

Once the strengths, weaknesses, opportunities and threats have been identified, the problem of implementation and co-ordination is rather a complex issue. Obviously, the organisation needs to begin with an overall strategy which can then be developed and applied to each area. One such set of approaches can be broadly defined as a growth and development strategy. Within this range of activity and application, we can identify three main ways of approaching the problem from a strategic base:

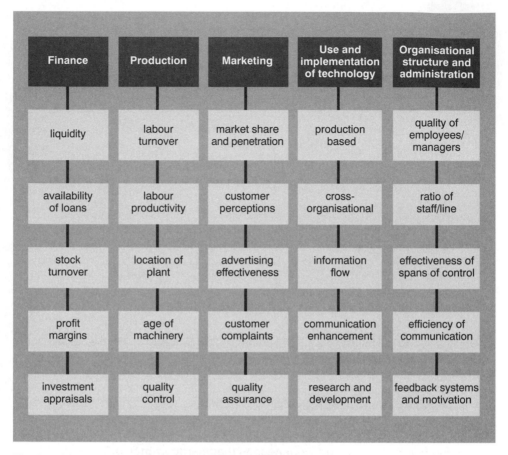

Fig 6.4 Diagnostic criteria by organisational operations

1 Business growth and development through the seeking of new markets for the current products offered (market development).

2 Business growth and development through an attempt to sell more products into existing markets (market penetration).

3 Business growth and development through the diversification and brand extension of current products catering for current markets (product development).

Whatever the approach, the organisation needs to be able to deploy all of the resources it has available to support the strategic plan. It is only at this stage that the organisation can identify the tactical considerations that will have to be employed in order to implement the strategic plan.

Decision making at functional and operational levels

Managerial decision making has its roots in the identification of a problem. It is, as we have seen, a complex process, no less so at functional and operational level. It is at this point that the objectives and strategies of the organisation as a whole have an impact on the day-to-day operations of the business. It is useful to visualise the decision making process as a stream of decisions, taken step by step (*see* Fig 6.5). It is also important to realise that this decision-making process is neither orderly or well planned in the majority of cases.

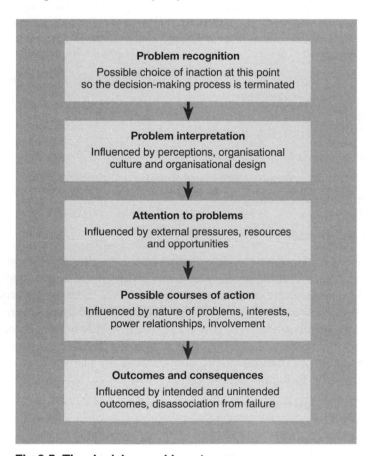

Fig 6.5 The decision-making stream

While we have correctly identified one of the major inputs into the decision-making process as company policy, the vast majority of decisions relate to 'hands-on' or fairly routine attempts to solve problems.

It is rare that the manager has the luxury of making a decision from the perspective of a totally new set of experiences. Previous decisions and experiences will always have a marked effect on the way the decision-making process proceeds. Indeed, previous experience will often determine whether the manager perceives that there is a problem that needs to be decided on in the first place.

Recognising the problem

Structured problems can be straightforward, where the manager is perfectly well aware of the steps that need to be taken in the decision-making process in order to ensure that the situation is rectified. For unstructured problems, the recognition of the problem is often a problem in itself. The majority of unstructured problems will arise when the organisation does not have a clear idea about the impact of changes that it has made, or developments in the marketplace that it has not considered to be important enough to devote any great amount of time and effort to. The simple development and transition of an organisation can bring about unstructured problems, not least the availability of new information as a result of setting up a research project or the commissioning of market research.

The recognition of the problem, whether it is structured or unstructured, should trigger a series of activities that would lead to a quick resolution of the situation. In some cases, the decision-making process will be a long and drawn-out affair, but this will depend on the complexity of the issue in the first place. As we will see, the problem needs to be addressed in the following way:

i) determine the reasons for the problem;

ii) implement a plan of action to solve the problem;

iii) assess the results of the action plan.

Interpreting the problem

The second phase of the decision-making process calls for a clear interpretation of the problem. This means that the problem needs to be given substance in terms of its definition and true meaning. As we can see from Fig 6.6, there are a number of ways in which the problem can be viewed. The options obviously range from not recognising that the problem exists (largely due to the manager being preoccupied with other concerns) to approaches which rely on 'gut reaction' or some notion of intuitively knowing how to handle the problem because the manager has encountered something similar in the past.

The main point which relates to problem interpretation is the notion that there is never a clear-cut way in which the problem is considered in an objective manner and in how it will be approached during the interpretation phase of the decision-making process. Above all, the most effective organisations, with strong organisational cultures, tend to be those which encourage active listening from their managers. If managers are more inclined to listen to employees, customers, suppliers and other interested and informed parties, they have a better chance of being more effective when it comes to problem interpretation.

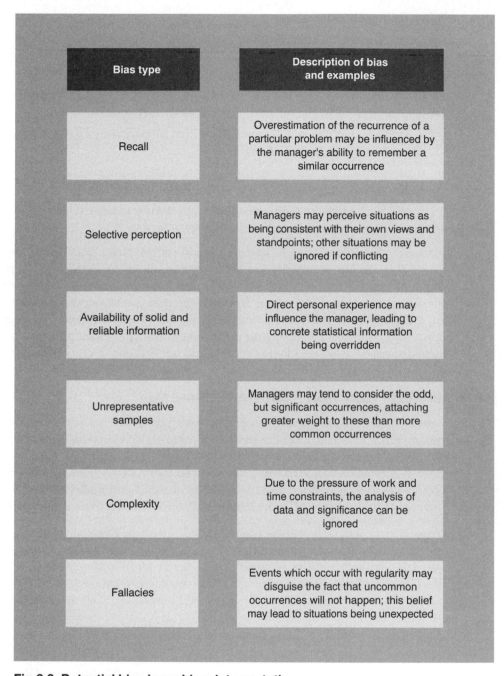

Bias type	Description of bias and examples
Recall	Overestimation of the recurrence of a particular problem may be influenced by the manager's ability to remember a similar occurrence
Selective perception	Managers may perceive situations as being consistent with their own views and standpoints; other situations may be ignored if conflicting
Availability of solid and reliable information	Direct personal experience may influence the manager, leading to concrete statistical information being overridden
Unrepresentative samples	Managers may tend to consider the odd, but significant occurrences, attaching greater weight to these than more common occurrences
Complexity	Due to the pressure of work and time constraints, the analysis of data and significance can be ignored
Fallacies	Events which occur with regularity may disguise the fact that uncommon occurrences will not happen; this belief may lead to situations being unexpected

Fig 6.6 Potential bias in problem interpretation

Prioritising the problem

When a particular problem has been identified, a judgement needs to be made regarding the priority or attention that it deserves. Managers cannot deal with all problems at the precise moment that they present themselves. They have to determine their relative priorities and give those with the highest priority their immediate attention. Examples of prioritising influences could include the following:

a) A problem that needs to be resolved within a specified period on the instructions of a line manager or member of the board.

b) A problem which can be handled immediately as the necessary resources or authorisations to use resources are currently available.

c) A problem which gives an immediate opportunity to solve it simply if handled now, but becomes more difficult if left for a period.

Obviously, the volume and variety of problems which face a manager at any given time will exceed their capacity to handle them. Indeed, new crises may throw the whole of the problem-solving and scheduling process out of line, requiring the manager to deal with the crisis as a priority. Broadly speaking, we can identify the fact that there are two distinct courses of action which will influence the manager's ability and willingness to deal with the problem. We will return to this concept and approach once we have looked at routine and non-routine decision making.

Routine and non-routine decisions

Most routine decision making can be made with reference to the rational decision-making model. Indeed, any step-by-step process of decision making is often called *normative* decision making. This means that the objectives are fully understood by the decision makers and that they have agreed them. In addition to this, the problems can be clearly defined and identified by the decision makers. There will also be a reasonable amount of information available on which to base decisions.

Well-defined and well-known problems will often be covered by the organisation's standard operating procedures (SOPs). These are rules and standards that have been set out in order to ensure that specific steps and actions are taken. In effect, this is a series of procedures that managers are supposed to follow in order to deal with a particular problem. It goes further than this: SOPs actually determine what the outcome of the decision will be.

Routine decision making, which is often repetitive and allows a more systematic approach, is sometimes referred to as producing *programmed* decisions. Company policy and standard rules and regulations would normally cover all of the various responses that could be open to the manager. On the other hand, non-routine or infrequent decisions can also be referred to as *unprogrammed* decisions. This is largely due to the fact that they are often unpredictable in terms of frequency and that they will have a different set of variables each time, requiring a separate response for each problem as it arises. For both sets of occasions, we can identify the sequences in Fig 6.7.

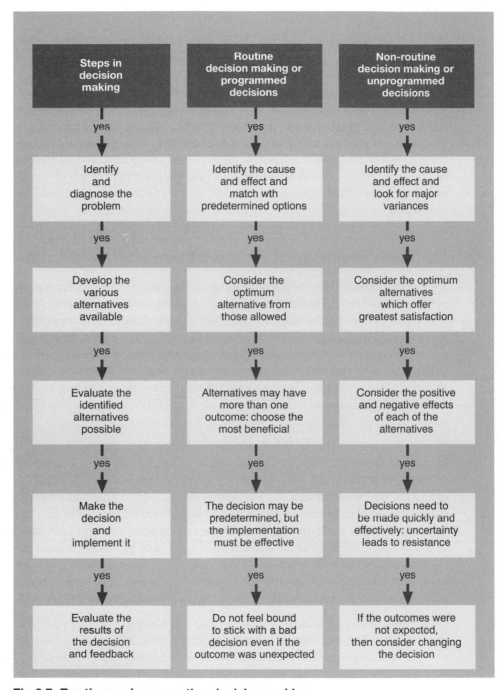

Fig 6.7 Routine and non-routine decision making

As we can see, many of the steps in the decision-making process which relate to routine problem solving have predetermined outcomes, at least as far as the responses of the manager are concerned. It should be noted, however, that the responses may not provide the manager with the expected outcome, as it may be impossible to predict exactly what will happen. This is particularly true of instances where predetermined responses based on SOPs are applied to new situations that, on the face of it, appear to be similar to predicted problems that have been encountered in the past.

For non-routine decision-making processes, the manager is faced with a set of unknown variables which may have predictable or unpredictable consequences. In this respect, although managers are more free to interpret the problem themselves, the probable outcomes of the decisions need to be more carefully analysed, and there needs to be a willingness to consider being more flexible and a preparedness to change the decision if the outcomes become more complex or unwanted. In both cases, the decisions need to be taken quickly to avoid the appearance of indecision and combat the probability of resistance to the decision.

Decision making within a problem-solving sequence

Trying to delineate between a decision and the process of problem solving can be problematic in itself. Naturally, the two interrelated acts fit very closely together. It is probably wiser to consider decision making as an integral part of the problem-solving sequence rather than the other way around. Decision making, therefore, can be seen as focusing on the choice of alternative courses of action. Problem solving, on the other hand, considers the wider process (including the recognition that there is a problem). The steps, as part of the problem-solving sequence, then include the interpretation, diagnosis and implementation that we have already outlined.

Before we consider the nature of problem-solving techniques, it is appropriate first to look at the two differing approaches to how individuals perceive situations, gather information and have insights. Using a variation of the Myers-Briggs Type Indicator, we can see that these are *sensing* and *intuition*. Those managers who rely on sensing tend to be more patient, practical and realistic individuals. On the other hand, those who focus on intuition tend to be rather more impatient, idea oriented and creative. There are no cut-and-dried, black-and-white reasons for an individual choosing to adopt these approaches; in fact we all use them both as the circumstances present themselves. In effect, we adopt the approach that we feel more comfortable with and trust. The differences can be typified as in Table 6.1.

In addition to this identification, we can also use Myers-Briggs' approach to explain the ways in which decisions are made. Again, there are two ways of looking at this, the first is known as *thinking* and the second is called *feeling*. Thinking managers tend to be more logical and rational, while feeling managers have a tendency to use their own values and beliefs, coupled with the beliefs of others, as a framework for their decision making. The differences can be typified as in Table 6.2. We have simplified the characteristics and focused on the precise nature of the individual in relation to the decision-making process. Readers are directed to the original work for a more in-depth explanation and discussion of these types.

Table 6.1 Isabel Myers-Brigg's sensing and intuition characteristics

Sensing types	Intuitive types
Dislike new problems	Like solving new problems
Prefer standard solutions	Dislike having to make the same decision
Prefer to use existing skills and techniques	Like to learn new skills
Steady workers, realistic idea of time required	Work in bursts with slack periods in between
Conclusions reached step-by-step	Quick to make conclusions
Patient about routine	Impatient about routine
Dislike complications	Like complex situations
Not very inspired by situations	More likely to be inspired
Very thorough and precise about facts	Apt to make factual mistakes
Prepared to spend time on making sure that they are precise	May skip precision in favour of speed

Source: Adapted from Isabel Myers-Briggs (1980) *Introduction to Type*, Consulting Psychologists Press.

Table 6.2 Isabel Myers-Briggs' thinking and feeling characteristics

Thinking types	Feeling types
Tend not to show emotion and have difficulties with others' emotional needs	Able to deal with own emotions and others
May have the capacity to hurt others' feelings without realising it	Actively avoid hurting others and try to please
Prefer order and logic	Prefer harmony at the expense of efficiency
Impersonal, pay little attention to individuals' wishes	Tend to base decisions on likes and wishes
Need to be treated fairly	Sometimes crave praise
Have the capacity to be harsh when necessary	Dislike being authoritarian
Analytical, respond to individuals' thoughts	People oriented
Tend to be more inflexible and firm about decisions	Tend to be flexible and sympathetic to others' views

Source: Adapted from Isabel Myers-Briggs (1980) *Introduction to Type*, Consulting Psychologists Press.

Putting these two pairs of dimensions together, we can begin to understand how the individual approaches decision making within a problem solving sequence. This is summarised in Table 6.3.

Remember that when we consider the importance of each of these approaches, we have to realise that the individual will favour one or more of the approaches to suit particular sets of circumstances. In this way, we will focus on one or more of the approaches as a matter of course. The others will not make a valuable contribution to the decision-making process.

Table 6.3 The four dimensions of problem solving and their impact on the decision-making process

Dimension	Impact
Sensing	Useful for developing and facing the facts about the problem as well as being able to be realistic about the nature of the problem
Intuition	Useful where the situation demands that the manager is able to be creative and able to recognise the opportunities
Thinking	Useful in helping the manager to focus on the impersonal, analytical aspects of the problem, to be able to weigh up the alternatives, consider the consequences (cause and effect)
Feeling	Useful for the manager to be able to consider the values, ethics and principles involved and how they will have an impact on the final decision

Review questions

1 Decision making often takes place in an environment of uncertainty and risk. To what extent is the decision maker able to influence the conditions under which the decision is made?

2 Why might the conditions under which decisions are made be referred to as *subliminal*?

3 Distinguish between routine, non-routine and adaptive decision making.

4 What are Standard Operating Procedures and what is their purpose?

5 What is *Kaizen*?

6 Describe innovative decision making.

7 What do you understand by the notion of a *hierarchy of objectives*?

8 What is stakeholder theory?

9 Describe what and how the rational model relates to decision making.

10 What do you understand by the term *bounded rationality*?

11 With reference to meeting objectives, what do you understand by the term *satisficing*?

12 Describe the political model of decision making.

13 What is an SBU and how does this relate to diversification?

14 How does the strengths and weaknesses diagnostic framework operate and what is its purpose?

15 How does functional or operational decision making differ from strategic decision making?

16 Outline the key stages in the decision-making stream.

17 What are the principal differences between structured and unstructured decision making?

18 Describe some of the biases which could affect decision making.

19 What is normative decision making?

20 How might the Myers-Briggs Type Indicator help us understand the process of problem solving?

Organisation factors

After considering the processes related to decision making at various levels within the organisation, we now need to turn our attention to factors within the company that can affect the way in which policy and decisions are made. We should also consider the various characteristics, roles and responsibilities of individuals within the organisation who may have a marked effect on the decision-making process. In this respect, we need to examine the nature of key decision makers and how their approach to this process can predetermine outcomes.

Policy conflicts

In its broadest sense, conflict is related to disagreements arising from incompatible objectives. This may manifest itself at organisational level, where separate companies may be at variance with one another, or, more seriously, within the organisation itself. We cannot assume that policy conflicts only occur at board level (*see* Fig 7.1). Before we consider the impact of conflict on the organisation, we need to examine the nature of conflict itself.

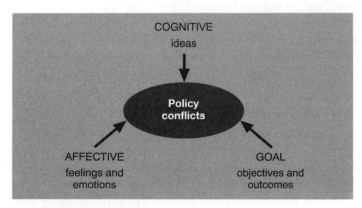

Fig 7.1 Policy conflicts

There are three main types of conflict which can be identified:

1 *Affective conflict* – where the feelings and emotions of the different groups are incompatible.

2 *Cognitive conflict* – where the ideas of the opposing groups appear to be incompatible.

3 *Goal conflict* – where the objectives and outcomes of the opposing groups are incompatible.

All of these apparent conflicts should be resolved by conflict management, where interventions are designed either to reduce or to increase the intensity of the conflict. We should bear in mind that conflict within an organisation, not to mention conflict between different organisations, is desirable, provided that it is controlled. Obviously, conflict arising out of racial, ethnic or gender incompatibilities is undesirable under any circumstances, but 'healthy conflict', which makes either grouping more attuned to the potential external environment, is often encouraged.

We should therefore not consider conflict to be purely negative. Traditionalists would disagree with this and work under the assumption that any conflict is undesirable. To this end, conflict used to be eliminated by the careful selection, training and division of work within the organisation. For many organisations, internal conflict can appear to be somewhat destructive. Others, with competing product lines, will openly encourage conflict in the hope that internal conflict will lead to a greater understanding and ability to deal with external competitors.

Intense conflict, of course, can mean stress, which can be expressed in terms of apathy, absenteeism and higher labour turnover. Above all, intense policy conflict will lead to distortions and bias within the decision-making process. Individuals will consider that winning a conflict is more important than the objectives and health of the organisation itself.

Alternatively, some organisations will actively encourage a degree of constructive conflict. It is hoped that individuals involved in this process will consider the environment more stimulating. This is particularly true of organisations at the cutting edge of innovation and creativity. A very careful balancing act has to be perfected in order to ensure that conflict stays within the bounds of acceptable control and behaviour.

 ## Values

Values are one of the main ways in which an individual's behaviour is determined. They also assist us in forming impressions about other people. Within the organisational context, the interrelationship of values between individuals and groups is extremely complex and is used to construct and maintain systems, and aid the selection of viewpoints and courses of action. Obviously, the different value systems within an organisation are not necessarily compatible with one another. The organisation's dominant values may be at odds with an individual's own value system.

The way in which value systems are constructed is often based on beliefs. Effectively we can categorise these beliefs in the following way:

◆ descriptive beliefs, where values are based on fact or reality and not opinion;

◆ evaluative beliefs, where values are based on judgement;

◆ prescriptive beliefs, where values are based on conditioned behaviour.

Out of these different forms of belief, and consequent values, individuals are able to group a number together to form a particular attitude. It is these attitudes which determine how an individual reacts in certain circumstances. For the outsider, the identification of an individual's attitudes will also assist them in being able to predict their particular response given a particular situation.

As we have said, within our attitudes there are a number of general preferences or values and these certainly affect behaviour. It is sometimes very difficult to distinguish between values and attitudes. However, values tend to be more positive, whereas attitudes can be both positive or negative. In reality, the true distinction between attitudes and values lies within an individual's own belief system. We can see that values form the foundation of our belief systems. Once we have established a series of values, many more of our preferences and attitudes are built on these. Even these values are not a permanent framework upon which individuals operate. They may, over a period, be affected or manipulated by outside forces and influences.

This is even more true when we consider the adoption of underlying values within the organisation itself. At first, an individual's value system or belief system may be at variance with the organisation's. Through induction, common practice and peer activity, not to mention managerial pressure and training, the individual will slowly adopt aspects of the organisation's values. For the organisation this is a deliberate strategy. Although it requires an individual to have a certain degree of independent thought, which would otherwise stifle good ideas and innovation, it does place considerable emphasis on gradual adoption of the organisation's values in order to ensure effective performance, both for the individual and for the organisation itself.

Deal and Kennedy (1982) identified three benefits and three risks attached to the establishment of shared values in an organisation. These are shown in Table 7.1.

Table 7.1 Establishing shared values in an organisation

Benefits	Risks
Managers are more likely to pay attention to issues which are part of the corporate value system	Unless the value system is continually upgraded there is a possibility that the whole organisation will be operating on the basis of obsolete values
Managers are more likely to make better decisions as a result of having this guidance	If managers slavishly follow the organisation's value system, they may find that they are resisting change
Managers are more aware of the company's value system, so they are more likely to work harder as they know what is expected of them	Over a period there may be a disparity between the known company values and the actual practice of management at various levels within the organisation

Managerial values

Having looked at the main aspects of broader value systems, we should now turn our attention to managerial values. It is interesting to ask the question whether managerial values are significantly different to the values of other individuals within an organisation. We could say that this would be true if all of the managers came from similar social or educational backgrounds. But, as we know, this is not the case in the majority of organisations. We could also, perhaps, identify the fact that managers' value systems might be similar if they all came from the same technical or scientific background, but again, this is not the case. The best that we can offer is a form of stereotyping, where managers are categorised according to very broad generalisations. More significantly, we can see a major difference between *operating* values (which are the actual ways in which managers handle real-life situations) and *intended* values (which are their espoused values). The reality is that an individual's intended values have little significance in most cases and it is their operating values which are more important. So, perhaps, it is these values that should form the basis of study and consideration.

Harrison (1981) made an attempt to rank operational values by different categories (*see* Fig 7.2). He noted that there were a considerable number of different groups of values or influences which would affect the way in which a manager reacted to, or considered, a situation. These were as follows:

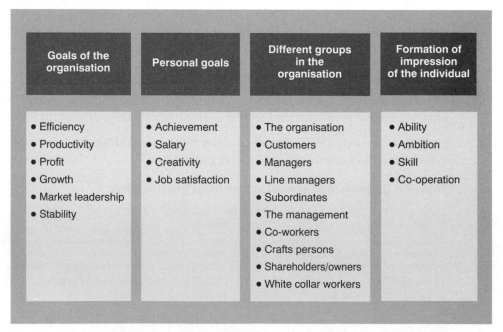

Goals of the organisation	Personal goals	Different groups in the organisation	Formation of impression of the individual
• Efficiency	• Achievement	• The organisation	• Ability
• Productivity	• Salary	• Customers	• Ambition
• Profit	• Creativity	• Managers	• Skill
• Growth	• Job satisfaction	• Line managers	• Co-operation
• Market leadership		• Subordinates	
• Stability		• The management	
		• Co-workers	
		• Crafts persons	
		• Shareholders/owners	
		• White collar workers	

Fig 7.2 E.F. Harrison's operational values

1 **Goals of the organisation**

  – organisational efficiency

  – increased productivity

  – maximisation of profit

  – organisational growth

  – market leadership

  – organisational stability.

2 **Personal goals**

  – achievement

  – success

  – creativity

  – job satisfaction.

3 **Different groups within the organisation**

  – the organisation

  – customers

  – line managers

  – other managers

  – subordinates

  – managers themselves

  – co-workers

  – technical or craftspersons

  – shareholders or owners

  – white collar workers.

4 **Formation of impressions of individuals**

  – ability

  – ambition

  – skill

  – co-operation.

5 **Attitude towards general issues**

  – change

  – competition.

As we can see from this list, managers have to operate under a number of different, potentially competing sets of values and influences. Not all of these will necessarily be compatible or, for that matter, desirable, if a manager is to be truly effective. Whether we can actually rank the different categories in any meaningful way is debatable, but certainly those which are related to the goals of the organisation itself will tend to be dominant.

An effective manager needs to be able to juggle, or hopefully resolve, many of the contradictions and conflicts which arise out of these different values. It is, perhaps, at this point that we need to consider the fact that a manager is more likely to be able to resolve these contradictions and conflicts if they broadly accord with the manager's own personal values. If they do, then effectively more values can be internalised, as they will reflect the manager's own personal aspirations.

Values and the decision-making process

So how do these values influence the decision-making process? We can certainly identify four ways in which the two aspects interrelate. First, values can operate at both a subconscious and a conscious level. This means that managers may not necessarily be aware that they are making value judgements during decision making. Even if managers believe that they are looking at the situation giving only due consideration to the facts, they will, in fact, be adopting some form of evaluation based on their own values. This is even more true of situations when there is an emotional or subjective slant to the decision making. In these cases, any attempt to claim that decision making rests on rationality or logic are completely untrue.

For the most part, managers are completely unaware that their value systems are affecting their decision making. They will subconsciously ignore certain information and will not actually perceive it as being relevant to the situation. This is known as *subconscious information rejection* and is a very common occurrence. Alternatively, if the information is actually perceived as being relevant, but is ignored all the same because it does not fit in with the manager's particular view of the situation, then we can describe this as being a non-conscious influence on the manager's behaviour.

The second way in which values can affect the decision-making process is that they will often influence the conscious process of a manager's choice of alternatives. Again, alternatives within a particular decision-making process will appear to be more or less viable to certain individuals. This viability aspect means that managers have evaluated the alternatives in some conscious way, but are also overlaying their own personal values, perhaps ahead of the organisation's values. Typical situations would include selecting an alternative which may have the fewest long-term consequences, or the least long-term effect on managers themselves.

The third way in which values can affect the decision-making process is when the manager considers that their own personal values are the normal or correct way of perceiving situations. Given the fact that individuals will tend to create an idea about other people's values by observing them, these observations are already biased by our own existing value systems. In other words, there is a natural tendency to select aspects of other people's values, through their behaviour, by looking for those which mirror our own personal value systems.

This selective perception is based on the assumption that our own values are the right ones. Behaviour which is contrary to our own value systems is often seen as a threat. The natural reaction is to challenge these contradictory values, reinforce our own and try to impose these on the other individual. It is very difficult for an individual to step back from their own values and realise that another's value system may be equally as valid as their own. It is not a common trait to be prepared to re-evaluate our own value system, as we do not perceive the alternative value system as being valid at all.

Within the decision-making process we can see that the adoption of another's value system is very unlikely, since our minds will be focused on the successful conclusion of the process in relation to our own value system, rather than examining or evaluating an alternative course of action.

The fourth way in which values can affect the decision-making process is when managers apply their value system to the choice of potential alternatives. Although managers may not be aware of it, certain situations will trigger particular aspects of their value system. This complex process involves individuals in systematically applying subsets of their value systems to a particular decision. Given any normal managerial situation, managers may apply their own values in relation to, perhaps, personal appearance with regard to another individual in the first instance, and then begin to apply their values related to personal ability, attitude or skill. Their view of the individual has already been coloured by their initial value application, and whether or not the values relating to other criteria are more dominant may affect this initial assessment. In any case, the initial impression which has been coloured by the manager's value system may cause them not to exercise perfect judgement in that situation. In addition to this, it may also influence the manager's ability or willingness to consider other criteria and may also limit their choices of courses of action.

 ## Bargaining and tradeoffs

It is inevitable that there will be certain sets of circumstances when potential conflict is unavoidable. The contingency model of conflict can help us to look at the different conflict-management approaches in a variety of situations. The model itself is based on two contingency variables, *distributive* and *integrative*. From this we can create four basic conflict situations. The distributive variable relates to the different objectives or goals of the individuals involved. We should see this variable as a continuum where at each extreme one individual's gain is another individual's loss. The integrative variable relates to the different objectives of the individuals and their compatibility. In this respect this variable identifies the fact that an individual may only gain if the team or organisation gains as well.

The *win–lose conflict* situation occurs when there is a high distributive and a low integrative relationship. This means that the situation has created a direct conflict in objectives. Organisations will be keen to avoid these types of situations, which are typified in the existence of 'office politics'. Some individuals will be self-serving and will actively oppose the goals and objectives of others in trying to create the ideal sets of circumstances to suit their own needs. In situations such as this conflict occurs on a very regular basis and at a very high intensity.

A *mixed conflict* situation occurs when both distributive and integrative variables are high. Management, for example, will focus on profitability, whereas employees will be more interested in their own remuneration. This is not to say that in all cases the two conflicting viewpoints are not compatible, often, however, they are not so.

The *collaborative* situation occurs when there is a high integrative and low distributive relationship. In these situations the actions of an individual will have positive effects on others. The objectives are compatible, reinforcing and attainable. Conflicts in these situations are not intense because of this compatibility. Conflicts do still occur, however, as a result of co-ordination difficulties and differing opinions regarding how goals should be attained.

A *low interdependency* situation occurs when both distributive and integrative variables are low. Conflict is virtually unknown because individuals and teams operate in a sufficient amount of space and with a greater degree of autonomy than in other situations.

Conflict-management styles

Broadening out the potential bargaining and tradeoff situations, we can look at more general conflict-management styles. Interpersonal conflict often occurs as a result of the following:

◆ disagreements
◆ incompatible interests
◆ distrust or fear
◆ rejection.

Creating a model of interpersonal conflict-management styles involves us in consideration of two basic criteria:

i) people's desire to satisfy their own needs, which could be measured at one extreme by assertiveness and at the other by unassertiveness;
ii) people's desire to satisfy the needs of others, which could be measured at one extreme by co-operativeness and at the other by lack of co-operativeness.

In turn, this allows us to create five conflict-management styles:

a) avoidance
b) smoothing
c) forcing
d) compromise
e) collaborative.

Avoidance

The avoidance style of conflict management is typified by individuals who seek to absent themselves or withdraw from possible conflict situations. At the very least they will put up a barrier between them and the other individuals involved in the conflict. Obviously, if this continues in the long term it will seriously affect the over-all performance of the organisation. This will often occur when an individual does not consider the conflict to be of sufficient importance to warrant spending any time on it. Equally, it may occur when the managers do not consider that they have sufficient information to deal with the conflict effectively. Finally, avoidance may occur when one individual has considerably less power than the other individuals involved in the conflict, as the weaker individual will consider that they have insufficient power to make any impact at all.

Smoothing

The smoothing style of conflict management occurs when the individuals involved attempt to minimise differences. In this respect the conflict is effectively dealt with as if the conflict is not actually occurring. People will try to co-operate in order to reduce tensions and stress. In most cases a manager using this technique will try to cover up their own feelings about a certain conflict and, as a result, is very ineffective when faced with a dominant individual who is forcing conflict. Harmony and disruption avoidance are the key aspects in this approach and the smoothing style is used to diffuse potentially difficult situations.

Forcing

The forcing style is used when one individual tries to dominate another by making them accept their appraisal of a situation. Naturally, the outcomes will produce circumstances when one individual gets exactly what they want and all the other individuals involved simply have to comply with their wishes. Referring back to the contingency model of conflict, we can see that the forcing style leads to win–lose situations which are typified by managers forcing decisions on their subordinates. This style is acceptable in as much as it provides an effective way of dealing with emergency situations, unpopular courses of action or situations where a manager needs to take a decision in order to protect themselves.

Compromise

The compromise style offers managers the opportunity to sacrifice some of their own interests in order to reach an agreement. Compromises allow a balance to be struck between assertive and unassertive individuals; in other words, a balance between co-operative and unco-operative behaviour. A manager should not adopt a compromise stance too early, as this will set the trend for all future negotiations. In most respects, the compromise style is ideal when there is no real possibility of being able to gain a complete 'victory' or for one side to 'win' and the other side to 'lose'. Since the conflicting objectives of the two parties will, effectively, block the progress of one another, there is no other real alternative but offering some form of compromise.

Collaboration

The collaborative style of conflict management is particularly effective when the actual objectives of the various parties are agreed, but the ways in which these objectives will be achieved are open to debate. A natural progression from this, quite clearly, is the fact that if the various parties can agree a common way in which the objectives are to be achieved, then there is every chance that the solution which will be arrived at (through consensus) is the best solution. It is common for collaborative decisions to be reached when there are a number of expert views offering different solutions to the same problem.

As we can see from these different approaches, the majority of managers and decision makers realise that there are times and places for full assertiveness and others for a more considered and balanced approach. Any good manager, regardless of their position within the organisation, should be open to discussion and compromise (at some level). It is not very likely that a manager will always be able to get their own way in every conflict situation; equally, relying on custom and practice (or SOPs) will not answer the question either. A continuous process of bargaining, offering alternatives and compromise (which help to form power blocs and alliances for the future) is advisable. Trading off one solution for possible collusion later is a viable tactic.

The best managers will realise that it is a fruitless task to fight every single battle as if it really counted. It is the important decisions and conflicts that need to be won. However, it is a delicate balance that determines whether the manager is able to identify and win the important battles while maintaining a strong and influential presence in decision making that does not really affect their long-term aims and objectives.

 Personality issues

Just as the situational and structural aspects of an organisation or a role can affect the way in which the individual approaches the question of decision making, the personality of that individual can also influence decision making. Exactly how the individual exercises the power they have in the organisation will depend on a number of different factors. Table 7.2 illustrates one way in which the personality of the decision maker can be identified in terms of their willingness to use or exercise this power.

If you have completed the questionnaire in Table 7.2, you may have identified the fact that you would be willing to be involved in internal organisational politics or at least be willing to use the power that you may have in an organisation.

The need to use power, which includes the following list of characteristics, is the most basic form of personality-based decision making:

i)   the need to influence others;

ii) the need to lead others;

iii) the need to control your own environment.

Table 7.2 Political orientation questionnaire

Respondents should indicate whether they agree (A) or disagree (D) with the statements.

		A	D
1.	I would not correct my boss's mistakes.	☐	☐
2.	I would hold on to information until I could use it to my advantage.	☐	☐
3.	I would never employ an individual who has a better education than I have.	☐	☐
4.	If I ever do someone a favour, I make sure that they pay me back sometime.	☐	☐
5.	It is important to try to make friends with the individuals who have the real power in the organisation.	☐	☐
6.	If I had a rival in my own department I would try to get them transferred elsewhere.	☐	☐
7.	I would have no problem about taking the credit for someone else's work.	☐	☐
8.	I would willingly give my boss personal assistance, even outside of work.	☐	☐
9.	I am prepared to show complete support to my boss at all times, even when it is not deserved.	☐	☐
10.	It is important to be seen at all organisational functions and events.	☐	☐
11.	If I sensed a weakness in one of the senior managers in the organisation I would be willing to exploit this.	☐	☐
12.	I would never dream of talking about politics to my boss before I knew his/her own political views.	☐	☐
13.	In order to highlight the mistakes of others it is essential that criticisms are put down on paper. I would use memoranda for this purpose.	☐	☐
14.	In order to get a co-worker to do something, I would be willing to threaten them with going to the boss.	☐	☐
15.	I would make a point of inviting my boss to a party or a meal at my home.	☐	☐
16.	I would try to have lunch or spend time after work with individuals who could further my career goals in the organisation.	☐	☐
17.	I do not think there is a dirty trick that I would not consider to further my own career goals.	☐	☐
18.	Power is important to me, especially the ability to exercise it.	☐	☐
19.	Striving to make a long-term impact on the organisation is incredibly important to me.	☐	☐
20.	Office politics are a fact of life and I enjoy being involved in them.	☐	☐

Give yourself one point for each of the statements that you have agreed with.

Over 16 points denotes that you have a strong inclination to use office politics to further yourself.

Between 10 and 15 points denotes that you are inclined to use office politics at the right time.

Between 6 and 10 points denotes that you may only use office politics in extreme circumstances.

Under 6 points denotes that you do not engage in office politics and are not very power oriented.

Successful use of power is very closely related to managerial effectiveness, since it means that the manager is able to control the activities of their subordinates and that they will be better motivated by having the ability to make decisions. The exercise of power leading to decisions needs to be tempered by restraint. Too strong a power drive may lead to decisions being made only with reference to the furtherance of the goals and objectives of the manager and not those of the organisation itself. In order to balance the power drives, the manager needs to be aware of the fact that there are two different aspects in play here. On the one hand, the manager needs to make decisions that are to the advantage of the organisation, creating an environment where subordinates can develop an understanding of the organisation and a loyalty towards it. On the other hand, the manager needs to be able to exercise power and decision making in such a way as to be able to feel that they are making a positive impact on the processes of the organisation and furthering their own career goals.

Machiavellianism (based on the writings of the sixteenth-century Italian philosopher and statesman Niccolò Machiavelli), recognises that there are three main traits or styles of behaviour:

1 The use of guile or deceit in personal relationships within the organisation.

2 The dominance of a cynical view about the nature of other individuals within the organisation.

3 The managers' apparent disregard for conventional morals in their activities within the organisation.

At whatever level these individuals operate, they are clearly manipulators of others. The following phrases and statements provide guidelines for individuals wishing to adopt a Machiavellian approach:

◆ Tell people what you think they expect to hear.

◆ Never trust anyone completely, otherwise you will be asking for trouble.

◆ Always disguise your real reasons for doing something unless this is what the other individual is hoping to hear.

◆ It is important to try to make friends with the individuals who have the real power in the organisation.

Locus of control

The *locus of control* refers to the extent to which an individual believes that they can control the events around them. Those who have a high external locus of control exhibit the belief that:

◆ other powerful individuals will have a high impact on their own fortunes;

◆ fate or chance will have a marked impact on their fortunes.

Those with a high internal locus of control have the following tendencies:

◆ the willingness to try to influence others as much as possible;

◆ the belief that their actions will be ultimately successful.

The use of overt political pressure and activity is far more likely in those who have a high internal locus of control.

Risk taking

Risk taking is an integral part of the manager's decision-making process. Some are willing to take risks; this is known as the *risk-seeking propensity*. Involvement in office politics can be seen as a risk-seeking activity but, more broadly, we must see this tendency as being very important in the manager's willingness to take decisions that could fail or not provide the safest returns. Other individuals are considered to be risk avoiders. This, at the extreme, will affect the way in which they approach the problem of decision making and may impair their ability to take decisions that could be considered as being risky.

 ## Decision takers and decision makers

On first impressions the distinction between decision takers and decision makers could appear to rest primarily on the level of management of the individuals concerned. It is certainly true that those at the strategic apex of the organisation are more likely to be the decision makers, since they are the ones that will frame the whole approach of the organisation and will have probably had a hand in establishing the SOPs. The decision takers, not merely restricted to slavishly following the courses of action predetermined by the decision makers, tend to make the decisions at operational level.

However, the differences are rather more complex than this. The key differences are:

a) Taking a decision infers something rather more positive than making a decision.

b) Taking a decision also infers that the individual involved is being rather more proactive than a reactive decision maker.

c) Given the fact that decision taking seems to infer a sense of speed and urgency, decision making may be considered as being a rather slower process that is the result of deliberation.

d) Decision takers may not consider the longer-term effects of their choice of action, but the decision maker (with a longer-term view) may be rather more considerate about the implications of the decision.

In any organisation there is likely to be a variety of different decision makers and takers at various levels. Whether there is an ideal way of making a decision will very much depend on the circumstances. In some cases, it is appropriate to take a more positive and speedy approach that will not involve detailed collaboration and consultation, in which case the decision-taking approach will be more appropriate. In other cases, a more laborious and considered approach of decision making, which could include a degree of consultation and group decision making, would be more appropriate.

Roles and responsibilities

The average large UK organisation's board is made up of about 30 per cent non-executives. The comparative figures for the USA stand at 75 per cent; the Japanese, on the other hand, have virtually none. The latter relies on a more rigid hierarchical structure of executives. This is one of the many reasons that the Japanese have developed their businesses quickly in the West. We can further identify the fact that British boards have a tendency to be more cautious and slow to respond, the Americans react violently to any possible change in the marketplace, with drastic and far-reaching results, whereas Japanese boards maintain their control by not only methodical planning, but encouraging goal-oriented participation at every level of the organisation.

Since we are concerned with the major roles and responsibilities of the decision makers in an organisation, we could begin by looking at the ideal characteristics of a board of directors:

1 They need to be able to analyse, evaluate and plan.
2 They need to be able to monitor and adapt these plans in a continuous cycle.
3 They need to have the strength and vision to appoint and fire the senior managers that will implement their decisions.
4 They need to have a firm grasp on the scope and availability of the organisation's resources, agree how they will be deployed and define the terms by which success or failure is measured.
5 They need to influence the structure of the organisation, taking account of the need to facilitate communications at every level of the organisation.
6 They need to be willing and able to contribute consistently to the decision-making process and realise the implications of their decisions.

At the head of the organisation is the chief executive, often known by a variety of different job titles. This role is pivotal in ensuring that managerial control runs smoothly up and down the organisation. The finance director needs to be very experienced; it is a key role and the organisation needs to get the best person that they can afford. Another director should be primarily concerned with the development of the business, able to react to market trends and ultimately make those market trends move in the direction that suits the organisation. Whether the organisation has a variety of functional directors within the board structure will depend on the nature of the business itself and whether they can make valuable (and regular) contributions to decision making.

Part-time directors are very useful. Not only do they not pose a threat to the full time directors, their independence enables them to make useful contributions that are not based on bias or membership of a particular power bloc.

The main executives have a vested interest in making the organisation a success, since this will largely determine the fortunes of their careers. The ideal mix would include a number of seasoned executives who know the business inside out, a smaller group of younger executives who are more pushy and aggressive, and some others who adopt a more cynical approach.

Perhaps the ideal size for a board of directors is around five. Once the board moves into double figures there is a tendency for it to split into different opposing camps. It has been said that all boards should have at least two non-executive directors, who have the ability to say things that executive directors do not dare to mention, otherwise there is a danger that the organisation will be too subjective. If the proportion of non-executives becomes too big, then there may not be room on the board for executive directors. In this respect, around 60 per cent should be seen as the maximum for non-executives. Whatever the proportion, non-executives need to have a keen interest in the organisation. Without this, there is the chance that whenever the organisation outlines or proposes a particular strategy that will need a decision to be made, the non-executives will not contribute fully or usefully.

Chairperson

The chairperson has two main functions, ceremonial and strategic (*see* Fig 7.3). The former function involves being the main focus of organisational unity and the latter is one of leadership. Although this is a basic definition of the role of the chairperson, it does allow us to identify the importance of this key role. It is crucial

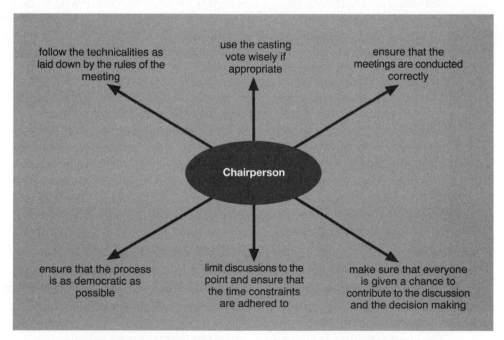

Fig 7.3 The role of the chairperson

to consider the fact that the chairperson is not chairperson of the company, but chairperson of the board. The role is a temporary one, in reality the chairperson only holds that position for as long as the board deems that person is fit. The key responsibilities are:

◆ to ensure that meetings are conducted correctly and in an orderly manner;

◆ to make sure that all members of the board have an opportunity to speak, but ensuring that discussions are limited to a specified amount of time where appropriate;

◆ to ensure that all the decisions made are majority ones in democratic circumstances;

◆ to ensure that all the technicalities of the meeting are followed, including proxy votes;

◆ to consider carefully the use of the casting vote when appropriate.

For the majority of larger organisations, the chairperson has become the spokesperson who leads the various discussions with external agencies and shareholders. In essence, this is in addition to the more common role of handling meetings. The chairperson needs to be a public relations expert, with the control of external relations given over to the position by the board of directors. In many cases, the role of the chairperson is combined with that of the chief executive.

Chief executive

While the chairperson leads the board, it is the chief executive who leads the management of the organisation. Individuals in this position are significantly more powerful than two individuals holding the posts separately; both roles taken together mean that the individual has enormous power to influence all areas of the organisation.

The concept of the chief executive was born out of necessity. Many organisations realised that they could not operate successfully with a board made up of part-timers and non-executives. It was therefore essential that they give the responsibility of running the organisation to a particular individual. More commonly, of course, the chief executive is referred to as the managing director. In law, the managing director can enter into contracts on behalf of the organisation without reference to the rest of the board. With this in mind, the board should not appoint a managing director without clearly defining the exact nature of the limits of the authority that they are prepared to give to the post. They should also clearly define the types of situation that they require the managing director to bring to the attention of the board.

There is some difference between the role of the managing director in most organisations and the exact nature of that of the chief executive in others. Essentially, the managing director is responsible to the chairperson, not to the board as a whole. The chief executive is also the chairperson in other organisations.

Board members

The remaining executives on the board have various specific functions that are related to the operations of the organisation. Some boards operate a two-tier system, where there is an upper supervisory board and a management board, with all members on either board operating as equals. This is a common board structure in Europe.

One of the principal problems of incorporating worker-directors or other members of the organisation who occupy lower-status positions is that they may feel inhibited during board meetings. In reality there should be no reason that subordinates cannot contradict their direct line managers. We should assume that in board meeting situations any adequately expressed point of view which has its merits has equal weight, regardless of the source of the suggestion.

Aside from the legal limitations regarding the choice of directors, some organisations may choose to identify certain categories of individuals in their Articles of Association whom shareholders do not wish to become board members. Many organisations will also limit board membership to those who hold shares in the company, but this can be easily circumvented by the ownership of a single share.

Above all, directors need to have a degree of independence, and this is particularly true of the non-executive director. They will be able to recognise situations where short-term decisions may prove to be the correct solution to a problem, but may bring long-term complications. Other executives may be co-opted on to the board for their specific skills and knowledge in particular areas. In most circumstances this will be on an *ad hoc* basis.

Company secretary

The law recognises a company secretary as an officer of the company. This individual will attend board meetings and draft the minutes on behalf of the chairperson. However, this individual may not necessarily be a director of the organisation. The primary concern of the company secretary is to maintain records of the board's deliberations, as well as being the principal individual responsible for legal advice. It is therefore difficult, in many circumstances, for the company secretary to combine the duties of an executive director's role. In some respects the functions may be at variance with one another. It is a difficult task to balance the vested interests of an executive director with the broader responsibilities of a company secretary.

Finance director

Obviously the primary candidate for the role of finance director would be an individual with long experience in accountancy. It is true to say that these individuals are few and far between, as many more general directors have avoided the intricacies of financial considerations and experienced accountants lack board exposure. Some organisations have chosen to enlist the services of a non-executive director to attempt to fill this role; however, this poses the very real problem of a lack of day-to-day access to this individual. If the finance director is not sufficiently strong and conversant with the organisation's activities, the company cannot hope to be in full control of its financial situation.

Marketing director

A relative newcomer to the board is the business development director, perhaps more commonly known as the marketing director. In a variety of different organisations directors responsible for sales and strategic planning assume similar responsibilities. Depending on the organisational structure, the most senior individual may be the sales director, the marketing director or the business development director.

Whatever the case, these roles are inextricably linked. At board level, strategic decisions related to investment or organisational direction need to be made with reference to all developments within the company. In essence, this role is one of co-ordination, where assessments can be made regarding competition, costs and timescales, and all are incorporated under the aegis of a named individual. This set of circumstances is even more crucial for holding companies, or those which have a number of definable divisions. A director needs to be conversant with all developments which are occurring at different stages and locations throughout the business. In this way the board can be appraised of the exact position of all developments.

Personnel director

In order to ensure that the board is aware of employee sensitivity, the personnel director has become a common member of the board. In the UK, personnel directors began to join the board in the early 1970s, at a time when new employee legislation was coming into force with the prospect of industrial action. During periods of high unemployment, when the board may be encouraged to take draconian steps to control the workforce, the personnel director would be able to offer a counter-balance to this extreme approach.

Technical director

Organisations with an industrial background will inevitably include a director related to the production or technical functions of the business. This is also a trend which has been encouraged by the adoption of Japanese philosophy, where production and productivity considerations are paramount.

Duties of directors

In all cases, directors need to act in good faith; in other words, in the interests of the company and not themselves. They must also operate in an honest and open manner, known as 'due diligence'. We should also realise that 'skill and care' are demanded of directors. This means that the approach and performance of all directors are under close scrutiny from their peers. The directors also need to ensure that they act with 'proper purpose', which means that they should operate in the *bona fide* interests of the organisation at all times and not for their own gains or needs.

Associate and alternative directors

An associate director is not normally a member of the board. These individuals are often given this title so that they can have an enhanced status both within the organisation and to those outside. A problem which arises as a result of this is that third parties tend to look on these individuals as fully fledged directors, expecting them to make decisions and commitments that are beyond their actual remit. Associate directors should not be confused with alternative directors, who are empowered by a director to represent them when they cannot attend to the duties of the organisation. In effect, this individual has the authority to act as a proxy for the absent director. This is a perfectly acceptable practice provided that the alternative is able to carry out the required functions fully and properly.

Non-executive directors

Organisations will either be fully behind the appointment of non-executive directors, or will positively state that this kind of director is useless and perhaps dangerous. The non-executive director is a part-timer who does not have a role within the organisation itself, but this does not mean that they do not have a valuable contribution to make to the organisation.

Ideally, an organisation's use of non-executive directors should have some of the following characteristics:

a) The non-executive directors should be very rigorously interviewed to see if they have the qualities demanded for the role. In many cases, the appointment of a non-executive director is more rapid and slap-dash than the appointment of a school leaver.

b) Clear criteria are laid down before the selection process, and some kind of monitoring and evaluation should take place during the tenure of the non-executive.

c) Although the majority of non-executive directors spend little or no time on the affairs of any one organisation, the actual pool of potential non-executives is very small. This needs to be considered when the organisation is considering the appointment of a non-executive.

Table 7.3 attempts to identify the key skills that can be offered and why non-executive directors are so important. It is worth remembering that organisations may have very different motives for bringing in a non-executive director, but we will return to this aspect later.

Table 7.3 Skills provided by non-executive directors

Skill or function	Why they can offer this
Objective evaluation of the business	They do not have a day-to-day role
Unprejudiced opinions and evaluations of the directors	The board may be dominated by certain individuals, ordinary members may not feel free to comment on this
Independent opinion on strategic considerations, such as investments and structure of the organisation	They are not concerned with the impact of their opinions on their careers or status
Experience of other similar organisations or environments	They will tend to have had a previous career
Expert managerial techniques to small- or medium-sized businesses	They will have had experience in the past
Specific skills relating to finance or technical areas	This will have been their area of interest in the past
A useful pool of potential chairpersons for the organisation	They will have made a valuable contribution to the organisation in their role as a non-executive
A link with various external organisations and stakeholders	They will be able to use their network of contacts

Hybrid directors

Geoffrey Mills (1988) identified the 'hybrid director'. These are individuals who offer positive assistance to the organisation for perhaps up to a week each month. In effect, the hybrid director works for the organisation in short, concentrated bursts of time so that their impact can be as effective as possible. The system seems to work quite well, as the hybrid comes into the organisation to input their expertise, withdraws for a period of time for the organisation to absorb their contribution and then returns to push the project further on. Ideally, these hybrid directors are particularly useful for some of the following:

◆ introducing new systems;

◆ adopting new organisational structures;

◆ building planning mechanisms;

◆ evaluating or implementing a specific marketing campaign;

◆ crisis management.

Professional directors

Peter Drucker and Bruce Henderson (part of the Boston Consulting Group) suggested that the most useful addition to any board would be a *professional* director. Obviously, an individual such as this would be in great demand by a number of different organisations. Having said this, the organisation considering taking on a professional director needs to ensure that these individuals are not sitting on too many different boards. They need to be flexible enough to shift their commitments from one organisation to another as needs arise.

These individuals can command considerable salaries; typically, their remuneration would be calculated in the following way:

1 Take the salary of the highest paid full-time director.

2 Double it.

3 Divide it by 200 (this nominally represents the number of realistically productive days in a year) to give the daily rate of pay.

4 Multiply this figure by the number of days the professional director has committed to the organisation per year.

The actual roles and responsibilities of a professional director will differ from organisation to organisation. However, their contribution can be measured in terms of their ability to offer a broad spectrum of different expertise, as well as to adopt a number of different roles within the organisation to suit changing circumstances.

Review questions

1 Outline the three main causes of policy conflicts.

2 Why might intense conflict distort or add bias to decision making within an organisation?

3 How are value systems created within an organisation?

4 Distinguish between values and attitudes.

5 Deal and Kennedy (1988) identified three benefits and three risks attached to the establishment of shared values in an organisation. Outline these benefits and risks.

6 What are the major differences between *operating* values and *intended* values?

7 E.F. Harrison (1981) made an attempt to rank operational values by different categories, briefly detail his suggestions.

8 How do values influence the decision-making process?

9 What do you understand by the term *subconscious information rejection*?

10 Potential conflict is unavoidable in some situations. How can bargaining and trade-offs alleviate this situation?

11 The smoothing style of conflict management occurs when the individuals involved attempt to minimise differences, i.e. the conflict is dealt with as if it is not actually occurring. Is this an effective way of dealing with potential conflict? What are the other alternatives?

12 Machiavellianism (based on the writings of the sixteenth century Italian philosopher and statesman Niccolò Machiavelli), recognises three main traits or styles of behaviour. What are these three traits?

13 What do you understand by the term *locus of control*?

14 What do you understand by the phrase *risk-seeking propensity*?

15 The percentage of non-executive directors sitting on the board of organisations differs widely from country to country, why might this be the case?

16 Outline the main functions and responsibilities of a chairperson.

17 How does the post of chief executive differ from those of the managing director and the chairperson?

18 What is the role of the company secretary?

19 Geoffrey Mills (1988) identified the *hybrid director*. What do you understand by this term?

20 Peter Drucker and Bruce Henderson suggested that the most useful addition to any board would be a *professional* director. What do you understand by this term and how does this role differ from other board-level personnel?

Decision-making styles

As we will see later in this book, the various techniques that can be employed to assist decision making only offer the organisation the ability to identify the possible outcomes of a decision. The identification of these possibilities is useful to the organisation, but it would be foolish to consider that this is the end of the story. In the first instance, the organisation's needs and objectives may not be clearly related to the possible outcomes. Second, the apparent value of these outcomes may be different for the various individuals within the organisation. They may simply not agree that the value of these outcomes is the same or as desirable as that of others. If one could say with certainty that if the organisation chose one course of action it would make a profit, whereas if it made another choice it would lead to a loss, then the decision would be very straightforward. However, situations are never as simple as this and require a much greater understanding of the short-, medium- and long-term effects of the decision.

It may be advisable for the manager or the organisation to create a decision-making model that takes the following into account:

i) understanding of the key variables in the decision;

ii) knowledge of the cause and effect, or pattern of influence that can affect the variables;

iii) understanding of how mathematical or quantitative formulae can be used to create the models.

In this chapter we will be focusing on the differences in, and the uses of, qualitative and quantitative decision-making styles and how they can be used to effect accurate decision making. We should remember that qualitative approaches tend to be related to individuals' own perceptions of the situation and the variables that they feel are relevant. More mathematical or quantitative approaches involve a more objective look at the variables and will include some measurement or comparison with other present or past events.

Quantitative and qualitative decision making

In order to make the distinction clear between these two approaches, Table 8.1 considers the three levels of modelling (descriptive, analogy and relationship) and how they relate to verbal (broadly qualitative) and scientific (broadly quantitative) approaches.

Table 8.1 Levels of decision-making model

Level of modelling	Verbal approach (qualitative)	Scientific approach (quantitative)
Descriptive	What the manager observes and perceives	Use of iconic models to represent reality
Analogy	Comparison between the present situation and one in the past	One set of properties are used to represent another (e.g. graph)
Relationship	An implied relationship is made between parts of the decision	Use of symbolic mathematical numbers and letters to highlight the relationship between parts of the decision

The model needs to incorporate both the variables and the parameters of the situation in order for the decision maker to understand all of the aspects that are involved. These can be explained in the following way.

A variable is an element of the decision that can have a different value at different times (such as the sales per day). The variables can be either inputs or outputs. The *input variables* (also known as the exogenous variables) are the independent aspects that can have an effect on the decision. They can either be controllable (i.e. the decision maker can have an influence over them, such as the minimum stock levels to be held) or they can be uncontrollable as far as the decision maker is concerned (such as the sales targets set by the sales director). The *output variables* (also known as endogenous variables) are generated as a result of the input factors (i.e. cause and effect) and are the consequences of the decision. Output variables cannot be considered as controllable as they only come into effect when the decision is made.

The uncontrollable input factors are the most problematic for the decision maker as it is very difficult to judge their value or potential influence on the decision. For this reason, the decision maker may consider these factors in terms of their probability distribution rather than by trying to give them a definite value.

 ## Cause-and-effect models

One of the simplest ways of showing the relationship between two different factors within a decision can be made by using arrows from the cause to the effect on a diagram. Rather than trying to create a diagram that traces the causes through to the effects, it is simpler to work the other way around. We know what the current situation is: in order to understand how we got there, we can build up the stages of the causes back to their origins. Eventually, we will have all the input and output variables detailed as well as any intermediate variables that have occurred in the sequence.

Although the cause-and-effect diagram is a useful tool in being able to describe the relationships between the various variables, it does not really show the nature of the relationships. In order to understand this, the decision maker needs to have a greater understanding of the relationships than the cause-and-effect diagram will reveal. Cause-and-effect diagrams can be seen as an initial step in the creation of more complex models to aid decision making; at some point there will be no alternative but to look deeper into the situation and consider a more complex mathematical model. Using a simple example, we can see how this process might work.

Example

An organisation knows that it needs to take a number of different variables into account when it is calculating the total costs involved in ordering stock.

The two variable inputs are:

◆ the order quantity; and

◆ the demand for the goods.

The immediate effect of these two variables is to cause the organisation to create an order, or more precisely it will determine the frequency of the ordering.

The final variable (which is a parameter, as it is a fixed cost related to the level of ordering) is the costs associated with ordering itself. This would include the administrative costs, delivery and other factors.

Taking these together means that the organisation can then calculate the total ordering costs (which is the output variable).

Converting this into a mathematical formula is quite simple in this straightforward example:

$$
\begin{array}{lll}
\text{Total costs} & = & T_o \\
\text{Organisational costs} & = & C_o \\
\text{Demand for goods} & = & R \\
\text{Quantity ordered} & = & Q
\end{array}
$$

Therefore:

$$T_o = C_o \times \frac{R}{Q}$$

Decision-making models

We can begin to see that decision-making models are very useful in helping the decision maker appreciate not only the probable outcomes of a situation, but also the causes of that situation in the first place. They also assist the manager in being able evaluate alternative courses of action. Above all, they help the manager simulate situations, allowing them to be more creative in their decision making.

Quantitative decision-making models are at the centre of operations research. They enable the manager to approach the problem of decision making through the use of models and, furthermore, offer a series of standard models that can be applied to various situations by the decision makers.

Linear-programming models

These models are particularly useful for situations when the decision maker has to make a series of choices related to the allocation of resources to a project or activity. Typically, this sort of model would operate under the following constraints:

i) They recognise that the resources that may be allocated to the activity may be limited.

ii) They recognise that the combination or allocation of resources to the activity may be limited or constrained as far as each of the individual components is concerned.

The rules which govern the model are often referred to as *constraints*, whereas the limitations regarding the combination of the resources are referred to as *objective functions*. The objective functions often occur as a result of the organisation setting precise objectives that must be achieved, whether this is maximising the situation or minimising a particular impact. Above all, linear programming is used when there is a clear linear relationship between the constraints and the objective functions. We can examine this further by referring to the following example.

Example

A marketing department has to decide where to allocate its £100 000 budget. Traditionally it has used national newspapers and regional television. The department knows the general costs of each advertisement, so the first task is to work out the constraints on the decision of where to allocate the budget. The number of advertisements that can be afforded if we assume that the budget is £100 000 can be shown in the following manner:

for national newspapers X_N
for regional television X_T

We can therefore show the choices as two different formulae:

$$\text{national newspapers} \quad = \quad 8X_N \quad \leq \quad \pounds100\ 000$$
$$\text{regional television} \quad = \quad 12X_T \quad \leq \quad \pounds100\ 000$$

Alternatively, the following combination could be used:

$$4X_N + 6X_T \quad \leq \quad \pounds100\ 000$$

There are other combinations that could be chosen, but the key constraint is the £100 000 budget total.

The objective function that is relevant here is the sales revenue that could be associated with the advertising. If we assume the following, we can extend the linear programming to its natural conclusion:

> newspaper advertising nets a sales revenue of around £20 000 per advertisement

> regional television advertising nets a sales revenue of around £14 000 per advertisement

The total gross contribution (sales revenue) can be expressed as one of the following formulae:

$$20X_N \text{ or } 14X_T = \text{total gross contribution}$$

In reality, the above formulae reveal that the contributions in cash terms are:

$$\text{for newspapers (8 advertisements)} \quad = \pounds160\ 000$$
$$\text{for television (12 advertisements)} \quad = \pounds168\ 000$$

Queuing models

Queuing models are useful to the decision maker as they can help describe the factors that relate to the interface of supply and demand (*see* Fig 8.1). In this respect, most organisations recognise the fact that there are short-term imbalances between supply and demand, they simply cannot predict what the demand will be for a product or a service over a period. The only thing that is predictable about the demand is that it is unpredictable! The key points to consider are:

a) The level of demand relies on the needs of the customer (whether they are internal or external).

b) The 'gaps' between demand are unpredictable, so the organisation cannot know exactly when the demand for the products and services will present itself.

c) The ability of the organisation to satisfy that demand is variable, regardless of the fact that it may have the resources to cope with that demand (i.e. the fulfilment of the demand is another variable that will change according to a number of different circumstances).

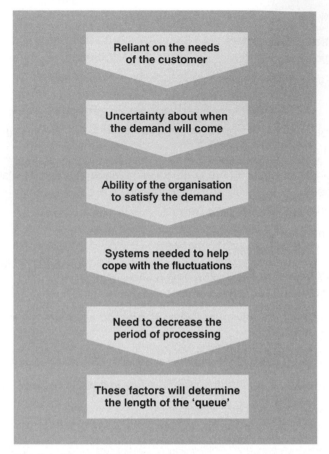

Fig 8.1 The relationships between supply and demand and queuing

d) A system which aims to provide the organisation with the ability to cope with a certain level of demand will, inevitably, be overstretched at times when the demand is high and idle when the demand is slack.

e) Systems that require a long period to process and fulfil the demand may well cause long delays in fulfilment if the demand increases.

f) As a result of this, a queue will form. How the demand (the input), the processing of that demand (the service) and the other support systems are organised will determine the length and the nature of the queue.

Queuing models are not designed to solve queuing problems, since the systems that are in place may be the only viable ways of dealing with the situation. What they can do is to try to predict the patterns of the demand and the queues. As a result of this, the organisation can attempt to predict the behaviour of the demand, the fulfilment and the associated services. In this way, the organisation or the decision makers will be able to try to work out the comparative costs of the various alternatives open to them, taking into account the fact that there may well be some limitations to the alternatives on offer.

Competitive models

Effectively, this is a version of 'game theory' that has been developed in order to assist the decision maker in identifying strategies and decisions that could be used in order to maximise the effect and the impact of the decision, while taking all of the reasonable variables into account.

These competitive models differ from linear-programming and queuing models in the following ways:

◆ Uncontrollable variables are directly related to the controllable variables. In this case, the uncontrollable variables are handled by another individual or a computer program which actively works against the interests of the 'game' player.

◆ The game player has to work systematically through all of the alternative actions to come up with a solution to the problem that best suits the current situation, optimising the gains and minimising the loses that are associated with the decision.

Heuristic models

Heuristic models are derived from the 'bounded rationality' concept, which aims to provide a framework that *satisfices* rather than offering an optimal solution to a problem. In this way the *sub-optimal* solutions should give a satisfactory resolution to a situation, and in some respects this is rather like adopting a trial-and-error approach to decision making. This means that the model allows the decision maker to learn about the decision, eliminating alternatives that do not provide a reasonable resolution to the problem. In other words, the model can be seen as being adaptive, identifying the parameters of the decision. The heuristic model is particularly useful in the following situations:

i) when the decision does not really suit a standard mathematical model as a result of it being unstructured or simply that it does not fit in with a range of basic assumptions about the situation;

ii) when the possible outcomes or solutions to the problem are so vast that it would be impossible to compute them by using a more formal mathematical model.

The potential drawbacks of this approach revolve around the fact that the model is only trying to satisfice and not to provide an ideal or optimal solution to the problem. The decision maker will be unaware of whether the alternative that has been chosen is the best one, given the circumstances that prevail at the time. The manager will not know whether it is the right thing to stop looking for a more ideal solution or whether they have (by accident or design) found the optimum solution. In order to answer these potential queries about the accuracy or efficiency of the solution, the decision maker would need to consider the following:

a) whether the identified solution actually offers a better solution or outcome than the present methods used to deal with the situation;

b) whether there will be any long-term savings or additional costs that can be identified with the adoption of this solution;

c) whether the search for a more efficient solution to the problem can be justified in terms of the effort and resources that will be need to be deployed to find it: will the decision maker simply be delaying the inevitable introduction of the currently identified solution just for the sake of searching for a better option that may not actually exist?

d) whether all of the necessary information is actually available at the point of decision about the solution to the problem: is the manager operating at a time when they are not in possession of all of the facts that are really necessary to make a reasonable choice between the alternatives?

e) whether the selected option offers the decision maker the opportunity to obtain information of a sufficiently high quality at the right time to solve the problem and assess whether the chosen alternative was, in fact, the right one;

f) whether, given all of the alternatives and variables that may operate within and outside the decision, the chosen option is more efficient and effective than the one that is currently under review or in need of change.

Simulation models

Simulation models are more accurately called *procedural models* since it is procedures that are integral to the model itself. Typically, these models rely on stating the exact relationship between the variables in the decision-making process. The model often takes the form of a very logical flow chart that accurately reflects the relationships and interrelationships between the various variables which are a part of the decision.

The simulation model is quite often seen as one of the most basic forms of decision-making model, but it does offer the decision maker the opportunity to investigate the decision by identifying the possibilities and consequences of the decision. Again, this model does not offer the opportunity to optimise decision making. Rather, it is concerned with attempting to predict what may or may not happen. Ideally, simulation models could be used for the following:

◆ prediction of the dynamic behaviour of systems;

◆ decisions which involve variables of a problematic nature, particularly when the variables are uncontrollable.

An organisation could create a simulation using the following procedures.

Example

Country Kitchens provides a full catering service for a variety of different social and business events. One of its major problems is ensuring that enough serving staff are available for the functions.

Many of the functions are booked well in advance, but the company is willing to take on extra work at very short notice.

It is this aspect of the business that causes the most difficulties. The company is aware from its records that over the past three months the number of staff required per day had the following frequency:

No. of staff required	Frequency of demand for staff
7	10
8	12
9	8
10	10
11	20
12	15
13	5
14	5
15	5
	90

In order to simulate the possible demand for staff, the company also needs to assess how much notice it is given by customers. Again, looking at historical records, the company is able to identify the following:

i) functions requiring less than 10 staff generally have a lead-time of at least five days;

ii) functions requiring more than 10 staff generally have a lead-time of eight days.

The only other aspect that needs to be considered is the actual number of orders received on a given day. On average, the company receives around four enquiries per day, but analysis has shown that this usually equates to about one firm order (either immediately or by the next day).

In order to simulate the possible demand for staff, the company would need to do the following:

1 Place a number of pieces of paper in a box with values written on them in the following proportions:

10 with 7 written on them;

12 with 8 written on them;

8 with 9 written on them;

10 with 10 written on them;

20 with 11 written on them;

15 with 12 written on them;

5 with 13 written on them;

5 with 14 written on them;

5 with 15 written on them.

2 Put 90 blank pieces of paper in the box in order to simulate an enquiry that does not lead to an order.

In this way, the organisation can simulate the average demand over a three-month period (90 days) and be able to predict the number of staff that would, theoretically, be needed on any given day. The lead-times from the order to fulfilment would be used to work out the maximum number of staff required on any given day: obviously this would be 30 if both of the pieces of paper drawn on a particular day required 15 staff.

In many respects, this approach to decision making avoids the potential complexities of mathematical modelling. However, the mathematical preparations required to carry out this form of modelling can be difficult in themselves. The principal areas for caution in using this technique are:

i) The conclusions drawn from it are only based on a sample of simulated customer behaviour.

ii) The more mathematical models tend to give more accurate solutions that can be proven.

iii) The data gathered for the simulation may not necessarily be representative of anything more than the period that was sampled.

iv) The assumptions based on the available data may be biased in some way and may not have taken into account all of the variables that were operating at the time. (In our example, the sample could have been taken over the summer period, which included a number of weddings and other seasonal functions. Trying to apply this data and the results to the spring or autumn period would be foolish.)

Financial simulations

Generally, these simulations are used to assist corporate, strategic-level decisions. In this respect, they are often referred to as either corporate modelling or financial modelling. Whatever the term used, or the purpose, they tend to have the following in common:

◆ they use conventional accounting measures and procedures;

◆ they will attempt to create a deterministic simulation that covers a relatively long period.

The type of information that is valuable for corporate planning and decision-making purposes tends to be related to measures such as the following, all of which have more of a macro feel about them rather than being grounded in the operational considerations of the organisation:

a) profitability

b) net cash flow

c) net present value

d) sales revenue.

The problem is that these output variables are very much removed from the measures that are used to calculate them. Seemingly 'distant' variables, such as capacity utilisation and unit price, are difficult to apply directly to these more global and generalised output variables. Obviously, the organisation can attempt to develop some kind of cause-and-effect model which seeks to explain the relationships between the 'micro' or incidental input variables and the more 'macro' output variables, but given the fact the input variables are numerous and perhaps unclear in terms of their relationships to the output variables, this becomes a difficult task.

The financial simulations will focus on the relationship between the more obvious variables, such as changes in price and consequent changes in demand. They do not tend to look at the underlying relationship between these two variables.

 ## Classifying and using decision-making models

Some of the decision-making models which we have looked at attempt to optimise the possible results or returns to the organisation. Others focus on satisficing, recognising the fact that the law of diminishing returns will come into play if the organisation spends too long contemplating the various options in the vain hope that it will find the optimum solution.

Deterministic models tend to use a single measure to estimate the value of each of the variables involved in the decision. On the other hand, probabilistic models use frequency distributions and other techniques in order to identify all the probable values of a variable in given sets of circumstances. At their most basic level, all decision-making models can be seen as being probabilistic in some way: after all, they often take the historical data as being representative of what may or may not occur in the future and they approach all aspects of prediction in a way that reflects the level of uncertainty that the modeller has in the given circumstances.

If models are so unpredictable and uncertain in their nature, why do decision makers consider that they are worth using? At one extreme, decision makers would state that intuition based on actual experience is worth far more than trying to create a mathematical model which attempts to reflect reality. At the other extreme, those who use models extensively are bound to support them, in the sense that they see that clear assumptions derived from the mathematical models in particular, can dispel all of the 'maybes' and 'given the right set of circumstances' quasi-experiential arguments of an intuitive decision maker.

Even the most complex form of linear programming cannot hope to reflect all of the subtle nuances of the decision and all of the associated variables. This model may provide the decision maker with a clear impression of the relative place of all of the variables concerned, but it does not guarantee that all of the variables have been included. After closer examination, the decision maker may well be forced to reconfigure the model to take these extra factors into account. As we will see, one of the key determinants revolves around the relative speed and convenience of the model. At the very least, the model should be simple to construct and understand, offering the decision maker the opportunity to consider the alternatives and concentrate on being creative about the options that are available.

As we have mentioned, there are a number of different factors that should be taken into account before settling on a particular type of model, regardless of whether this is qualitative or quantitative. In fact, if some of the questions cannot be adequately answered, then the decision maker may choose not to use a model at all. These principal considerations include the following:

1   Are the costs of developing the model justified in terms of the potential uses to which the model will be put by the organisation in general? Although some of the mathematically based models can be purchased 'off the shelf' for computer use, most qualitative models will require the services of a consultant.

2   Do the development and use of the model fit within the timeframe in which the decision maker is forced to operate? The development of a 'bug-free' or error-free model may be precluded by the deadlines imposed on the decision maker.

3   Will the time, effort and resources which will need to be ploughed into the model and its subsequent use give the decision maker and the organisation positive benefits as opposed to decisions made without reference to the model?

4   Does the decision, in itself, actually need or justify a model at all? Key considerations of this will include the following:

◆   Are there large amounts of resources at stake? The more resources that will need to be committed as a result of the decision, the greater the argument for using a model. On the other hand, if the decision does not involve the widescale use of resources, then there may not be a compelling argument to use a model.

◆   Is the decision, in itself, a complex one? Given the fact that the majority of decisions (particularly at higher levels) are very complex they may be beyond the scope of even the most comprehensive and sophisticated models.

◆   Is the data available on which to base the model sufficient to be able to produce a feasible and relevant answer to the questions surrounding the decision? Naturally, the more in-depth and complete the data, the greater the chance that the model will be able to produce a solution that is based on the realms of probability and reality.

 ## Top-down and bottom-up processes

Although a large number of organisations have successfully developed a variety of different empowerment schemes within the workplace, we still find that the vast majority of decisions derive from the more traditional top-down approach. Having said this, certain organisations will actively look to individuals who occupy relatively junior positions within the organisation for the 'hands-on' or practical touch that may be required to understand and implement a decision. The more complex and macro the decision, the more likely it is still to be grounded and implemented according to the hierarchy of the organisation. For practical solutions to day-to-day problems which require a decision, the organisation will be more inclined to consider employing the opinions of subordinates.

The success or failure of a decision-making model or process will be very much influenced by the following:

a) whether the organisation has the right type of environment;

b) whether the modelling process is undertaken in a logical and systematic manner;

c) whether the nature of the finished article, in terms of the parameters and uses of the model, is appropriate for the organisation when it actually attempts to use it.

We will need to investigate these factors rather more closely as they will determine the basic decision to use a model, its implementation and the general involvement of individuals in the framing of the model, use and post-use reactions.

Having the right organisational setting or environment is the first key consideration. Within this aspect of modelling use, the organisation needs to look at the following:

1 To what extent is management offering its support to the decision modellers? This will obviously be a major concern, particularly if the key decision makers show that they do not have particular confidence in the model or those involved in its development. Some may also feel that the model may both undermine their own freedom to make decisions or force them to take decisions within an 'alien' framework that does not appear to be relevant or useful. They may also not understand the timescales involved in the development of a decision-making model or the constraints under which the developers are having to operate.

2 Whether the decision makers choose to, or are asked to, be involved in the development of a workable model may well have a significant effect on whether the model is adopted by them. This involvement should attempt to go beyond common courtesy and the decision makers should feel that they have a very real stake in the formulation of the model. Linkages should be formed with everyone who will be invited to use the model once it has been developed. Equally, there is a strong argument for the modellers to incorporate the views of those who will be directly affected by the decisions made by management.

3 Is it clear at what level the model will be operating within the organisation? This follows on from the last point, but specifically addresses the proposed universality of the model and its appropriateness at different levels of decision making. Above all, the model needs to have strong supporters at some level in the organisation (arguably not at the top level of management, as this may mean that the

rest of the organisation feels that the model is being imposed on them). The involvement of all interested parties is essential to ensure that the model at least appears to be consistent and widely usable throughout the organisation. The modellers and those directly involved will be able to draw on the collective experiences and views of the relevant parties, regardless of their status within the organisation.

4 Do those involved in the creation of the model have a good reputation within the organisation (or as a result of work carried out elsewhere), regardless of the fact that they may be fully supported by senior layers of management? For experiments in the creation of new models it may be advisable to consider choosing areas of activity and decision making that will produce tangible results for the modellers, rather than trying to tackle situations that have so far eluded all attempts to categorise or control them.

What these points suggest can best be summarised in Table 8.2.

Table 8.2 Using decision-making models

Client groupings	Consultant groupings
Major decision makers	*Principal consultant*
The individual who will take ultimate responsibility for the decisions needs to have an extensive dialogue and ongoing involvement with both the principal consultant and the modeller as well as managers who will operate underneath the decision maker in the organisation itself.	This individual will need to consult with all of the consultant team as well as the major decision makers in the client's organisation and those managers who will be using or be affected by the implementation of the model.
Managers	*Modellers*
Working closely with the consultant team, these individuals will act as vital linchpins between the major decision makers and the actual users of the decision-making model.	These individuals, working under the direction of the principal consultant, will have to incorporate all relevant needs and views suggested by the client groups.
Users	*Technicians*
On a day-to-day basis, these individuals will use the decision-making model or framework in order to aid their work. They will have to ensure that they have made their needs perfectly clear to the managers and the team of consultants. The success or failure of the model may well rest on their willingness or ability to use it.	These are the individuals who will, ultimately, create the working decision-making model that will be used by the different client groups. Although they will be working under the express instructions of the principal consultant, they will have to liaise closely with the managers and the users in the client organisation to ensure that the model mirrors their day-to-day requirements and needs.

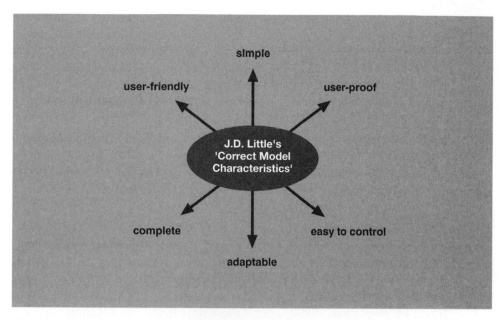

Fig 8.2 J.D. Little's 'correct model characteristics'

The six main characteristics of a correct model for a particular organisation were suggested by Little (1970) to be as follows (*see* Fig 8.2).

1 The model needs to be as simple as possible. This will facilitate understanding of its use and application at various levels of the organisation. In addition to this, a simple model will only focus on the really important issues and considerations that have to be addressed by the decision maker.

2 The model needs to be 'user-proof' in the sense that the day-to-day users of the model may lose confidence in it if they discover that there are gaps in its coverage or inconsistencies in its assumptions. At all costs, the model should never be capable of producing a result that is either ridiculous or unusable.

3 The model should be easy to control in the sense that the users should understand the impact of changes in the input variables or the output variables. Provided that the users understand the relationships between the inputs and the outputs, there is a better chance that they will trust the construction and the applications of the model.

4 The model needs to have the capacity to be adaptable and usable in a variety of allied contexts. The model needs to be constructed in such a way as to ensure that unexpected changes in the input variables are incorporated into the overall structure of the model. If the user discovers that the model is incapable of being used because the parameters of the variables have changed beyond its scope, the model will no longer be a viable alternative to the intuitive approach to decision making.

5 The model needs to be complete in respect of addressing all of the basic variables that may come into play within the decision. The users will lose confidence in the model if they discover that it is unable to incorporate all of the variables and considerations that they would feel appropriate when making the decision in another way. This means that there is a complex balance between simplicity and completeness, but this problem should be avoided if the users are fully consulted throughout the framing of the model.

6 The model needs to be 'user friendly' in the sense that an impenetrable model will prove very difficult to use. This can again be avoided if the modellers try to involve the users at every stage of the development of the model. Above all, the model needs to use the same language as the users and not that of the modellers.

 ## Impact of culture

Essentially, organisational or corporate culture is the organisation's personality. It is the way in which the organisation thinks and how it does things. The culture is something that most members of that organisation share. The culture is gradually learnt by employees as they spend more time in the organisation.

The management will try to create a particular organisational culture. Some organisations do have very strong cultures. Perhaps the best way of expressing the core values which lie at the root of these cultures is to examine some of the work-related values which are shared by all. There are four basic core values as identified by Hofstede. These are:

i) *Power distance* – this addresses the fact that individuals accept the way in which the organisation is structured. It also includes the realisation that not all members of the organisation have equal power. The subordinates trust the management and in turn receive that trust back.

ii) *Uncertainty avoidance* – this is a measurement of how individuals within the organisation feel in situations when they are unsure of themselves. An integral part of this is to encourage employees to take part in decision making through empowerment. This will greatly reduce the uncertainty and allow for greater expression and participation.

iii) *Individualism* – certain organisations stress the importance of personal initiative and achievement. Indeed, they reward employees for personal performance. On the other hand, other organisations will stress the importance of co-operation, but will positively encourage competition between departments or subdivisions of the organisation.

iv) *Masculinity or femininity* – masculinity puts forward the notion that all men should be assertive and that women should be present in order to encourage males to show dominance. This form is particularly common in US organisations. On the other hand, some organisations favour femininity, because they feel that this approach is more employee-oriented. Further, it also suggests that the organisation positively nurtures its employees.

Examples of organisational cultures

Having looked at the core values, we can now turn our attention to some particular examples of organisational culture.

Clan culture

Clan culture is a type of organisational culture which is based on teaching employees to share values. Organisations that favour this form of organisational culture will develop their ability to pass on this particular culture from one employee generation to the next. These organisations are far more traditional, with a distinct history and origin. All members of the organisation have a particular style and manner of conduct.

Market culture

A market culture is rather less formal. The individuals within the organisation conform to the culture, which offers rewards for performance. There is little pressure from the organisation to conform; in fact, the culture almost demands that individuals remain different. It thrives on differences. The market culture does not generate loyalty or co-operation, but it does generate initiative, responsibility and entrepreneurial approaches.

Two key theorists, Harrison (1972) and Handy (1985), developed and proposed four different types of organisational culture.

Power culture

The first is known as power culture, which has a central source and depends on trust and personal communication. Within these organisations there are few rules; however, the central power of the organisation controls the individuals and the decisions. Typically these organisations would be controlled by a charismatic leader. They are strong and effective in most cases.

Role culture

Role culture is based on logic and rationality. All individuals are controlled within their roles and by the rules of the organisation. The only way to achieve in an organisation such as this is to attain a certain level of performance. The organisation is stable and predictable. Individuals who thrive in this kind of environment will be efficient. It is not, however, an organisation that adapts well to change.

Task culture

In these organisations power is based on ability and expertise. Project teams are the most important aspect of the task culture. Typically, the organisation will be structured as a matrix. These organisations are strong and flexible. Teams established to handle certain situations can be changed, adapted and redeployed.

Person culture

The person culture emphasises the importance of the individual. In these organisations there is a tendency for like-minded people to co-operate. Power is shared and based on ability. Organisations such as these find it difficult to control the various individuals within them. In many cases, person cultures can be found within larger organisations which are predominantly role or power culture oriented.

Changing culture

If employees share the organisation's cultural values, then they will often be more committed to it than is the organisation itself. However, organisations need to be able to adapt and change their culture if they intend to remain competitive and adaptable. There may be a degree of resistance to any change proposed since employees may feel that their status within the organisation will be affected by the change. Equally, employees get into the habit of certain forms of behaviour and approach. They will feel less secure and may consequently fear the unknown.

Review questions

1 Distinguish between qualitative and quantitative decision-making styles.

2 Define the term *variable* and give an example.

3 'The uncontrollable input factors are the most problematic for the decision maker as it is very difficult to judge their value or potential influence upon the decision.' Why is this the case?

4 What is the purpose of a cause-and-effect diagram?

5 What is meant by the following equation? $T_o = C_o \times R/Q$

6 What is a linear-programming model?

7 Describe the queuing model with an appropriate example.

8 Competitive models are a version of game theory developed to assist the decision maker in identifying strategies and decisions that could be used to maximise the effect and impact of the decision. How do they differ from linear programming and other forms of model?

9 Simulation models are more accurately called *procedural models* since it is the procedures that form the integral part of the model itself. Describe the model fully with an appropriate example.

10 Financial simulations are used to assist corporate and strategic level decisions. How do they achieve this?

11 Distinguish between probabilistic and deterministic decision-making models.

12 Explain the key differences between the top-down and the bottom-up approaches to decision making.

13 The six main characteristics of a correct model for a particular organisation were suggested by J.D. Little (1970). What are they?

14 How can the culture of the organisation affect its decision-making processes?

15 Two key theorists, Harrison and Handy, developed and proposed four different types of organisational culture. Briefly outline these four types.

Decision-making techniques

This chapter considers the various ways in which an organisation or particular managers can use specific techniques to aid their decision making. The majority of the techniques covered rely on some kind of data being available to managers. Although most of the techniques do rely on data or information from which the decision can be analysed, there is often a degree of qualitative appraisal involved. It is worth remembering that although the techniques begin with pure data, the sources may not be completely reliable (which could cause some inaccuracies) and, more importantly, the application and interpretation of the resulting data may be open to qualitative analysis. The various weightings that are attached to the data or the outcomes of the techniques may not be clear enough to allow the manager to make a positive assessment of the situation. It is at this point that seemingly quantitative approaches are overlaid with qualitative assessments and appraisals.

Some of the techniques are drawn from the work of accountants (such as investment appraisal), others have a economics background (such as cost–benefit analysis) and others have more general usage in the strategic and operational planning areas of the organisation (such as decision trees).

Investment appraisal

Any expenditure within an organisation is made in order to gain some kind of benefit. One of the principal factors surrounding this is how fast the expenditure pays off, either in terms of covering the costs of the investment or turning a profit. The reasoning behind any capital expenditure is that it should mean that the organisation will benefit in the future. Although the returns may take a while to be realised, eventually (and over a number of years) the funds will come to the organisation. In many cases, the capital expenditure programme may involve hundreds if not millions of pounds.

Benefits will be expected either in financial or non-financial terms. It is not necessarily the case that the benefits will be financial. Typical forms of capital expenditure include:

◆ the purchase of land;

◆ the erection of buildings;

◆ the purchase of plant and machinery.

The key objectives of any quantitative appraisal need to address the following:

i) Can the project be justified in terms of the potential benefits?

ii) Are there alternative proposals that could give a better return on the investment?

Payback

Payback is a method of investment appraisal that aims to calculate the period it will take to recover the expenditure. It therefore enables the organisation to determine whether the investment is likely to be profitable.

The organisation needs to determine the likely contribution that the investment will make to the organisation. This can be calculated either on a monthly or yearly basis, depending on the nature of the investment. The formulae are:

$$\text{payback period} = \frac{\text{investment outlay}}{\text{contribution per month}}$$

or:

$$\text{payback period} = \frac{\text{investment outlay}}{\text{contribution per year}}$$

While payback is one of the more simplistic ways of calculating the viability of a project, it is one of the more common. The organisation would normally set a period within which the investment would pay for itself. After this period, often two years, the project would then move into profit.

The calculations can be relatively simple, provided that the cash flows are either predictable or constant. We can illustrate the payback methodology by looking at the following examples in practice.

Example

A printing works invests in a new print machine, for which the total investment cost is £500 000. The organisation believes that the new machine will generate some £180 000 per year in income (or contributions). We can express this in the following manner:

Investment (purchase)	Cash in	Cash out
		£500 000
End year 1	£180 000	
End year 2	£180 000	
End year 3	£180 000	

Working out the monthly contribution is simply:

$$\frac{£180\ 000}{12} \ = \ £15\ 000$$

Therefore the payback period (in months) is:

$$\frac{£500\ 000}{£15\ 000} \ = \ 33.3 \text{ or } 34 \text{ months}$$

The investment will have achieved a payback situation before the end of the 34th month.

Similarly, it is possible to calculate the relative payback periods for a number of competing projects or investments. Remember that all investment is made at the expense of another project. This means that the organisation needs to know which, potentially, will be the best investment to go for. Bearing in mind that this is a question of opportunity cost, we can address the choices in purely cash terms. However, not all investments are made just to get the quickest cash return. There may be other motives in making the investment: perhaps the organisation is looking further into the future in terms of a return on its expenditure. Whatever the case, payback does allow you to look at a number of competing projects and at least ensure that a decision is made regarding the best option in purely monetary terms.

Example

A retail chain has the option of setting up a number of new outlets in a variety of different locations. After extensive market research, it has arrived at the following set of figures. The choice now has to be made about the best location.

	Leicester	Bristol	Birmingham	Glasgow
Set-up costs	£150 000	£120 000	£160 000	£140 000
Income yr 1	£50 000	£40 000	£50 000	£40 000
Income yr 2	£50 000	£60 000	£50 000	£40 000
Income yr 3	£50 000	£80 000	£50 000	£60 000
Income yr 4	£50 000	£80 000	£50 000	£60 000
Total income	£200 000	£260 000	£200 000	£200 000

Leicester would achieve payback at the end of the third year and move into profit in the 37th month after the investment.

Bristol would achieve payback during the third year (contribution £6666 per month in year 3), so three months into the third year, or the 27th month, would be the payback period. So profit is achieved in the 28th month.

Birmingham has not reached payback by the end of the third year (only £150 000 of the original £160 000 has been contributed). Therefore with a monthly contribution of £4166, it would take nearly three more months to move into profit. This gives a payback period of 39 months.

Glasgow reaches its target precisely at the end of the third year, so it moves into profit in the 37th month.

From these figures we can see that Bristol provides the best opportunity to receive an early return on the investment. It is also clear from the projected figures that in turnover terms, Bristol also provides the better set of figures.

Payback is essential for organisations which have to make considerable investments in machinery. This is particularly true of situations when the organisation has to make its current machinery payback before it can replace it with a more up-to-date model. It is also extremely helpful in the sense that it provides the organisation with the opportunity to take a close look at its cash flow. Difficult investment decisions can be made based on the payback approach. If the organisation is forced to look ahead at its cash flow, it can reduce the uncertainty. Payback is designed to get the most out of the investment in the short-term. As it is a forecast over a short period, the guesstimates are likely to be more accurate.

Payback is often criticised for focusing too closely on time as opposed to profit. Those using payback often state that if the calculations are not made in conjunction with other investment appraisal methods, such as average rate of return, then profit is ignored. Although some believe that the short-term focus is a good idea, others will state that this encourages 'short-termism'. In other words, the organisation is simply interested in rapid results, these are given the number one priority and nothing else seems to matter.

Average rate of return (ARR)

The average rate of return is a means by which the annual profit on a particular investment can be calculated as a percentage of the original amount paid. The formula is:

$$\text{ARR (\%)} = \frac{\text{total profit over project life/number of years} \times 100}{\text{capital outlay on project}}$$

Alternatively, the formula can be expressed as:

$$\frac{\text{net return (profit) per annum}}{\text{capital outlay (cost)}} \times 100$$

We can see how these formulae can help to evaluate the work of a particular investment.

Example

	Project A	Project B	Project C
Cost	£100 000	£60 000	£50 000
Return in yr 1	£20 000	£15 000	£15 000
Return in yr 2	£25 000	£20 000	£15 000
Return in yr 3	£35 000	£20 000	£15 000
Return in yr 4	£40 000	£25 000	£20 000
Totals	£120 000	£80 000	£65 000

To compare projects A–C we need to deduct the original investment, then calculate the average annual profit. We can then work out the annual profit as a percentage of the investment.

Project A

$$£120\ 000 - £100\ 000 = £20\ 000$$
Average annual profit = £20 000/4 = £5000
Therefore $\dfrac{£5000}{£100\ 000} \times 100 = 5\%$

Project B

$$£80\ 000 - £60\ 000 = £20\ 000$$
Average annual profit = £20 000/4 = £5000
Therefore $\dfrac{£5000}{£60\ 000} \times 100 = 8.3\%$

Project C

$$£65\ 000 - £50\ 000 = £15\ 000$$
Average annual profit = £15 000/4 = £3750
Therefore $\dfrac{£3750}{£50\ 000} \times 100 = 7.5\%$

It is therefore clear that project B is the most profitable investment. Obviously, the longer the lifespan of the project, the better the opportunity to receive a decent return on the original investment. The other main consideration is the difference between the average rate of return and the interest rate. If the interest rate exceeds the possible annual rate of return, then it is not prudent to make the investment. However, provided that the interest rate is lower than the average rate of return, then it is worth the investment.

By working out the average rate of return for a particular project, the organisation can clearly see whether it would be more profitable to put the money into a bank account that will pay a higher rate of interest than the project would repay. The cost-conscious and investment-aware organisation might wait until the interest rate drops to a figure below the probable ARR. Using the ARR together with the interest rate enables the organisation to identify the opportunity costs of the investment in one particular project instead of another, or, for that matter, the possibilities of leaving the cash in the bank for the time being.

Internal rate of return (IRR)

The internal rate of return is the discount which, when used in cash flow, makes the net present value equal zero. The organisation needs to discover the rate of return where the net present value is zero. This is used in order to compare the market rate of interest with the internal rate of return in order to make a decision about the potential investment. As the rate of interest represents the cost of the capital, if the internal rate of return is higher then the project is worth investing in. However, the organisation may set its own discount rate, which could be higher than the interest rate. So, even if the project looks as if it will be at the interest rate, it still may not be accepted as it does not meet the minimum discount rate set by the organisation.

Example

If we assume that an organisation wishes to invest £30 000 in a new project, it can calculate the probable yield for the first year. It may decide that the investment will bring in some £40 000. At the time of the decision, the market interest rate is 12 per cent.

In order to work out the internal rate of return, we will use the following calculations:

$$\text{cost} = \frac{A}{(1 + x)^1}$$

$$\text{or } £30\,000 = \frac{£40\,000}{(1 + x)^1}$$

$$(1 + x) = \frac{£40\,000}{£30\,000}$$

$$1 + x = 1.3$$

$$x = 1.3 - 1$$

$$x = 0.3 \ (30\%)$$

Therefore the internal rate of return is 30 per cent. Given that the market interest rate is 12 per cent, the investment should provide a much more attractive return than keeping the money in a deposit account.

As we mentioned, there is an alternative way of calculating the internal rate of return. This uses the net present value approach.

Example

If an organisation makes a £100 000 investment which should show a five-year return, then the calculations would look like this:

Year	Income	Present value of income at				
		10%	8%	5%	4%	3%
1	£10 000	£9 091	£9 259	£9 524	£9 615	£9 709
2	£10 000	£8 264	£8 573	£9 070	£9 246	£9 426
3	£20 000	£15 026	£15 876	£17 276	£17 780	£18 302
4	£40 000	£27 320	£29 400	£32 908	£34 192	£35 540
5	£40 000	£24 836	£27 224	£31 340	£32 876	£34 504
Totals	£120 000	£84 537	£90 332	£100 118	£103 709	£107 481
NPV		–£15 463	–£9 668	£118	£3 707	£7 481

At the discount rate of 10 per cent, the NPV is less than zero (at –£15 463). The NPV at 8 per cent is still less than zero (at –£9668). At 5 per cent, the NPV is fairly close to zero (at £118). We can therefore say that the internal rate of return is about 5 per cent.

The discount rate directly affects the NPV. The higher the discount rate, the lower the NPV. The internal rate of return is when the discount rate shows that the NPV is almost zero.

Discounted cash flow

Discounted cash flow seeks to address two vital considerations in investment appraisal. The interest rate and time will determine the return on a particular project. The concept states that the money that is earned in the future, or paid in the future, is worth less than today.

Example

If you were to invest £100 in a deposit account, with a rate of interest of 10 per cent, the value of that investment at the end of the first year would be £110. At the end of the second year, assuming that the interest rate remains the same, it would be £121. This is known as compound interest. Let us see just how and why the money grows:

Year	Calculation	Interest rate	Value of £100
0	–	10%	£100
1	£100 + 10%	10%	£110
2	£110 + 10%	10%	£121
3	£121 + 10%	10%	£133
4	£133 + 10%	10%	£146
5	£146 + 10%	10%	£161
6	£161 + 10%	10%	£177
7	£177 + 10%	10%	£195
8	£195 + 10%	10%	£214
9	£214 + 10%	10%	£236
10	£236 + 10%	10%	£259

This sounds great: a worthwhile investment that shows a return of over 250 per cent in ten years. Unfortunately, this is not the whole picture. The actual value of the money in future is not quite what it seems.

In order to analyse a potential capital expenditure in the future, it is necessary to convert all of the various cash inflows and outflows to their value at one point in time. This is achieved by converting the future values of each of the cash inflows and outflows to their present values. This is done by using a discount factor, based on the relevant interest rates.

Example

We have shown how, with an interest rate of 10 per cent, the value of £100 gradually increases over time. We now need to look at the present values of £100 using discount factors, *see* Table 9.1.

Table 9.1 Discount factors

Interest rates (%)	1	2	3	4	5	6	7	8	9	10
1	0.9901	0.9803	0.9706	0.9610	0.9515	0.9420	0.9327	0.9235	0.9143	0.9053
2	0.9804	0.9612	0.9423	0.9238	0.9057	0.8880	0.8706	0.8535	0.8368	0.8203
3	0.9709	0.9426	0.9151	0.8885	0.8626	0.8375	0.8131	0.7894	0.7664	0.7441
4	0.9615	0.9246	0.8890	0.8548	0.8219	0.7903	0.7599	0.7307	0.7026	0.6756
5	0.9524	0.9070	0.8638	0.8227	0.7835	0.7462	0.7101	0.6768	0.6446	0.6139
6	0.9434	0.8900	0.8396	0.7921	0.7473	0.7050	0.6651	0.6274	0.5919	0.5584
7	0.9346	0.8734	0.8163	0.7629	0.7130	0.6663	0.6227	0.5820	0.5439	0.5083
8	0.9259	0.8573	0.7938	0.7350	0.6806	0.6302	0.5835	0.5403	0.5002	0.4632
9	0.9174	0.8417	0.7722	0.7084	0.6499	0.5963	0.5470	0.5019	0.4604	0.4224
10	0.9091	0.8264	0.7513	0.6830	0.6209	0.5645	0.5132	0.4665	0.4241	0.3855
11	0.9009	0.8116	0.7312	0.6587	0.5935	0.5346	0.4817	0.4339	0.3909	0.3522
12	0.8929	0.7972	0.7118	0.6355	0.5674	0.5066	0.4523	0.4039	0.3606	0.3220
13	0.8850	0.7831	0.6931	0.6133	0.5428	0.4803	0.4251	0.3762	0.3329	0.2946
14	0.8772	0.7695	0.6750	0.5921	0.5194	0.4556	0.3996	0.3506	0.3075	0.2697
15	0.8696	0.7591	0.6575	0.5918	0.4972	0.4323	0.3769	0.3269	0.2843	0.2472

Using Table 9.1, we can now calculate the present values of amounts received in the future.

If we receive £100 000 at the end of 5 years at an interest rate of 5 per cent, the present value is £100 000 × 0.7835 = £78 350.

If we receive £54 835 at the end of 3 years at an interest rate of 8 per cent, the present value is £54 835 × 0.7938 = £43 528.

Comparing these different projects, we can see the potential returns.

Project 1, costing £200 000, is expected to make returns of £320 000 over the next six years. The prevailing interest rate is 12 per cent.

Outflows	End of year	Future value	Discount factor	Present value
	0	£200 000	1.0000	£200 000
Present value of outflows				£200 000
Inflows	1	£30 000	0.8929	£26 787
	2	£50 000	0.7972	£39 860
	3	£60 000	0.7118	£42 708
	4	£60 000	0.6355	£38 130
	5	£60 000	0.5674	£34 044
	6	£60 000	0.5066	£30 396
Present value of inflows				£211 925
Less capital expenditure				£200 000
				£11 925

From these calculations, we can see that the project has a net present value of £11 925. This means, in other words, that once we allow for the organisation's cost of capital, the present value of the cash inflows arising from the project exceeds the outflow by £11 925.

Project 2 will again cost the organisation some £200 000. The interest rates, hence the discount factors, remain the same, at 12 per cent. The project is expected to produce inflows of £320 000. At first glance, the returns look likely to be the same as Project 1, but the inflows are structured differently.

Outflows	End of year	Future value	Discount factor	Present value
	0	£200 000	1.0000	£200 000
Present value of outflows				£200 000
Inflows	1	£60 000	0.8929	£53 574
	2	£60 000	0.7972	£47 832
	3	£60 000	0.7118	£42 708
	4	£60 000	0.6355	£38 130
	5	£60 000	0.5674	£34 044
	6	£60 000	0.5066	£30 396
Present value of inflows				£277 080
Less capital expenditure				£200 000
				£77 080

Project 2 is more financially viable using these calculations because the earlier inflows are higher than in Project 1. As such, they are subject to lower discount factors and are worth more to the organisation. The lower inflows are affected by the discount factor but do not have so drastic an affect on the overall inflows.

Project 3, again working on £200 000 is expected only to have returns over the next four years. Again, the interest rate, or discount factor calculations are based on 12 per cent. The total inflow is expected to be some £240 000.

Outflows	End of year	Future value	Discount factor	Present value
	0	£200 000	1.0000	£200 000
Present value of outflows				£200 000
Inflows	1	£60 000	0.8929	£53 574
	2	£60 000	0.7972	£47 832
	3	£60 000	0.7118	£42 708
	4	£60 000	0.6355	£38 130
Present value of inflows				£182 244
Less capital expenditure				£200 000
				–£17 756

This means that over the four-year period, despite the estimated £240 000 worth of inflows, the actual present value of the inflows is just £182 244. This means that the project is likely to show a loss and consequently the organisation should think very hard before actually committing itself.

Taking the three different projects, obviously Project 2 offers the best opportunities to make a profit. A positive present value is an indication that the project is worth the investment. A negative net present value shows that the project is not a good investment. Under this criteria, Projects 1 and 2 are acceptable, while Project 3 is not.

You can, of course, work out the discount factors yourself. The process is a little laborious, but you may have to calculate them based on figures provided.

Remember that the discount factor is the adjustment which you need to apply to the estimated cash flow in order to arrive at the present value. It is unlikely that you will have to calculate these in an examination, but they are invaluable aids if you are required to work out a cash flow for a small business enterprise project.

Discount factors are merely the inverse of the compound interest that you would receive if you had invested the money in a deposit account over a period of time. In other words, if you invested £1000 at 10 per cent, you would expect to receive £1100 at the end of the year. In subsequent years, the calculation would be based on the amount that has accrued at the end of the previous year:

initial investment	£1000
amount at end of year 1 at 10%	£1100
amount at end of year 2 at 10%	£1210
amount at end of year 3 at 10%	£1331

In order to work out the inverse, we must make the following calculation:

$$\frac{£1000}{£1331} = 0.7513$$

We can use this figure in order to calculate the true value of £1000 at the end of the third year. This discount factor, in effect, shows us what we have lost in terms of interest by not investing the money in an interest-bearing account:

$$£1000 \times 0.7513 = £751.30$$

 ## Break even

One of the most straightforward decision-making models is derived from economics and is known as *break even*. We discussed the break-even point in Part 1 of the book but it is useful to consider it here as a method of helping the organisation to make decisions. The key to understanding break even is to appreciate the importance of the following equation:

$$\text{total costs} = \text{fixed costs} + \text{variable costs}$$

or, more commonly:

$$TC = FC + VC$$

The technique is best understood by using it to work out a particular problem as outlined below.

A firm of solicitors has a number of local clients and feels that it is more efficient to sub-contract the delivery of legal documents to a local courier company. After some discussion, considering the volume of work, the courier company has offered to provide the service for a basic fee of £100 per month, plus a standard charge of £50 for 10 deliveries or part thereof. The FC is £100, while the VC is £5 per delivery (or, more clearly, £50/10). The variable here is the amount of deliveries in a given month, so we need to include this in the equation, to this end we will insert an *X* to denote this. The simplified equation is:

$$TC = 100 + 5X$$

This equation will allow the solicitors to work out the total costs incurred for any number of deliveries in a month. This can be transferred on to a graph (see Fig 9.1).

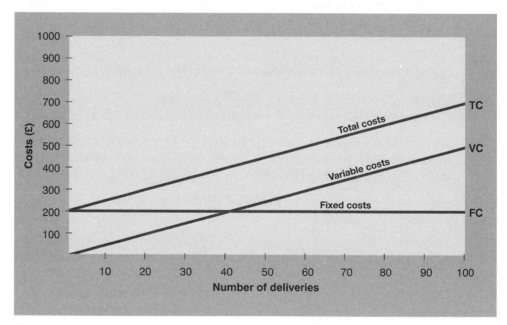

Fig 9.1 Break-even graph

The FC line is fixed across the graph regardless of the number of deliveries that are actually made. The VC line starts at zero, as the solicitors will not incur any extra costs if they do not have any deliveries in a given month. The TC, starting at the FC line, is effectively £200 more at each point than the FC line. It is therefore clear that the solicitors will have to find £700 if they want the courier company to deliver 100 documents in a given month.

This is the first part of the analysis. Obviously, the service could work out to be quite expensive, so the solicitors realise that they will need to pass this cost on to their clients. They set the delivery charge per document (or parcel) at £10. They estimate that this will help to cover the standing charge made by the courier company. Although they do not intend to make a profit from the service, they realise that if 100 deliveries are made at a cost of £700, they will be receiving a revenue of £1000. However, they do not expect to be sending out 100 sets of documents every month, so they need to know how many deliveries would mean that they could break even. This is achieved by using the same information as before, retaining the TC line on the graph, but adding a revenue line based on the assumption that they will be charging their clients £10 per delivery. By referring to the graph in Fig 9.2, you will see that it is comparatively easy to calculate that they need only send off 40 sets of documents per month in order to break even. This is rounded to take into account of the fact that the courier company charges in multiples of 10 or part thereof. Therefore, the solicitors need to base their decisions on this and not the individual cost/revenue of each delivery.

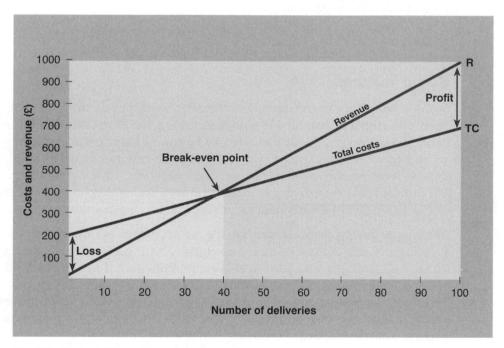

Fig 9.2 Calculation of break-even point

Cost-benefit analysis

Several of the decision-making techniques which we have investigated so far have their roots in finance, in other words, they aim to weigh up the potential financial costs and the financial benefits of a particular decision. Naturally, the majority of organisations would always choose a route that offers them the best potential in terms of positive benefits either in the short-term or the long-term, depending on the actual nature of the decision.

Cost–benefit analysis requires the organisation to take a broader view of the potential costs and benefits associated with a decision. This means that the traditional 'private' or internal costs and benefits are only one part of the overall equation. Aside from these internal considerations, the decision may create a series of external costs and benefits that are either unavoidable if a certain course of action is taken, or desirable as a natural by-product of the decision. Negative impacts on the environment are seen as being the most tangible way that the social costs involved in business decision making can be measured; at the same time, the social benefits that can be associated with a decision could include higher levels of local employment or an enhanced road system (the cost of which has been underwritten by the organisation). In order to quantify the social costs and the social benefits, the following formulae are generally used:

$$\text{social costs} = \text{private or financial costs} + \text{external costs}$$
$$\text{social benefits} = \text{private or financial costs} + \text{external benefits}$$

Social auditing

So how would these considerations actually work in practice? Inevitably this means that the organisation will need to develop some form of social auditing. The earliest references to social auditing can be traced back as far as the late 1960s when organisations sought to expand their conventional financial reporting to include some features of 'corporate social expenditure'. By the late 1970s, particularly in the USA, the majority of large organisations had begun to devote at least one or two pages in their annual reports to their social expenditure.

The biggest developments occurred in the 1980s, perhaps as a direct response to the growing strength of the consumer movement. Any organisation that professed to be ethically minded was keen to show the public that it not only talked about social considerations but was actually doing something about it. These were the first real attempts to offer some kind of benchmark measurement system that would enable the public to judge the activities of the organisation against a set of predetermined or espoused criteria.

The 1990s have seen a new move in the field of social responsibility and auditing, with organisations beginning to state clearly that they wish to appear both ethically minded and positively active in developing a strong moral stance. Finally, the question of social auditing has come of age: it is no longer driven by external agencies and interest groups, it is driven by the organisation itself which can see the positive benefits of adopting such a stance.

Ethical accounting approaches encourage stakeholders to propose changes in the organisation's operational practices, although some organisations do not yet incorporate external verification of the published statement by independent auditors.

There are a number of different approaches and understandings of the social and ethical accountability concept. Essentially, the differences can be categorised as in Table 9.2.

Table 9.2 Social and ethical accountability

Social/ethical approach	Social audits	Ethical accounting	Social evaluation
Multiple stakeholder perspective	Yes	Yes	Yes
Systematic policy assessment	Yes	Yes	No
Internal monitoring of social performance indicators	Yes	No	Yes
Monitoring of stakeholder accounts	Yes	Yes	Yes
Ongoing commitments	Yes	Yes	Yes
Independent external verification	Yes	No	Yes
Public disclosure	Yes	Yes	Yes

Placing a value on the externalities may be very difficult. An example will clarify this.

Example

If a city council has decided to make a considerable investment in the installation of a comprehensive tram system in the centre of the city, there are a number of potential costs and benefits that can be associated with this policy. The costs include:

1 The disruption of the city centre during the construction period, leading to time wasted for commuters and businesses.

2 The chaotic appearance of the city centre, making it a less attractive place for visitors, shoppers and tourists.

3 The impact on the existing forms of transportation, with a possible consequent loss of jobs.

4 The investments that will need to be included in the overall package such as education of the commuters and other users in how the system works and setting up tram sheds and allied support services (including repair and maintenance).

5 The long-term impact on access to the city centre for other, more conventional modes of transport (whether personal or business).

6 The actual financial cost of the whole project. Assuming that the council manages to attract central government funding, European funding or the partnership of private contractors, it will have to divert a certain amount of its funds from other projects to this one.

7 Individuals or areas of the city that had hoped to be able to attract council funding for other projects may find that the council is fully committed financially for a number of months, if not years. For the council, this is a question of priorities, but for those affected by the switch in funding, it will be difficult for them to understand why they have lost out.

8 The eighth cost will very much depend upon the sources of finance that the council is proposing to use (or for that matter what options are available to it). If it will have to fund the majority of the project, then business rates will have to be increased in order to pay for the project and the inhabitants of the city will also be expected to make a contribution through an increase in council tax.

However, the benefits include the following:

i) the immediate increase in employment in the city to carry out the work needed to construct the tram system;

ii) reduced congestion, pollution and damage to the city centre by the reduction of conventional forms of transport;

iii) the need to employ local people to staff the tram system, support services and other maintenance contracts;

iv) the enhanced nature of the city centre in terms of its opportunities to attract more shoppers, visitors and tourists once the system is up and running.

Even though we can identify these potential costs and benefits to the city in the long- and short-term, it is very difficult to quantify some of them. Perhaps the most easily quantifiable are the implications (short- and long-term) for the employment prospects in the area. It could be argued that the long-term prospects offered to the new staff for the tram system are at the expense of the employment prospects for the employees of the present forms of transport. Equally, the fact that the city will need to employ a number of contractors to carry out the work on the system may be offset by the fact that the majority of the workers will need to be specialised and probably not local people at all. Whatever the choice, the employment for these individuals is only likely to be short-term.

Financial considerations can be quantified to some degree, but the council will have to assess the probability of each of the options in order to see what the consequences of particular decisions will be, both in the short- and long-term. The council would argue that whatever the short-term costs, either to its budget, the city centre or local businesses and dwellers, the long-term benefits will be enjoyed by all for a considerable period of time.

Assessing the impact of a decision

The human impact of a decision is very hard to quantify in any meaningful manner. It is not always likely that the organisation has even thought about the costs to, say, the local community or the general public in a wider sense. This is why any attempt to use cost–benefit analysis should be preceded by a period of consultation with those parties which could suffer some form of cost as a result of a decision being made by the organisation.

Perhaps the best way to approach the question of cost–benefit analysis is to consider the fact that benefits will be enjoyed over a period and that immediate returns or benefits should not be expected.

Example

If an organisation states that an investment of £100 000 today will bring it returns of twice that in five years' time, we should view this with a degree of scepticism. If we assume that inflation is running at 5 per cent over each of the years, the actual £100 000 investment looks very different:

End of year	Actual value of investment
1	£105 000
2	£110 250
3	£115 762.50
4	£121 550.625
5	£127 628.156

Rather than actually doubling the value of the investment, the organisation will net less than £75 000 at the end of the fifth year. Having said this, it is still not a bad return on the investment, given the fact that the organisation could have chosen another alternative which may have meant that it lost the investment.

Whatever the criteria used, or the purpose of the cost–benefit analysis in the first place, the fact is that the system is very imprecise. It is extremely difficult to place a precise value on some of the more intangible aspects of costs and benefits. In any case, the expected benefits in the future need to take into account the fact that the value of the returns in the future will be eroded by inflation, or at least offset by the potential gains that could have been enjoyed had the organisation made a different decision about the investment. As a result, any cost–benefit analysis needs to be viewed with a degree of scepticism, and the assumptions need to be clearly stated in order to understand the basic foundations of the analysis. In an ideal world, the organisation should carry out a series of cost–benefit analysis tasks to look at the variety of different long-term implications of a decision made today. It should also take into account the fact that, despite all attempts, certain social costs simply cannot be measured in purely monetary ways. Cost–benefit analysis, although used fairly widely, is only one of the range of tools and techniques used to assist decision making.

Expected values and decision trees

Before we investigate the nature of these two allied techniques, it is prudent that we spend some time looking at the foundations that will need to be laid in order to get the most out of them. Given the fact that organisations operate, or more precisely decisions are made, in conditions ranging from *certainty* to *total uncertainty*, there is a tremendous amount which is unknown between these two extremes.

In conditions of certainty, the decision maker can be sure that one of the following is in operation:

i)   the conditions themselves cannot change as they are always the same (such as knowing that a supplier will always deliver the next day);

ii) the variables that could affect the conditions under which the decision is made are never significant enough to affect the overall outcome of the decision under the majority of circumstances (such as minor changes to the specification of a product that may not be immediately apparent to the customer, or, in fact, affect the use or function of the product).

At the other extreme, the organisation or decision maker may be operating in conditions that are wholly uncertain. In this case, the following may be relevant:

i) the decision maker cannot actually predict the outcome of a decision at all (such as the actual effect on sales if the prices were increased by 10 per cent across the board);

ii) the decision maker does not have any confidence in the fact that the sets of circumstances that relate to the decision today will hold good during the implementation of the decision, or for that matter, after the decision has worked through to all of the relevant parties (such as a building society considering a change in its interest rates at a time when interest rates are volatile and unpredictable);

iii) the decision maker is not sure that the assumptions that are being made in relation to the decision are actually true or relevant, or, for that matter, will still be so when the decision is implemented.

Obviously, these are two extremes and, although they are possible, they are comparatively unlikely to occur. The fact is that the majority of decision makers will recognise the fact that, no matter how well prepared they may be, there is always the chance that an unforeseen occurrence may throw out all of their well-laid plans.

As we will see in the last part of this book, decision makers will nearly always have to make their decisions in situations of uncertainty and risk. This is the very nature of decision making and is unavoidable. How can uncertainty be incorporated into any kind of attempt to make a decision, particularly if the fundamental nature of the decision means that uncertainties are commonplace?

In effect, there are only three ways of doing this, which are:

a) to make the best possible guess based on the information available. In this case, the existence of uncertainty should be ignored as the decision maker cannot know the unknown.

b) to follow the approach above, but to include some form of *contingency* in the decision-making process in case the best guesses are too optimistic. In other words, what would be the course of action if the decision brought about severe consequences?

c) to attempt to bring the uncertainty into the equation itself and incorporate it fully into the modelling.

Probability

This brings the question of probability back into the discussion. Using and understanding probability are critical to creating effective decision trees and working out expected values.

An organisation is developing a new product that it hopes to have ready for June of next year. After consultation with all of the relevant parties within the company, it arrives at a 70 per cent probability that it will meet the deadline. This assumes two very critical points:

i) The organisation is stating that the launch will either happen by the deadline, or it will not. This is cut and dried, there are no other possible alternatives; in other words, the two alternatives are *exhaustive*.

ii) The organisation is stating that if one alternative occurs the other cannot; in other words, the two alternatives are *mutually exclusive*.

So far, the organisation has only stated that it will or will not meet the deadline. There are, of course, other variations here, perhaps a 'near miss' of the deadline is possible. If this is the case, then the following may be the true set of probabilities:

Product development completed ready for launch in June as required   = 70%
Product development completed ready for launch in July
(one month too late)   = 20%
Product development not completed until at least two months
(or more) later than the required June date   = 10%

Again, this can be refined even further as the organisation breaks down these initial probabilities to incorporate all of the possible variations. Let us begin with the figure related to completion by June:

Product ready one month before the deadline   = 30% ⎫
Product ready in the deadline month   = 40% ⎭ 70%

Following this approach, the whole of the problem can be broken down in the following manner:

Product ready more than one month early   = 0% ⎫
Product ready one month before the deadline   = 30% ⎬ 70%
Product ready in the deadline month   = 40% ⎭

Product ready in July   = 20% ⎫
Product ready in August   = 5% ⎬ 30%
Product ready in September   = 5%
Product ready later than September   = 0% ⎭

The cumulative probability distribution can be created directly from the information that we have already gathered. This will show us the total probability of an event occurring by a particular date:

Product ready more than one month early	=	0%
Product ready one month before the deadline	=	30%
Product ready in the deadline month	=	70%
Product ready in July	=	90%
Product ready in August	=	95%
Product ready in September	=	100%

In order to use probabilities in situations where there is a degree of uncertainty, the probability estimates will need to be manipulated. Before we can do this, it is important that the three key laws which allow the decision maker to combine the probabilities of different events are understood.

The first law of probability

If X_1 and X_2 are exclusive events, then the probability of X_1 or X_2 occurring will be the sum of the probability of X_1. This can be shown as:

$$P(X_1 \text{ or } X_2) = P(X_1 + X_2)$$

Let us expand this by looking at the following set of percentages and probabilities.

Example

An organisation wishes to make an assessment of the probable impact of an advertising campaign in order to be ready with sufficient stocks of products in the warehouse for dispatch. The organisation has calculated the following from previous experience of similar campaigns.

Advertising effect on demand	% chance	Probability
Nil	0	0
+ 5%	10	0.1
+ 10%	5	0.05
+ 15%	5	0.05
+ 20%	20	0.2
+ 25%	10	0.1
+ 30%	10	0.1
+ 35%	5	0.05
+ 40%	10	0.1
+ 45%	10	0.1
+ 50%	10	0.1
more than 50%	5	0.05

Remember that all of these events are mutually exclusive. The organisation really needs to be able to show at least a 25 per cent increase in sales in order to justify the investment in the advertising campaign. So if we look at the cumulative percentages up to and including the 30 per cent sales increase, we arrive at the following figure:

$$10\% + 5\% + 5\% + 20\% + 10\% + 10\% = 60\%$$

This means that there is a 60 per cent chance of the organisation meeting the target of an increase in sales of 30 per cent.

The probabilities should give us a similar answer:

$$0.1 + 0.05 + 0.05 + 0.2 + 0.1 + 0.1 = 0.6$$

By simply converting this probability into a percentage, we can see that the prediction is still 60 per cent.

The second law of probability

In many situations the decision maker is faced with a more complex problem than just having to work out the probability of one event occurring. Often, the decision maker will be asked, 'What is the chance of being able to reach the targets that we want and stay within the budget?' This added level of complexity is at the root of the second law of probability. In these cases, when we have to calculate the probability of two events occurring, the individual probabilities are multiplied to produce a third probability that is the estimate of that happening.

In order to illustrate this, we will expand our example.

Example

Based on experience, the advertising manager is able to tell the key decision maker that, under normal circumstances and everything being equal, they would have a 70 per cent chance of staying within the budget that has been assigned to the campaign. The advertising manager stresses that this is based on the assumption that the media owners are not going to put up their advertising rates and that the preferred spaces and slots are available.

The decision maker must now merge the two probabilities together in order to work out the probability of returning a 30 per cent increase in demand within the budget:

$$P \text{ (required sales increase in budget)} =$$
$$P \text{ (required sales increase)} \times P \text{ (within budget)} =$$
$$60\% \times 70\% \text{ or } 0.6 \times 0.7 = 0.42$$

There is, therefore, a 42 per cent chance of the required increase in sales volume being reached within the predetermined budget set for the campaign. It is important to note that the probability is gradually dropping as we add in the extra criteria that need to be taken into account. The decision makers may not have the same level of confidence about the decision that they had at the start of the investigation.

The third law of probability

Potentially, this is the most complex of all of the laws, but it is a logical progression all the same. We already know the following:

$$P(X_1) \quad = \ 0.6$$
$$P(X_2) \quad = \ 0.4$$
$$P(Y \mid X_2) \ = \ P \text{ (target reached within budget)} = 0.7$$
$$P(Y \mid X_2) \ = \ P \text{ (target not reached outside of budget)} = 0.12$$

It is important to remember that in all cases the following is true:

$$P(X_1) = 1 - P(X_2)$$

Therefore, if X_1 and X_2 are exhaustive and mutually exclusive, then the probability of another event (Y) can be estimated using the following formula:

$$P(Y) = P(Y \mid X_1) \times P(X_1) + P(Y \mid X_2) \times P(X_2)$$

Example

Inserting the figures from the example into this equation we have the following:

$$P(Y) = 0.7 \times 0.6 + 0.12 \times 0.4$$
$$\text{or: } P(Y) = 0.42 + 0.048$$
$$\text{or: } P(Y) = 0.468$$

This is a more accurate and slightly more appealing 46 per cent or 47 per cent probability that the required sales revenue is reached within the budget.

Decision trees

As we will see, the more complex the number of variables and possibilities that need to be incorporated into the decision, the greater the need to use a decision tree to illustrate the problem.

A decision or outcome matrix can be used to attempt to quantify the relationships between the various *states of nature* (which means listing as many of the uncertain events as possible) and the options open to the decision maker. In effect, the matrix will look something like Table 9.3.

Note that the outcomes will always be recognisable by virtue of the fact that they will have the numbers of both the option and the uncertain events attached to them.

This identification of all of the possible outcomes for all of the relationships between the two principal criteria (options and states of nature) may be useful, but in practice the organisation will have to try to quantify each of these values.

Table 9.3 Decision matrix

Options	States of nature									
	N_1	N_2	N_3	N_4	N_5	N_6	N_7	N_8	N_9	N_n
S_1	O_{11}	O_{12}	O_{13}	O_{14}	O_{15}	O_{16}	O_{17}	O_{18}	O_{19}	O_{1n}
S_2	O_{21}	O_{22}	O_{23}	O_{24}	O_{25}	O_{26}	O_{27}	O_{28}	O_{29}	O_{2n}
S_3	O_{31}	O_{32}	O_{33}	O_{35}	O_{35}	O_{36}	O_{37}	O_{38}	O_{39}	O_{3n}
S_4	O_{41}	O_{42}	O_{43}	O_{44}	O_{45}	O_{46}	O_{47}	O_{48}	O_{49}	O_{4n}
S_5	O_{51}	O_{52}	O_{53}	O_{54}	O_{55}	O_{56}	O_{57}	O_{58}	O_{59}	O_{5n}
S_6	O_{61}	O_{62}	O_{63}	O_{64}	O_{65}	O_{66}	O_{67}	O_{68}	O_{69}	O_{6n}
S_m	O_{m1}	O_{m2}	O_{m3}	O_{m4}	O_{m5}	O_{m6}	O_{m7}	O_{m8}	O_{m9}	O_{mn}

Key
S_1–S_m are the options open to the organisation
N_1–N_n are the uncertain events that may effect the decision or will be a consequence of the decision
O_{11}–O_{mn} are the outcomes of the relationships between the options and the uncertain events

Example

A small kitchen furniture manufacturer has been approached by a major home builder to supply purpose-built kitchens to a common size and standard for its three new estates in the area.

The construction company is confidently expecting to be able to sell all 300 of its new starter homes, but the kitchen furniture manufacturer is not entirely convinced that all of the houses will be sold. It needs to incorporate this into the equation, as the kitchens will not be needed for a particular house until it has been sold.

The kitchen furniture manufacturer realises that it cannot possibly make all of the kitchens that are needed by the builder, so it has two main options:

◆ to subcontract the work to another company, or range of companies, at a fixed rate, but still to fit the kitchen into the house;

◆ to buy in 'off-the-shelf' kitchens from a supplier and then convert the units to look like its own kitchens.

In deciding which option to use, an organisation will have to consider whether it has a real chance of being able to achieve the desired optimum level of sales or profit. In order to do this, the organisation will have to consider the following four rules which apply to decision making of this type:

i) the optimistic decision rule;

ii) the pessimistic decision rule;

iii) the regret decision rule;

iv) the expected value decision rule.

We will use our previous example to illustrate how all of these different rules apply to the decision-making process.

Example

Optimistic and pessimistic decision rules

Construction method used		Sales volume and profit from the contract with the builders	
		50% supplied	100% supplied
Method 1	*Revenue*	£600 000	£1 200 000
	Profit	£75 000	£150 000
Method 2	*Revenue*	£600 000	£1 200 000
	Profit	£150 000	£300 000

The optimistic decision rule leads the organisation to consider all of the potentially most favourable sets of circumstances that could occur. For the kitchen manufacturer, the best level of profit occurs when it chooses construction method 2 and assumes that all of the kitchens will be ordered by the builders. This analysis, although simple, involves finding the maximum profit outcome and cross-referencing it with the construction option that provides that maximum profit.

The pessimistic decision maker will look at the information in a very different manner. Each of the options will be examined and the worst possible outcome for that option will be identified. The option selected will be the one that shows the lowest possible profit in the worst set of circumstances. In this case, the kitchen manufacturer will choose the first option that works on the assumption that only half of the homes will be sold and consequently only 50 per cent of the kitchens will be needed.

Regret decision rule

Optimistic/pessimistic calculations incorporating regrets are as follows:

Construction method used		Sales volume and profit from the contract with the builders		
		50%	100%	Maximum regrets
Method 1	*Revenue*	£600 000	£1 200 000	
	Profit	£75 000	£150 000	
Regrets		£75 000	£150 000	£150 000
Method 2	*Revenue*	£600 000	£1 200 000	
	Profit	£150 000	£300 000	
Regrets		£0	£0	£0

Although this is a very simple rule, it does lie at the very centre of the decision-making process. Effectively, the decision maker must ask a question that demands a degree of 'crystal-ball gazing'. In other words, if the decision maker settled on a particular course of action, how much would they regret having made that decision if one of the other alternatives turned out to be a better one? In our example, there are regret situations attached to the first method of construction of the kitchen units. For the 50 per cent supply of the units, the kitchen manufacturer would stand to lose £75 000, but for the 100 per cent order, it would lose £150 000. This gives the kitchen manufacturer a very clear indication that the second method is a far more (potentially) profitable option.

In some cases the regret situation is far less clear than our example. At low production levels, the profit may not be very high for one method, but as economies of scale come into play, the profit on higher production levels offers a greater profit return. On the other hand, a production method may offer higher profits for short production runs (for example, the organisation may be buying in the product from a third party at a fixed rate), but even with the higher demand, the fixed rate paid to the supplier keeps the profit level down.

What the organisation is looking for is to minimise the maximum regrets that may occur as a result of making a decision. In many respects, we should consider the use of the regret rule as being very closely allied to the concept of *opportunity cost*. You may recall that this looks at what an organisation will forgo by choosing a particular alternative. In other words, the first method for the kitchen manufacturer may be more straightforward and easier to control, but it is forgoing the potential profits that the second method offers.

Applying this decision rule is fraught with dangers and complications, not the least of which is the point that the regrets will very much depend on the other options which have been considered. Let us consider this potential logic problem with another example. The choices or alternatives here have been designed so that the potential problems are fully highlighted and show the dangers facing the decision maker in applying this rule in all cases that may present themselves.

Inconsistency in the regret rule worked example

Supply method	Annual sales volume		Maximum regrets
	Low	*High*	
1	120(00)	155(25)	25
2	100(20)	165(15)	20*
3	95(25)	180(0)	25

*minimum of the maximum regrets

For the low demand, the third method offers the lowest profit, followed by the second method. The first method is clearly the best: with no regrets at all, it offers the highest potential profit. If we turn our attention to the high demand column, we can see that we will have to change our minds entirely. The first method, which had appeared to be so attractive at a low level of demand, now gives us the highest level of regret. The second method also provides us with regrets. The most attractive option now appears to be the one that looked the worst at low demand, the third.

This illustrates the inconsistency in the regret rule, indeed the basic problem behind opportunity costs. The choice will very much depend on the options that the decision maker is comparing and will change if the scope of the choices is increased.

Expected value decision rule

So far we have looked at rules that will help the decision maker to clarify and identify the nature of the different options or alternatives in a particular situation. What has not been considered, up to this point, is the probability of certain events actually occurring. In order to do this the organisation will have to apply *expectation weights* to each of the possible outcomes. In other words, it will need to decide on the likelihood of the events taking place. With all decisions, no matter how careful the decision maker is in working out the possible profit returns, there is always a chance that they will sell nothing at all. In the case of the kitchen manufacturer, for example, the construction company may decide not to build the houses in the area and invest elsewhere. Alternatively, it may give the contract to another supplier.

Example

For this worked example, we will use our second organisation, which has identified three ways to produce its products, since this gives us the opportunity of investigating the relationships and comparisons between three different sets of figures:

Supply method	Annual sales volume		Maximum regrets
	Low	*High*	
1	120(00)	155(25)	25
2	100(20)	165(15)	20*
3	95(25)	180(0)	25

The organisation places a probability against the low and the high sales volumes, arguing that there is a 0.4 chance of only low-volume sales being achieved and 0.6 for the higher-volume sales. This means that we can now work out the expected value for each of the three methods:

Expected profit for method 1 =

$$(120 \times 0.4) + (155 \times 0.6) = 48 + 93 = 141$$

Expected profit for method 2 =

$$(100 \times 0.4) + (165 \times 0.6) = 40 + 99 = 139$$

Expected profit for method 3 =

$$(95 \times 0.4) + (180 \times 0.6) = 38 + 108 = 146$$

From this assessment of the situation, the third method offers, marginally, the better bet. The enormous note of caution here is that these figures are, of course, hypothetical. These profit figures will never occur, the expected values are merely an indication of the relative worth of each of the options. In reality, the real profit figures can be anything up to and including the maximum profit that is associated with the preferred choice of alternative.

Using decision trees

Real management decisions are based on a series of choices or situations that present themselves over a period. At each point, let us call this a decision point, the decision maker will have to choose between two or more options. The net result of all of the decisions is the true outcome of all of the twists and turns that have had to be made through the maze of decisions necessary (*see* Fig 9.3). The decision tree allows the decision maker to see how the decision points operate in the sequence in which they presented themselves and how their input into the decision-making process had an impact. It is also useful to see how the choices at each of the decision points will have an effect on decisions that will be made in the future. In order to illustrate the ways in which decision trees can be useful to the decision maker, we shall use another worked example.

Example

An organisation which produces a hand-held device which measures the emissions from vehicle exhausts has a serious dilemma. With a view to providing a product that conforms with new legislation regarding the measurement of emissions from older vehicles, it has produced a new product that can more accurately measure the nature and composition of the various gases involved.

The organisation currently supplies, on a contract basis, £700 000 p.a. of the existing product to current customers. The new product, ready for launch, has been market tested, but not to existing customers. The sales force has predicted that the pre-release contracts that could be signed will be worth around £500 000 p.a. of new business.

The organisation faces a number of alternatives:

1 It launches the new product. However, the existing customers find out about it and discover that it is better than the one that they are using. They cancel the current contracts with the supplier, so they only pay up to their outstanding commitments of £350 000. The total income for this option would be £500 000 + £350 000 = £850 000.

2 It launches the new product. However, the existing customers find out about it and discover that it is better than the one that they are using. They cancel the contracts, then switch across to the new one. The total income for this option would be £500 000 + £350 000 + £250 000 = £1.1 million.

3 It launches the new product. However, the existing customers find out about it and discover that it is better than the one that they are using. Despite this, they stay with the old product. The total income for this option would be £500 000 + £700 000 = £1.2 million.

4 It launches the new product. However, the existing customers find out about it and discover that it is better than the one that they are using. They continue buying for the rest of the year, then terminate their contracts with the supplier. The total income for this option would be £500 000 + £700 000 = £1.2 million. Bear in mind that this is for one year only. The £700 000 would be lost in year 2.

5 It launches the new product. However, the existing customers either do not find out about it, or do not react at all. The total income for this option would be £500 000 + £700 000 = £1.2 million.

6 The product is not launched at all. The total income for this option would be just the £700 000 of existing sales to current customers.

We can see how these options would look by transferring all of the information on to a decision-tree format.

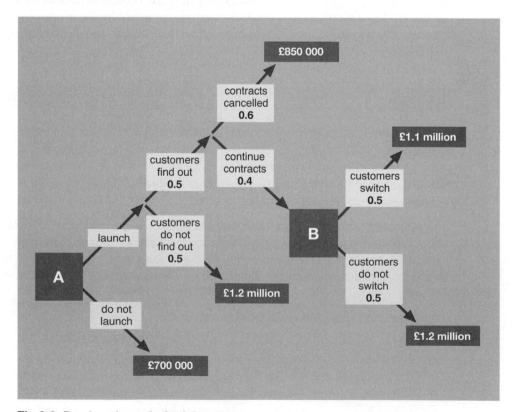

Fig 9.3 Product launch decision tree

By referring to the decision tree in Fig 9.3, it can be seen that the organisation has assigned the particular probabilities of each of the different events occurring at each of the decision points. The normal convention in the construction of the decision tree is to show the decision points clearly and have the nature of the choices at these points described in brief detail. Obviously, at the end of each of the series of connections and consequences, the value of the decision is also included.

The profits on the basic decision tree are the gross amounts that relate to the outcome being 100 per cent possible in each of the cases. Remember that each of the final totals is mutually exclusive and the organisation would only expect to reap the benefits of one of the totals for a particular alternative. At decision point B, there is a 50 per cent (0.5) chance that the existing customers will transfer their contracts over to the new product and a 50 per cent (0.5) chance that they will not. This could be expressed in the following manner, based on the concept of expectation:

$$(£1\ 100\ 000 \times 0.5) + (£1\ 200\ 000 \times 0.5) = £1\ 150\ 000$$

Outcome balance

The final piece in the jigsaw relates to what is known as the *outcome balance*. This relates to the possibility of identifying the magnitude and likelihood of the outcomes at a particular decision point. Although the outcome that may yield the highest profit is the most common one to look for, it may not always be the easiest to obtain or the most obvious to recognise. We should remember that the probabilities that are placed along the route of the decision tree are cumulative and may have a direct impact on the final profit outcomes. Referring back to our example we can illustrate this point.

Example

The combined probability of the customers finding out about the new product launch, continuing their contracts and not switching over to the new one is:

$$\frac{0.5 + 0.4 + 0.5}{3} = 0.46$$

The probability of the customers finding out and then cancelling their contracts is:

$$\frac{0.5 + 0.6}{2} = 0.55$$

Working out the outcome for these two alternative series of consequences gives:

$$(0.46 \times £1\ 200\ 000) + (0.55 \times £850\ 000) = £552\ 000 + £467\ 500 = £1\ 019\ 500$$

Again, this is a hypothetical figure, but it gives a clearer indication of the possible variances in the outcomes. Remember that the previous outcome totals were based on

100 per cent of the customers doing one particular thing and did not take into account the fact that some would do one thing and others would choose a different course of action.

Decision trees and the cost and value of information

The decision tree is still merely a diagrammatic representation of the decision maker's subjective assessment of the probabilities of uncertain events occurring. In order to use the decision tree as a more objective means of calculating or assessing probabilities, we will need to incorporate some aspects of probability law. Again, this is best understood with the use of an example.

Example

Although AquaMin Limited is a relatively small manufacturer and bottler of infused carbonated drinks, it is quite well known in the health food market. It has recently been approached by a large American bottling company to manufacture and bottle its leading brand of carbonated 'health drink', *Vermont Vitamin Vitae*. AquaMin is very interested in the proposition and sees it as an excellent opportunity to expand its sales into the mass market. In the US, the brand sells well throughout the many thousands of outlets that stock the product. It is not seen there as being a niche market product and is very much a part of the mainstream of carbonated drinks, competing directly with the enormous multinationals that dominate the marketplace.

The owners of *Vermont Vitamin Vitae*, Vermont Drinks Corporation, have a number of conditions that they feel that they must place on the deal. They will expect AquaMin to guarantee that it will assign a high level of expenditure in promoting the product in the UK and, if the product launch is successful, they will consider offering AquaMin the sole European rights to produce the product. This does mean that AquaMin has to make sure that the product does well on a national basis. It will have to cope with very high fixed costs as a result of the advertising expenditure to which it will have to commit itself.

Considerable deliberations have taken place at board level within AquaMin. It is very much impressed with the level of sales that the product has achieved in the US market. After enlisting the advice and opinion of marketing specialists, AquaMin believes that the product has about a 60 per cent chance of being successful in the UK. If it proved to be successful, then the profit over the licence period would be around £3 million. The company accountant, not well known for his optimism, has assessed that if the sales are poor, then AquaMin stands to lose around £1.5 million. This level of loss would all but cripple the company.

The basic decision tree can be seen in Fig 9.4.

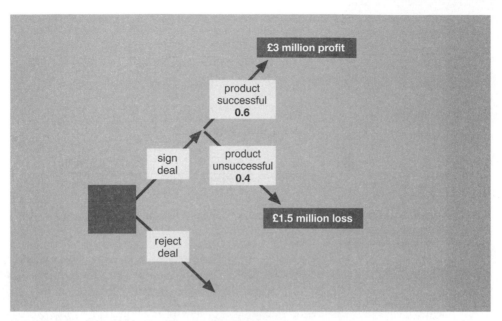

Fig 9.4 Accepting or rejecting the contract

The board decides to defer the offer until it has more concrete evidence that the product has a real chance of success in the UK. Although it trusts the judgement of the marketing manager, even she admits that she is working from a 'best guess' basis. The real alternative is to commission some market research and get a better, objective, view of the situation. The marketing manager approaches a number of different market research agencies on behalf of the company, outlining the scope and the nature of the research to be undertaken. Given some variance in the cost, the market research agencies quote around £100 000 to carry out the research for the company. They suggest that the research will be around 80 per cent accurate and reliable. AquaMin needs to decide whether this 'investment', as the marketing manager puts it, is actually worth following up. In other words, will the results of the marketing research seriously alter the guesstimates that have already been made by the organisation?

In order to work out the value of this information, the organisation will have to use the following:

> The probability of the product being a success,
> given that the marketing research indicates a success   = 0.8
> The probability of the product being a failure,
> given that the marketing research indicates a success   = 0.2
> The original estimate of the probability that the product will be successful   = 0.6
> The original estimate of the probability that the product will be a failure   = 0.4

This can be applied to a formula:

$$\frac{0.6 \times 0.8}{(0.8 \times 0.6) + (0.2 \times 0.4)}$$

or:

$$\frac{0.48}{0.48 + 0.08}$$

$$= 0.85$$

This means that the board and the marketing manager can upgrade their original esti-mate of the success of the product from a 60 per cent (0.6) chance to a more reassuring 85 per cent (0.85) chance. Revising the original or *prior* probability can be shown diagrammatically in Figs 9.5 and 9.6.

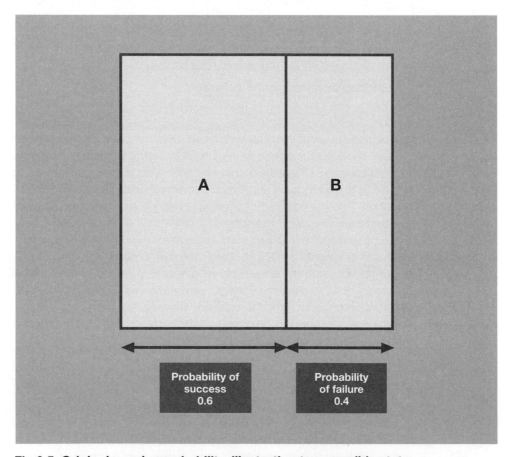

Fig 9.5 Original or prior probability, illustrating two possible states

Note that Fig 9.5 aims to represent the possible probabilities as a square. A represents the product being successful and B represents the product being unsuccessful. We can express the probability of success, $P(X)$, as:

$$P(X) = \frac{A}{A+B}$$

In other words:

$$\frac{\text{the event that is in question}}{\text{all of the possible events}}$$

Deciding to carry out some form of market research adds a further level of complication to this. We will have to subdivide the events further, so that they are represented in the following manner:

A_1 = the research shows that the product will be successful and the product is successful

A_2 = the research shows that the product will be successful but the product is not a success

B_1 = the research shows that the product will be unsuccessful, but despite this it is a success

B_2 = the research shows that the product will be unsuccessful and the product fulfils this prophecy

The net results of this addition to the estimates of probability are shown in Fig 9.6.

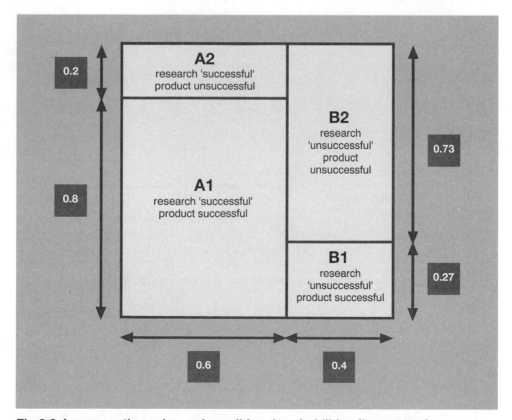

Fig 9.6 Incorporating prior and conditional probabilities (four states)

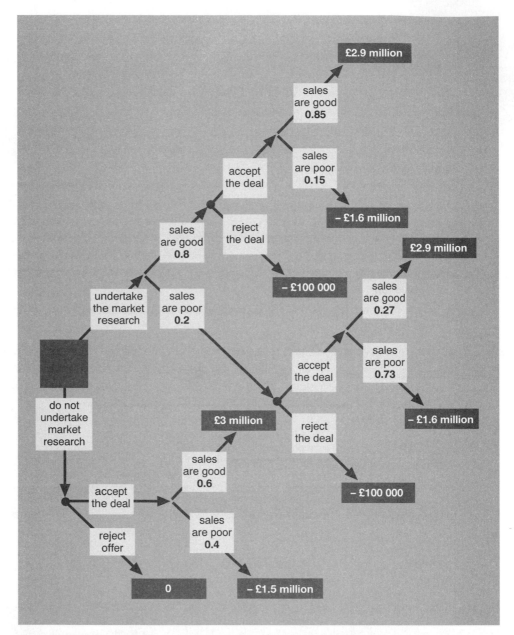

Fig 9.7 Decision tree incorporating all possible outcomes

Calculations to establish the new probabilities include the following. To show the probability of the product being successful given an unsuccessful prediction from the market research would be:

$$\frac{A_2}{A_2 + B_2}$$

$$= \frac{0.6 \times 0.2}{(0.6 \times 0.2) + (0.4 \times 0.8)}$$

$$= \frac{0.12}{0.12 + 0.32} = 0.27$$

We can now transfer this information on to a more complex and comprehensive decision tree to show the net results and outcomes of each of the decisions and the options (*see* Fig 9.7).

At the end of the day, the organisation will be able to judge the true value of the information in the light of what it could have lost as a result of not having undertaken the market research. For the outlay of £100 000 the organisation could stand to just lose that if it decides not to go ahead with the contract. If it does decide to go ahead and the product ends up being a failure, then this £100 000 will have to be added to the projected loss of £1.5 million. On the other hand, if the product is a success in the UK, then it will have to reduce the profit that it will make (£3 million) by £100 000. This is a small price to pay to be reasonably sure that the proposal is a good one and will not cripple the organisation.

Ishikawa diagrams

Effectively, this is a variation of the cause-and-effect diagram. It has found widespread popularity in the study and implementation of TQM in particular. However, given the universality of the technique, not to mention the simplicity of the fishbone structure, it has found numerous advocates in other areas of management.

The construction of the diagram, clearly enough, begins with the known (observed) effect. The convention is to place this effect on the right-hand side of the page. This is the aspect, situation or problem that the decision maker or organisation is considering. All of the major causes or factors which the organisation feels have brought about this effect are then added to the diagram, as can be seen in Fig 9.8.

The main factors (where applicable) are grouped under the following headings:

◆ Manpower – staffing and allied topics etc.
◆ Methods – production, procedures and company policies etc.
◆ Measurements – how costs and profits are allocated etc.
◆ Machinery – utilisation and capacity etc.
◆ Materials – sources, wastage and storage etc.

Once the key headings have been placed on the diagram, the organisation can then identify the precise aspects relating to those headings as appropriate. Under

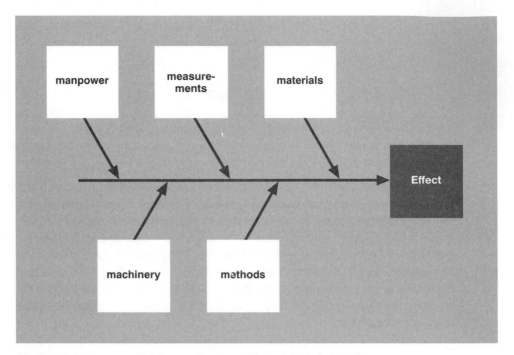

Fig 9.8 Ishikawa or fishbone diagram illustrating the 5 Ms

the manpower heading, for example, the organisation might cite a shortage of trained labour, or a high labour turnover, or perhaps the fact that employees of different grades within the organisation find it difficult to communicate within the systems provided.

Although the Ishikawa diagram appears to be very simplistic, this is something of a false impression. If it is used in the correct manner, the decision maker will be able to identify all the causes of the effect and will not only be able to make a judgement about the effectiveness of current/past policy and decision making, but also the probable causes and effects in future situations.

In identifying the key causes that can be related to an effect, the decision maker will be able systematically to tackle the roots of a problem. Each of the subsets of causes can be prioritised in terms of issues that can be dealt with easily or perhaps with some considerable amount of time and effort. In this way, the decision maker can make positive appraisals of what can and cannot be looked into and solved. In cases when the causes are more complex and do not offer the opportunity for a simple solution, the decision maker always has the option of being able to create another Ishikawa diagram to discover what the root causes of that problem actually are and whether they have to be addressed first.

The main advantage of grouping the causes under the headings already mentioned is that each of the specific issues can be delegated to individuals or teams which specialise in that area of work. In order to ensure that the problem is tackled in a concerted manner by the different parts of the organisation, the creator of the original diagram would be wise to have included these different parties in the formation of the original diagram. In this way, all of those who will be expected to react to the issues raised by the diagram will have a sense of ownership and would, therefore, be more likely to respond to it in a positive manner.

The final point regarding the Ishikawa diagram is that it can also be used for effects that are seen as being positive or successful. The technique does not have to be applied only to situations that appear to be a problem. In using the diagram to analyse how the success was achieved, the decision maker and the organisation can move towards creating a blueprint to ensure that similar goals and objectives are approached in the same manner.

Review questions

1 Outline the main features of investment appraisal in terms of the support it offers to decision makers.

2 Detail the two variants of the pay-back equation and give a worked example of how it operates.

3 How does ARR differ from IRR?

4 Describe the purpose of discounted cash flow.

5 What is the purpose of calculating the net present value?

6 Describe the purpose and the methodology of break even.

7 What is meant by cost–benefit analysis and how can this be useful to an organisation in terms of effective planning?

8 Negative impacts on the environment are seen as the most tangible way of measuring the social costs involved in business decision making. Why might this be so?

9 Distinguish between social audits, ethical accounting and social evaluation.

10 How do expected values and decision trees relate to one another?

11 How do organisations seek to cope in situations ranging from total certainty to absolute uncertainty?

12 Outline the laws of probability.

13 What do you understand by the term *states of nature*?

14 What is meant by the term *opportunity cost*?

15 Distinguish between expectation rates and maximum regrets.

16 What do you understand by the term *outcome balance*?

17 In the context of a decision tree, what is the value of the best guess?

18 What is the purpose of an Ishikawa diagram?

19 How might an Ishikawa diagram be used in the TQM context?

20 'The Ishikawa diagram can be used for detailing both successes and failures, it can also act as a blue-print for the future.' In what respects do you agree with this positive assessment of its potential.

Part 3

CONTINGENCY PLANNING

This section aims to enable students to:

◆ identify and evaluate how organisations plan for contingencies;

◆ compare and contrast pragmatic as compared to planned approaches to contingencies;

◆ identify and evaluate alternative strategies for coping with risk;

◆ prepare and evaluate contingency plans.

Planning

By contingency planning an organisation can attempt to reduce the risks and uncertainties that are an integral part of the decision-making process. Basically, this involves identifying all the alternatives arising out of future possibilities and drafting an action plan to deal with them. While it is impossible to plan for all eventualities, contingency planning should really be restricted to anticipating and responding to:

◆ events that cannot be foreseen with any real degree of precision or certainty;

◆ events that are really beyond the control of the organisation in any direct kind of way;

◆ events that will inevitably lead to a major positive or negative impact on the organisation;

◆ events that are not really based on any particularly valid set of criteria, but are simply assumptions. These assumptions may be based on beliefs, but are important since they may have a marked effect on the organisation.

Without doubt, the organisation needs to be very careful about the number of contingency plans that it has in mind at any period. There may be a tendency for the organisation to overplan, leading to a form of paralysis of action through over-analysis. It may not decide to take a particular course of action, as it may believe that it is moving into territory that has been investigated in a contingency planning session and identified as a problem area that should be avoided. In this chapter we will be investigating the nature of contingency planning and how it is applied at the various levels of an organisation, the timing and sequencing of the parts of the contingency plan, and the ways in which the plan can be monitored and reviewed in order to ensure that it meets the requirements and needs of the organisation. It should be remembered at all stages, that the contingency plan, above all, aims to identify and evaluate the alternative strategies that can be adopted by the organisation and is very much related to the organisation's willingness to adopt and embrace the uncertainties of risk.

In 1973 Vroom and Yetton proposed a contingency theory. They recognised that there is a very broad sweep of different styles of management within organisations, from the very autocratic styles to the more democratic and participative. They linked different management styles to the notion that all problems need to be addressed and solved in rather different ways. The adoption of a particular management style in relation to the problem is crucial in ensuring that the problem is settled and dealt with successfully. Some of the problems require 'leadership from the front', which means that the wishes and opinions of the employees do not play a key role in the solving of the problem. On the other hand, there are situations that require the full participation of employees and, to this end, a more participative approach needs to be adopted.

There will always be a rational solution, not necessarily to the problem, but to the adoption of the right management approach to the situation. Some situations may require there to be a degree of goal sharing, but others may have to be approached without any real attempt to resolve or avoid conflict. Whether we think that this rather obvious and simplistic approach from the theorists is acceptable or attached to any degree of reality, we need to establish the fact that the framing of contingency plans needs to come from some quarter of the organisation. Obviously, a predetermined set of measures to cope with a particular problem would be more effective if there was a degree of co-operation and goal sharing, but in many circumstances this is either impossible or not desirable and other courses of action need to be adopted.

Application of contingency planning at different levels in the organisation

Any contingency approach recognises the fact that there may not be an ideal way in which to tackle and resolve a particular problem. The contingency approach hopes to incorporate the fact that there are a number of different variables involved, not to mention situational factors, that could influence the choice, implementation and outcome of the decision. Adopting a contingency approach and installing a comprehensive contingency plan will show that the organisation is aware of the need to be flexible when it tackles a particular problem or opportunity.

The contingency approach, and the plan in particular, will attempt to analyse the situation and incorporate an understanding of the relationships between aspects and variables of the situation. The plan will, further, attempt to ensure that there is a *fit* between the structure of the organisation, the management systems used, the range of resources and the variables which relate to the problem. In other words, the deployment of the resources, physical and human, will be *contingent* on the particular variables which relate to a given set of circumstances.

Classical approaches to decision making

Classical approaches to decision making revolve around the need to establish a clear linkage between the objectives and the purposes of the decision and a logical or rational approach to the solution. In other words, the organisation will have established a range of different (predetermined) approaches to the solving of problems within a given set of principles. Perhaps these would be the standard operating procedures or some other form of more formal rules and regulations regarding decision making. The organisation would measure its effectiveness and efficiency in terms of decision making by having clearly identified the roles and responsibilities that each individual may have in the decision-making process.

Human relations school

The human relations school, while focusing on the informal relationships within the organisation, still assumes that the majority of individuals are committed to the organisation in terms of the general achievement of objectives. In this respect, the organisation is less likely to have developed a range of predetermined responses and approaches to decision making. It will rely on loyalty and a joint desire to meet the objectives, and will more willingly allow the decision makers a greater degree of flexibility.

If contingency plans exist at all in this type of organisation, they will be on an individual basis, but nevertheless grounded on the principle that the individual's desires are very similar to those of the organisation. Any more formal attempt to determine the way in which individuals plan for contingencies will be viewed as not attending to the social and psychological needs of the decision makers. It is also worth remembering the fact that organisations adopting this approach will tend to avoid the use of overprescriptive controls as this would be seen as alienating individuals and restricting their ability to perform in an effective manner for the good of the organisation.

Systems approach to decision making

Organisations which adopt more of a systems approach to decision making will have placed a great emphasis on some form of sociotechnical solution. An organisation that has created a number of subsystems which have a large degree of interrelationship and interdependence will be more prepared for the opportunities that exist in the external environment. To this end, these types of organisation will have the subsystems in place to be able to identify areas of expertise within the organisation that can be deployed to deal with a particular problem. Whether they are able to deal with the alternatives and create effective contingency plans will depend on the flexibility of the systems and the availability of individuals with the time and the resources to devote to the creation of separate alternatives, should the need arise.

We have deliberately left the systems approach to last as this is much more clearly related to the contingency approach itself. As we have said, the organisation may have a series of subsystems in place that are designed to cope with the variety of different situations that may occur. At the same time, the organisation is aware of the fact that some external influences may have brought about a set of circumstances that will have a direct bearing on the decision and the variables that relate to it.

Identifying alternatives

Given the fact that the contingency approach recognises the fact that there may not be an ideal or best way of dealing with a situation, it also takes note of the fact that all of the aspects, criteria and other variables have to be examined before making a decision. In this way, the organisation will need to identify, quantify and evaluate the various possibilities and alternatives before settling on a preferred course of action. At the same time, the contingency approach also incorporates the fact that a particular 'best' or preferred choice will be completely contingent on the outcome of the analysis of all of the variables and other related issues. In other words, the organisation and its decision makers have to accept the fact that there will never be a model of decision making that can be universally applied to all sets of circumstances or problems.

Most organisations, given the fact that they will have developed (to some extent) in an organic manner, will have differing approaches to the solving of problems and the framing of decisions. It is only when the organisation has developed a very tight form of hierarchical structure that relies very heavily on a handful of decision makers who all approach the process of decision making in the same manner that there will be a degree of consistency across the organisation. Even in these cases, the development of contingency plans may differ. This is an essential part of the organisation's ability to cope with and handle the problems of decision making as they are presented.

At its most basic, the contingency plan is merely a system by which the organisation can ask itself a series of 'if what' or 'if then' questions. There are, of course, some general ways in which the problem of predicting the possible outcomes or alternatives can be addressed. Let us first look at a specific example of how the organisation and the decision makers could use existing systems to predict the nature of the 'what ifs'.

Example

In order to ensure that the business is holding sufficient stock to cater for immediate production requirements, many organisations have prudently integrated their production systems with stock control. Systems which would facilitate this streamlining include:

i) Computer-aided design, which aims to allow designers to store and retrieve their work. At an early stage estimates can be made regarding the nature of materials and components required for this product. The business can then ensure, through cross-checking, that the stock is either in place or can be ordered in sufficient time for production.

ii) Computer-aided manufacture. The use of robots on the production line is one of the more commonly associated applications of CAM. However, a fully integrated system incorporates stock control and ordering facilities.

iii) Computer-integrated manufacture. This system enables the business to co-ordinate all production from design through stock control to actual production. A series of sophisticated schedules and controls is incorporated in order to maintain flexible and efficient production.

iv) Computer-numerical control machines. Using numerical instructions programmed into memory, these machines are able to undertake a series of automated tasks during the production process. Typically, they would be programmed to produce a definite number of products in a single production run.

v) Manufacturing resource planning II (MRPII), a computer system which aims to co-ordinate the full production process. Essentially it covers the following abilities:

◆ to translate sales forecasts into the purchasing requirements for particular materials and components;

◆ to establish and set production schedules;

◆ to produce individual work instructions;

◆ to set deadlines.

The principal aim of the MRPII system is to maximise capacity utilisation. The system will be able to identify the fact that in order to meet specific deadlines, the business may have to request employees to undertake overtime. Alternatively, it may have to instruct the business to tell its customers that deliveries will be delayed.

Although setting up an MRPII system takes time, the business will find it invaluable, since it will contain a comprehensive computer model of all its operations. The managers will be able to ask 'what if' questions, allowing them to experiment before actually risking any resources.

MRPII replaces the MRP (material requirements planning) system which is still used to calculate materials requirements for the completion of a particular order.

Situational factors, including the various variables that may come into play, will cause additional variables to be taken into account by the organisation. So, for example, if the organisation is trying to make some decisions related to its restructuring, we can see that the following 'if' and 'then' relationships come into play:

◆ *if* the organisation takes into account the current size, configuration, technology used and the external environment;

◆ *then* it will have to consider the fact that these will have an impact on the intended organisational structure and the systems of management that will have to be deployed in order to control them.

Size, structure and performance

Clearly, there is a relationship between the size and the structure of an organisation and its ability or willingness to create a series of contingency plans that will come into operation when required. The larger the organisation, it can be argued, the greater the need for the organisation to have contingency plans. The very essence of the larger organisation does imply that the situations and the problems it may face will be all the more complex. Simple answers or solutions to problems may not be as appropriate for these larger organisations as for a smaller company. The scale and implications of the problems and their attendant solutions may have equally lasting effects on both sizes of organisation, but the larger organisation is bound to face situations that can have a more catastrophic effect if the solution is not the correct one. The more formalised relationships and the greater level of control that may be exercised in the larger organisation may also tend to mean that it is less able to deal with problems that are out of the normal scope of its understanding and procedures. At the same time, the larger organisation may be blessed with access to decision makers and experts who are perfectly capable of handling the situation if they have the benefit of a contingency plan (developed at least to some stage of clarity).

The size of the organisation is a very important variable and deciding factor with regard to the availability of contingency plans. Given the fact that relationships between individuals in the smaller organisation are bound to be more informal and perhaps more productive (although this becomes a problem at times as the organisation grows), mechanisms, behaviour and attitude may not foster the need to develop any consistent or comprehensive range of contingency plans. It could also be argued that the nature of the management system in the organisation will have a marked effect on the willingness to develop and indeed the existence of contingency plans. The more formal organisation, perhaps typified by bureaucracy, will almost certainly insist on the development of contingency plans as this 'pre-prepared' approach lies at the very centre of the nature of the organisation.

Does this linkage between size, organisational structure, management style and the existence of contingency plans mean that the organisation is more likely to perform well in the market? Probably the simple answer to the question is yes. Child's study (1988) regarding this very relationship seems to infer that organisations (particularly bureaucratic ones) do perform well, but only in cases when the organisation is large and has a considerable number of employees. For the smaller, less formal organisations, the ability to handle contingencies and perform well seems to revolve around their very informality and flexibility rather than having a distinct set of rules, regulations and standard operating procedures.

Is it possible to extend this debate and consider the overall performance and efficiency of organisations in terms of their creation of contingency plans? Certainly, the research that has been undertaken by a variety of different theorists and consultants is, at best, contradictory. The most fruitful areas which would allow a degree of objective comparison are related to the profits made as a result of capital expenditure. However, this information is very difficult to obtain and notoriously hard to quantify or verify. The search for comparable data needs to be considered a little more carefully in the light of this, and other factors would need to be taken into account. Perhaps a more basic investigation into the nature, management type and structure of the organisation would provide the necessary information.

Arising out of the work carried out by Joan Woodward (1980), we can summarise the information as in Table 10.1. It is worth bearing in mind that only 100 organisations were included in this study and the results, as can be expected, may not be applicable to the majority of organisations. Nevertheless, the information does give us some useful pointers as to the relationships between these different aspects.

Table 10.1 Relationship between organisational type and structure

Type of organisation	Management levels	Spans of control	Organisational structure
Unit/small batch	2–4	average of 23	Simple Line
Large/mass production	3–8	average of 49	Line Staff
Process production	4–8	average of 13	Line Staff

Type of organisation and contingency planning

The next step is to try to establish whether the generalised characteristics of these types of organisation can be superimposed on the existence or absence of some degree of contingency planning. Perhaps if we extend the investigation in line with the findings of Woodward, we will be able to ascertain whether the manufacturing cycle itself allows the incorporation of contingency planning. One thing which may be clear about this is that the precise order in which the events or activities within the organisation are positioned will trigger the appropriateness of particular forms of contingency planning at different levels of the organisation (*see* Table 10.2).

Table 10.2 Order of priorities in different types of production organisation

Type of organisation	Marketing function	Product development	Production function
Unit/small batch	First	**Second**	Third
Large/mass production	Third	First	**Second**
Process production	**Second**	First	Third

Note: the critical function is shown in bold.

Unit/small batch organisation

The inter-relationships between the different functions of the smaller batch or unit organisation lead to constant interchange of information regarding the tasks in hand as well the discussion of opportunities and their associated decisions. In this respect, the smaller organisation would not place a great emphasis on contingency planning, as all of its associated roles and functions are in close contact with one another at all times. The relevant individuals would be able to plan and react with very little forward knowledge or predetermined patterns of action. Since the critical function for these types of organisation revolves around the development of the products and the services offered, the organisation should be well appraised of the possibility of having to consider alternative courses of action should the initial plan not prove to be very successful or viable.

Large/mass production organisation

For the large batch or mass production organisation, the key function is the production of the product or the facilitation of the service itself. In this respect, the organisation is far more tied to 'feeding' the production machinery and would be well advised to have a series of contingencies in place at various levels of the organisation in order to ensure that it is able to react to potential opportunities and threats that may affect production levels and production efficiency.

Given that the organisation's separate departments or divisions would only routinely communicate as a direct result of activities already in progress or in the joint development of new products and services, the independent decision makers (at least at operational level) may not have a macro view of the situation. It is far more important, in these more complex organisations, to consider the importance of having contingency plans developed that can be implemented by those decision makers at the strategic apex of the organisation. They, and only they, will have the opportunity to consider all of the factors and the ramifications of opportunities and threats. As a result of this, they will have been able to develop a series of key contingency plans that seek to address at least the most commonly presumed sets of variables that may have to be considered when looking at alternative courses of action.

Process production organisation

For organisations involved with process production, we will find that again the departments within the organisation will communicate and exchange information as a matter of course, primarily as a result of the fact that all of the functions of the organisation are geared to support the process function. Contingencies are vital for these types of organisation, at all levels, as the complexity of the sales and marketing effort must be mirrored by the ability of production and allied support functions to ensure that the systems operate in an effective manner.

Levels of contingency planning

In each of the above classifications of organisation we can see that the priority or critical areas of importance will vary, but this does not mean that the organisations will not attempt to create their own, personalised means of planning for contingencies. For the most part, organisations will endeavour to have contingency plans *in situ* at the following levels of management, decision making and responsibility.

Strategic level

At a strategic level, decision makers will be expected to make contingencies to compensate or react to problems and situations that may affect the organisation as a whole. Decisions at this level will have to incorporate plans which are able to redeploy resources, and switch organisational emphasis in different markets and activities, as well as coping with the forward financial planning of the organisation.

Director or executive level

At director or executive level, as distinct from strategic (or board) level, individual decision makers who have specific responsibilities for certain actions and activities must have very clear contingency plans prepared that they can put in place. As they will be directly answerable to the board, these individuals will have to offer viable alternatives when called on to do so. In this respect, these decision makers will need to have rather more complex and comprehensive contingency plans as the majority of activities (and ultimately the success or failure of the organisation) will rely on their judgement. Naturally, these individuals will have to present their alternatives to the board, as appropriate, but will be expected to be able to implement the contingency plan as soon as they are given the go-ahead.

Operational level

At operational level, decision makers may be guided by the plans and policies of senior managers, but to a large extent they will need to have a series of contingency plans ready to cope with a variety of different situations. If the situation is not too complex, then these individuals will probably be able to follow the plans and procedures that have worked for the organisation in the past.

Typically, contingency plans at this level will involve the deployment of human and physical resources, coupled with the maximisation of the production facilities and other means of production and output. For the most part, given the potential level and complexity of the work that needs to be carried out, these decision makers may rely on the guidance and direction of their senior line managers.

For organisations which have devolved decision making to separate, semi-autonomous units, separate contingency plans should be developed in order to mirror this independence. Again, the contingency plans will have to be presented to senior management (where appropriate) in order to ensure that they are consistent with the overall objectives and strategy of the organisation.

Supervisory or junior management level

At supervisory or junior management level, the degree and complexity of contingency plans may not seem as important or difficult compared to many of the other levels. However, this assumption presupposes that the organisation does not rely on supervisory or junior management structures to make complex operational decisions that may not fall within the bounds of normal or contingency planning. These decision makers, albeit at a lower level, will have the responsibility of ensuring that the smooth running of the departments, teams and other groups is ensured at all times. To this end, the development of contingency plans is essential to this process. They will have to know exactly what the options or alternatives are in cases when the standard procedures and the demands on their subordinates present problems in terms of operational control and flow of work.

Junior level

Even at the lowest levels of the organisation, the individual will be expected to have some contingencies in mind, particularly in terms of managing work flow and the allocation of time and effort. Obviously, these individuals would defer judgement and final decisions to their immediate line managers. For the most part, experience and knowledge of the work itself would allow these junior members of staff to develop a series of contingencies, perhaps some of the more formal manifestations of which would arise from appraisals and discussions with line management.

Technology and contingency planning

So far we have restricted our investigations into contingency planning to organisations that are production based. Our appraisal now needs to incorporate the probable affects of technology. In this respect, technology can be seen as another layer of complication for the decision maker and the contingency plan. After all, many alternative courses of action will need to be identified for organisations that are heavily reliant on technology.

C. Perrow (1970) suggested that there are two main ways in which the decision maker should view technology in terms of contingency planning. This is particularly relevant if we consider the fact that organisations do depend, to a greater or lesser extent, on technology as either an essential part of their production efforts, or as a support mechanism that provides vital back-up (administratively or technically) to the production function. Perrow's two considerations are as follows:

1 To what extent is the work associated with the technology predictable or variable? In this respect, an integral part of contingency planning would have to revolve around the fact that some problems will be unpredictable (such as the difficulties in interfacing different technologies into a streamlined process) or that they are exceptional (such as the occasional need to terminate production or use of the technology to carry out routine maintenance or upgrading). Given the fact that the predictable problems will fall within the bounds of normal decision making and standard operating procedures, the organisation would have to be aware of the exceptional and unpredictable cases, since these would need to have associated contingency plans.

2 To what extent does the actual technology lend itself to detailed analysis? If the organisation is using technology that has a high degree of complication and integration, it may be difficult to pinpoint the exact nature of a problem within the overall process. For organisations that use technology to carry out simple and clearly identifiable tasks and work functions, the identification of problem areas and difficulties will be much more straightforward. To this end, contingency plans need to be incorporated into the overall strategy of the organisation, particularly in terms of coping with, identifying and solving problems of a complex nature. The standard problems will, again, be handled by the standard operating procedures of the organisation. Certain technological difficulties will be expected to present themselves, but perhaps only the straightforward ones will have preplanned solutions.

The other relevant area of interest as far as technology is concerned is the fact that organisations will use technology to carry out a series of routine and non-routine functions. For the routine functions, the organisation will have a series of solutions in mind, but when the non-routine functions fail, the organisation may not have the understanding or the expertise to cope with the problem. The possible solution to these problems will lie with the availability of expert help from consultants or technical support. The source of this assistance, particularly in the framing of an unforeseen contingency plan, may come from the supplier or maintainer of the technology. At the very least, the organisation will need to have a basic contingency plan that incorporates the acquisition of this assistance at the earliest possible point.

Perrow goes on to suggest that there is a very definite relationship between the technology used in an organisation and the predictability of the work tasks that are associated with the technology. In this way, we can attempt to categorise the key differences between the routine and the non-routine in terms of the need to establish contingency plans (*see* Table 10.3).

Table 10.3 Routine and non-routine functions

Routine functions	Non-routine functions
Little decision-making discretion at supervisory or technical level	High dependency on supervisory and technical staff to make decisions
High degree of decision-making responsibility at middle management level	Middle management's primary function is to co-ordinate and direct overall operations
Low interdependence between supervisory and technical staff and middle management	High dependency between supervisory and technical staff and middle management
Fairly bureaucratic nature	Tendency for the organisation to be more organic in nature
Little need for supervisory and technical staff to consider the importance of contingency planning	Since much of the power and responsibility is related to supervisory and technical staff, the need for them to develop contingencies is much greater
Greater need for middle management to have contingency plans in place to cope with potential problems	The need for middle management to develop broader contingencies still exists

Before we move on to investigate the timing and sequencing of contingency planning, it is worth considering some case studies.

Case 1

For an organisation that produces products by hand or perhaps using traditional (basic) forms of technology, the occurrence of problems that defy close examination is likely to be very rare. In these cases, the organisation will not be likely to encounter problems that have not occurred before, therefore the need to develop contingency plans will be low.

Case 2

For an organisation that is either at the 'cutting edge' of technology or is dealing with a variety of different products and services to a wide range of customers, the occurrence of problems that have not been encountered is likely to be high. In these cases, although contingency planning would be desirable and perhaps advisable, the organisation may find it very difficult to predict the types of problems that could occur. As a result, the organisation will not be able to develop contingencies as it will not know the parameters of the potential problems that may be encountered. In other words, the time and effort expended on the framing of contingency plans will not be cost effective. The organisation would be far better advised to try to deal with the problems as they arise, perhaps drawing on past experience as a framework to begin its analysis of the situation and the implementation of a solution.

Case 3

Organisations that use 'routine technology' to produce products or support the production function will encounter a series of problems that can be easily predicted and analysed. As a consequence of this, they will be able to develop a range of basic contingencies that will solve the problem with the minimum of confusion, time and effort. As long as the organisation is involved in the production of products and services of a standard nature, it will not encounter very many 'unforeseen' problems that cannot be covered by existing contingency plans.

Case 4

For organisations that use technology either to produce or to underpin the development of new products and services, it is probably not the technology that needs to have discrete contingency planning. It is the matching of the technology to the needs of the customer or the particular product/service that would require a degree of contingency planning. To this end, the problems, although unpredictable in nature, may be able to be tackled with reference to previous experience with similar products and services in the past.

 Timing and sequence of contingency planning

As you may recall from our investigations into the setting and achieving of objectives in the first part of this book, we should link the timing and sequencing of contingency planning to the framework which determines the way in which the organisation sets out to achieve its objectives.

Given the fact that the majority of objectives identified by an organisation will tend to be linked to an overall strategy or direction in which the organisation intends to move, it would be prudent for it to consider the ramifications of the potential failure of an objective and how it will affect the overall strategy of the business.

In order to see how contingency planning fits into the context of objective setting and accomplishment, we will refresh your memory concerning the *hierarchy of objectives* and attempt to identify where contingency planning would fit in (*see* Table 10.4).

Table 10.4 The Hierarchy of objectives and the timing and sequencing of contingency planning

Level/nature of objective (common example only)	Probable timing and sequence of contingencies
Organisational (corporate) To increase profitability by achieving more efficient utilisation of resources and production facilities.	Immediate identification of the key steps to be taken and the main responsibilities of individuals in achieving these aims. There would be a need to frame the main aspects of the contingency plans and assign individuals within the organisation to develop the alternative plans.
Divisional To reduce manufacturing costs in line with the strategic objectives outlined at corporate level, with specific savings targets.	Not only the need to create workable plans to meet the objectives as demanded by the corporate decision makers, but also to have a series of identifiable and implementable contingency plans that will be understood by the various subordinate levels of management. The required contingency plans will have to be ready for approval at board level and this tier of management will be answerable for the success or failure of the plans.
Departmental Specifically to examine the nature and efficiency of the various systems of production and create plans which will ensure that the maximum output is achieved by all workers and machinery.	An immediate response to the guidelines and instructions received from the divisional managers, coupled with a number of contingency plans that can be implemented at departmental or operational level. The contingency plans will have to be fairly detailed in order to ensure that individual workers and key technical personnel appreciate the timing of the stages of the contingency plans.
Technical and maintenance To ensure that the downtimes experienced by the organisation are minimised, to reduce the need for specialists to carry out routine maintenance of the machinery and to make effective savings on the wage bills associated with maintenance and technical support.	Considered and workable alternatives to current practice would be required immediately, but the identification of contingency plans would probably need greater attention to detail. Given the expertise at this level of the organisation, in terms of the knowledge of machinery, workable contingency plans would not be too difficult to identify. They would need to have the flexibility to be able to be implemented with minimum disruption to the production process.
Shop floor (supervisory) To ensure that machine operators have the capacity and the expertise to carry out routine maintenance on their machines. Also to make sure that workers are meeting specified targets and to take remedial action if this is not being addressed.	An immediate response in terms of workable alternatives to the main strategies to meet the objectives. Close co-operation between supervisors and key factory floor workers would enable the organisation to identify the main alternatives and allied contingencies that will have to be considered.

Remember that all of the objectives have some degree of linkage with those at the different levels of the organisation and that the organisation attempts to see all of the objectives as an integral part of the whole. While the identification of objectives may be comparatively easy, it is more difficult to judge the scope and detail of the contingency plans that could be incorporated into the strategic plans. Remember that an essential part of the overall structure of the strategic plan will be the identification of strengths, weaknesses, opportunities and threats (SWOT analysis) as well as detailed examination of the social, legal, economic, political and technological factors (SLEPT analysis). How comprehensive these investigations are will depend on the complexity and importance of the objectives and how they are will affect the internal operations of the organisation and be influenced by the external environment.

Decision-making models and contingency plans

In order to appreciate the timing and sequence of contingency plans more fully, it is useful to compare three of the decision-making models that could be adopted by an organisation. For our purposes, we will be considering the following:

1 The rational model, which aims to allow individuals to obtain the maximum level of achievement within the limitations of the decision itself. In other words, it attempts to address the means by which the objective will be achieved and not, necessarily, the ends themselves.

2 The bounded rationality model, which attempts to explain why different individuals will come up with radically different alternatives to the same problem. This points out that some individuals will not always select the 'best' alternative (they will seek to satisfice), some will only make a limited search for alternatives, and others will be constrained by a lack of information or understanding of the ramifications of factors in the external environment.

3 The political model, which attempts to describe decision making in terms of the interests and objectives of particular individuals. Specifically, it focuses on the relative distribution of power, how the problem is defined, how choices are made and implemented in the light of interest groups with differing levels of power and influence.

We have attempted to summarise the stages of decision making related to each of these different forms of decision-making model, with the aim of identifying how and where contingency plans will fit into the overall strategy that is being adopted to cope with or solve the problem (*see* Fig 10.1).

From Fig 10.1, we can see that for the rational and political models, the search for alternative solutions would identify a number of contingencies that could be used should the preferred plan of action fail. The fact that the organisation has eliminated these alternatives at this point and chosen another way of achieving the objectives in no way invalidates the potential of these alternatives. What is perhaps true is that the alternatives would be applicable at the pre-implementation stage, but would need to be amended to take account of the changing conditions arising

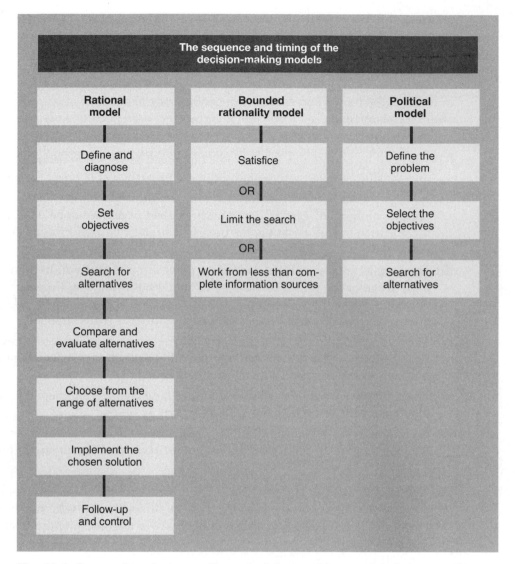

Fig. 10.1 **Comparison between three decision-making models incorporating contingency planning**

out of circumstances and situations created by the implementation of the main plan. In other words, the conditions which exist when the organisation originally sets the objectives will be different from those that will exist after the preferred plan has either failed or has only been partially brought into action. To this end, the assumptions and framework of the contingencies will need to be reconsidered with a view to using them with an imperfect understanding of what may have changed. This will demand that contingency plans are rather more flexible and capable of immediate amendment.

The bounded rationality model does not really give the organisation the ideal conditions to offer a viable set of contingencies. However, given the potentially poor nature of the chosen strategies that may derive from this approach, the use of contingencies may be far more critical.

Using contingency plans

In terms of the timing and sequence of contingency plans, both in respect of their original creation and the probable point when they will need to be implemented, we can identify the following:

i)   The majority of contingency plans will be created as a result of decision makers investigating the alternatives and settling on a particular course of action.

ii) Having chosen a particular strategy, the decision makers will 'set aside' a number of different approaches that can be held in reserve to be used as contingencies in the future should the preferred strategy be ineffective or deficient in some way.

iii) The decision maker will have a review point in mind that will help to determine whether the preferred strategy is operating in the way expected. If the preferred plan has not lived up to the expectations of the decision maker, one of the contingencies will be selected and the situation reinvestigated.

iv) The contingency chosen to replace the original strategy will need to have the ability to be implemented at short notice with the additional ability to 'pick up' from where the preferred strategy ended or failed.

v)   The contingency will have to reflect the ongoing changes and new conditions that are applicable at the point of replacement.

vi) The contingency will also reflect the predetermined objectives and move the organisation forward to successful resolution of the problem or strategies.

The actual decision to use one of the contingencies will, of course, have to be considered very carefully. Perhaps the organisation will be wise to consider a re-evaluation of the conditions and the present circumstances very much in the same way as it investigated the options in the first place. Consequently, this would involve the following processes:

a)   seeking any additional information that may be relevant to the situation;

b)   creatively thinking about the problem and how the contingency could be employed to provide the solution required;

c)   using expert opinion to test the viability of the contingency given the present set of circumstances;

d)   if necessary, carrying out some research in order to assess the contingency and the prevailing conditions in which it will be expected to operate;

e)   reassessing similar activities and operations that have been undertaken in the past in order to identify any probable problems that may affect the contingency plan.

There is a final note of caution that should be sounded at this point which concerns the actual framing of the objectives of the organisation or the intended objectives of a particular decision maker. Some objectives do not have an immediately identifiable or feasible strategy to meet them. In this respect, the organisation or the decision maker may have set objectives that are impossible, so despite the complexity and the in-depth considerations of the alternatives (including the contingencies), there is little or no hope of being able to achieve the objectives. Ultimately, the stress and the disappointment, not to mention the apportioning of blame, will cause the organisation radically to rethink its strategies.

No degree of preplanning or framing of contingencies will get around this problem. The fault does not lie with the solutions and the alternatives, more clearly it rests on the shoulders of the key decision makers at strategic level who have made impossible demands on the organisation and its resources.

Ad hoc and planned approaches

Clearly, the environment in which the organisation operates, coupled with internal considerations such as structure and type of management, will have an impact on the need for and the comprehensive nature of contingency plans. For external considerations, we can categorise probable environments from the 'stable and predictable' to the 'unstable and unpredictable'. Obviously, there are many shades of environment that lie between these two extremes.

The need to have contingency plans ready for implementation would be far more important for organisations that operate in a stable and predictable environment. It is obvious to assume that these organisations will tend to be faced with a variety of technological, competitive and operational challenges that demand a high degree of precision and timing in terms of identifying and implementing contingency plans.

In order to identify precisely the probable timing and sequence of events related to contingency planning activities, it is important to consider the nature of the organisation and how its structure and operations may affect the processes. For our purposes we will focus upon some of the conclusions drawn from Burns and Stalker's studies in the 1960s. Despite the age of the studies, their basic assumptions and conclusions still have more than a ring of truth and applicability to modern organisations. The main considerations are drawn from their book *The Management of Innovation* (1996). The main points can be described as follows:

Mechanistic/bureaucratic system or structure

1 Since the majority of tasks and activities are carried out by specialists, it is presumed that the majority of problems and situations that require some degree of decision making will be well known to the individual.

2 As the majority of duties, responsibilities and methods of carrying out tasks are clearly defined, the organisation will almost certainly have prepared a number of standard operating procedures to handle recurrent or predictable problems.

3 These organisations, with their tendency to have a very distinctive hierarchical structure, will demand that planned approaches to contingency planning are an integral part of the overall planning process.

4 Given the fact that most of the power and responsibility rests at the strategic apex of the organisation, the board will demand that there is a comprehensive assessment and identification of planned responses (in the form of contingencies) by all subordinate levels of management.

5 These organisations do tend to encourage the development of vertical integration and co-operation between managers and subordinates. To this end, planned responses are more likely to be developed as the manager and the team of workers will have a closer working relationship. In terms of the need to develop *ad hoc* contingency plans, the relationship that has been developed will also help facilitate this approach when necessary.

6 Since the majority of the activities, tasks and duties are clearly defined by a particular manager, the contingency plans associated with operational difficulties will also have a tendency to be planned rather than to be *ad hoc*. In this way, the understanding of the standard operational procedures and other rules and regulations which govern how subordinates carry out their duties will tend to have 'in-built' contingencies that can be implemented when required.

7 The bureaucratic organisation makes considerable demands in respect of loyalty and obedience from subordinates. This aspect can greatly assist the organisation in ensuring that planned contingencies are followed through, thus reducing the need to come up with *ad hoc* approaches to decision making.

Organic system or structure

1 A more fluid structure should be able to cope with problems that may arise. This is the particular strength of this organisational structure in as much as unforeseen circumstances are dealt with as a result of less defined job roles. The structure of this type of organisation often reflects the fact that the business operates in an environment that demands actions and contingencies that lie outside normal operating procedures.

2 The organisation will tend to have a number of specialised individuals who can contribute in a more open and free manner to the contingencies as they arise. In this respect, the organisation expects, and is able to cope with, *ad hoc* decision making by developing alternative plans of action.

3 Given the fact that the job roles are less defined than in a bureaucracy, the individual members of the organisation must be able to cope with constant changes to the parameters of their responsibilities. On an individual basis, as well as collectively, the staff must be able to incorporate a degree of contingency planning that takes this aspect of their job role and definitions into account.

4 The networks of communication, control and authority are easily adaptable to encompass both planned and *ad hoc* contingency planning. There will be positive benefits for the organisation in terms of being able to pool the resources and the individual abilities of the workforce in order to frame these planning strategies.

5 As a result of the organisation developing in an organic manner, there will be a number of key individuals at various levels of responsibility and status in the organisation that have the necessary experience and ability to cope with both planned and *ad hoc* contingency planning.

6 The technical or business knowledge is quite evenly spread throughout the organisation and does not tend to be concentrated at the strategic apex. In other words, the experience and ability of individuals are not always necessarily linked to their particular position in the organisation.

7 Arising out of the networks that are encouraged within the organisation, the business is able to develop the ability to call on advice and experience from a variety of individuals from different parts of the organisation. This will allow the organisation to draw on the expertise and knowledge of individuals so that they can quickly develop an *ad hoc* contingency plan without needing to use the skills of outside consultants.

8 Common commitment to objectives and the strategies of the organisation is encouraged. In this way individuals are more willing to contribute to both planned and *ad hoc* contingency planning when requested.

9 Since advancement and promotion will be based on individual contributions to the operations and planning of the organisation, individuals will be more likely to offer workable contingencies that can be associated with them. This will help to facilitate both the planned and the *ad hoc* approaches to contingency planning.

Implementing contingency planning

Regardless of the fact that the organisation may prefer planned or *ad hoc* approaches to contingency planning, we can see that the main underlying principle is that there is a high degree of commitment to the organisation from those who can effectively contribute towards contingency planning. If the organisation is one that prefers to concentrate the power and authority in the hands of relatively few individuals, the broader ability of other individuals to make a contribution, either in times of great urgency (typified by the *ad hoc* approach) or pre-prepared (planned approach), will be diminished.

It is also interesting to note that the fact that the organisation has adopted a formal or informal structure does not seem overly to influence the way in which the business approaches contingency planning. In the formal structure, the organisation will have developed a series of measures that are designed to create contingency plans (standing interdepartmental or interdisciplinary teams or committees), but with the structure in place to be called on to create *ad hoc* contingency plans if required. For informally structured organisations, these groups, teams or committees may not have the clearer definition that exists in the formal organisation, but nevertheless still have the ability to create both types of contingency plan.

As long as the organisation expends some efforts to ensure that the staff have internalised the goals, beliefs and values of the organisation, it will find that it has a willing (although not necessarily able) pool of individuals that can be drawn on for both approaches to contingency planning. Co-operation, monitoring and review, as we will see, form the vital foundations for successful development and implementation of contingency plans.

Monitoring and reviewing contingency plans

Regardless of the nature of the contingency plan, both before, during and after its implementation it should be reviewed and monitored at regular intervals. Specifically, the organisation and the relevant decision makers should consider the following.

Continuing relevance

They should review and evaluate the appropriateness of the contingency plans that have already been developed in the light of the prevailing conditions in which they could have to be used. In other words, a contingency plan framed in respect of a particular body of understanding or knowledge in the past may not still be relevant to the current situation. If the review and evaluation are not carried out, then the organisation may discover that it will be relying on contingency plans that bear no real relation to its needs. The contingency plans that are being 'held in reserve' should reflect the direction in which the organisation is moving. They may not require a great deal of modification, but adjustments may need to be made. The review and evaluation should incorporate the 'closeness of fit' to the corporate activities, relevant alternative strategies that are being used and whether they can realistically accomplish what the organisation hopes they will achieve.

Appropriateness of underlying assumptions

During the implementation and use of the contingency plan, the organisation will be able to assess the appropriateness of the assumptions and processes that underpin the plan. In this way, additional or supplementary contingencies may be framed in order to take account of the changes that have occurred. These changes, both in terms of the situational modifications created by the use of the contingency plan and other changes brought about by the natural progressions and actions, both internally and externally, will mean that the organisation can no longer rely on the plans that have been set aside for later implementation. Organisations would have to incorporate the normal processes of review and evaluation in the contingencies in just the same way as they would carry out these vital functions as part of any revision or evaluation exercise.

Identifying the next stage

Once the contingency plan has been implemented and seen through to its logical conclusion, the organisation will need to be able to identify the next stage of measures designed to carry objectives and the strategies forward. In this way, the organisation will be able to review and evaluate the contingency in the light of the definable outcomes that have been achieved. The organisation will also be able to consider, with the benefit of hindsight, the wisdom of actually using the contingency plan and whether any other course of action would have been more appropriate or successful given the circumstances. While the contingency plan may have dealt with the immediate problems and addressed the identified gaps between the original strategies and the requirements of the organisation, it may have created a number of new problems that will have to be examined, leading to the need to develop new contingencies as the organisation's current set of contingency plans become inappropriate.

Monitoring and review process

The investigations which lead to the identification of gaps between the existing strategies and the organisation's objectives, whether these strategies are contingencies or not, must be based on what can be realistically achieved. If the organisation cannot identify a gap between the strategies and the objectives, this may mean that the contingencies do not have to be employed. What is also clear is the fact that some of the contingencies may, in fact, offer a more efficient means of matching the strategies to the objectives. Regular review and monitoring of both the current strategies and the existing contingencies will give the organisation some useful insights into this possibility.

The actual monitoring and review process should give the organisation the opportunity to appreciate the fact that changes and improvements are an integral part of the reality of running a business. Organisations should not shirk from the decisions that may require them to develop or implement contingencies. The use of these plans does not infer that the organisation is not able to create coherent plans that do not require amendment.

Any improvement to the information-gathering exercises or analysis of the market will be bound to uncover strategic considerations that have been omitted from the organisation's main plans. Any review or monitoring process that arises out of these investigations should always be made with reference to the corporate values or the basic principles that lie at the heart of the organisation. These review or monitoring activities will help the organisation address whether the current policies and strategies match or support its perceived values.

For the most part, the monitoring and review process will be carried out within the framework of the organisation's view of 'how it does business'. In this way, the organisation can be the best judge of whether the contingency plans, however created (planned or *ad hoc*), match the preferred way of doing things. There may be cases when either planned or *ad hoc* contingencies are implemented without serious regard to this point. The organisation may not have a choice, but the monitoring and review process will give it the opportunity to re-adjust the balance and try to bring the contingency back into the parameters of normal operational procedures.

At the very least, review and monitoring should be able to identify whether the organisation is being consistent in its avowed intentions to address issues such as equal opportunities, ethical behaviour, social responsibility or general environmental concerns. Equally, the organisation will also be able to judge whether the use of the contingencies has drawn it away from the normal business practices and perceptions that are related to its area of business activity. In this sense, the organisation will have the opportunity to assess the reactions of its stakeholders to apparent changes in the operational or strategic approaches that have been adopted as a result of the use of contingency plans.

Review questions

1 What circumstances might occur to force an organisation to develop a contingency plan?

2 Vroom and Yetton proposed a contingency theory. Briefly outline their thoughts.

3 'Any contingency approach recognises the fact that there may not be an ideal way in which to tackle and resolve a particular problem.' If this is the case, what is the point of creating a contingency plan?

4 At its most basic, the contingency plan is merely a system by which the organisation can ask itself a series of 'if what' or 'if then' questions. How can an organisation begin to quantify these questions?

5 What is MRPII?

6 Summarise the work carried out by Joan Woodward (1980).

7 How do the needs of large-scale or mass production-based organisations affect their ability to control their basic functions?

8 How does the complexity of contingency planning differ at the various levels of an organisation? Why is this the case?

9 Perrow (1970) suggested that there are two main ways in which the decision maker should view technology in terms of contingency planning. Describe the main features of these two views.

10 How does Perrow distinguish between routine and non-routine functions?

11 How does the hierarchy of objectives relate to the timing of the contingency planning?

12 Some objectives do not have an immediately identifiable or feasible strategy to meet them. This is true of both original and contingency plans. What are the possible solutions to this problem?

13 What are the main points which can be drawn from Burns and Stalker's book *The Management of Innovation* (1996)?

14 Outline the main methods employed to monitor a contingency plan.

15 What are the main differences between *ad hoc* and planned contingencies? Why do some organisations prefer to use a combination of these two approaches?

Alternatives for coping with risk

A prudent decision maker should always attempt to develop a series of alternative solutions to problems. If the choices open to the decision maker have not been explored properly, then there is the danger that the problem will have to be handled without sufficient preparation which ensures that the situation is given the correct degree of importance. Without an alternative plan, at least in the mind of the decision maker, there is the very real possibility that the decision maker will act without thinking and will simply choose another course of action that may have dire consequences. If the main solution to the problem does not work, then decision makers will either find themselves faced with the prospect of having no plan at all or, perhaps worse, the need to install an alternative that is the exact opposite of the intended one.

Problems rarely present themselves in such a way as to allow the decision maker to identify a clear right or wrong approach to them. Nothing as complex as a business-related problem is clear cut, with the opportunity for the decision maker to rule out all of the obvious 'no hope' solutions and arrive at the one and only true solution to the problem.

The dangers of not thinking about the alternative courses of action are enormous. The organisation, having identified the way in which it proposes to deal with a situation, will often wait until the last possible moment, only to discover that its intended way out of the problem will not work. Following on from this is the fact that the organisation may not look at the solution to the problem right through to its logical conclusion. The long-term impact of a bad solution to a problem can have far-reaching effects. Without correctly defining the true nature of the solution and the possible impact it might have, the organisation is effectively ignoring all of the other options and their (perhaps) relatively less drastic impact.

Finding out the implications of a solution and investigating the alternatives can, of course, be very time consuming. In many cases, the level and complexity of the problem and its associated solutions do not warrant any real in-depth consideration. However, for those decisions that have taken on a more important status, perhaps affecting the whole of the organisation and its long-term viability, the decision makers need to be very careful about the final choice of the solution and its attendant implications. For this reason, organisations would be very wise to consider developing a series of contingency plans which would help them in the following areas:

1 Is there a need to do anything about the problem? Perhaps it needs to develop further before any real solution can be offered. This approach is often known as the *take no action* stance.

2 Should the organisation settle on one solution rather than another? Perhaps the situation at present demands a rather more subtle approach. The organisation at this point may decide that it is more appropriate to consider trying out a series of different approaches and seeing which one is more suitable for the situation. This approach is often known as *hedging*.

3 Do the organisation and its decision makers need to obtain more information before they can make a valid and relevant decision about the choice of solution to a problem?

4 Has the organisation encountered similar problems in the past and tackled them with a different solution? At the very least, there may be a depth of knowledge and understanding in the organisation on the part of individuals who have had experience of these types of problems before. In this case, the organisation needs to assemble all of the alternatives before launching into one of the solutions as the saviour of the situation.

Obviously, the organisation needs to consider these alternatives in the light of the urgency or importance of the decisions that will need to be made. Equally, the decision maker may face situations when there is little or no time to devote to the seeking of new alternatives once the preferred solution has either failed or appears not to work. The identification and development of alternatives needs to take place at a point when the decision maker has the information available, the time to devote to them and sufficient time to put them into action if this appears to be the right way of approaching the problem.

Take no action or hedging – alternative ways of coping with risk?

Contingency plans and the application or implementation of methods to deal with change are very much a fact of life for the majority of decision makers. Just how they choose to approach the problems associated with the exploration, choice and implementation of viable contingencies will differ from organisation to organisation and, as importantly, from individual to individual. Before we consider the place of these two strategies, it is appropriate to begin by looking at the scope of the changes that may require the decision maker to make efficient change-management decisions. We will begin by considering the possible changes to the scope of the problem or the situation that faces the decision maker.

Types of change

Clearly, changes in the scope of the problem can be categorised in terms of the degree of change. Initially we can identify the following probabilities (*see* Fig 11.1):

◆ that the problem or current situation has some additional considerations that will need to be taken on board

◆ that the problem or current situation has been changed in either the way in which the organisation needs to approach the problem (either through internal changes or the influence of the external environment) or as a result of additional information or considerations coming to light;

◆ that the problem has been reduced in some way by the 'deletion' of a consideration or an assumption that used to underpin the decision-making approach normally used.

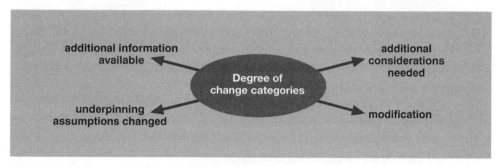

Fig. 11.1 Degree of change categories

We will need to be rather more precise in our assessment of the potential changes in order to identify why an organisation may choose to adopt a particular response to the change. We can best explain the potential changes with reference to the five most likely recurring changes (*see* Fig 11.2).

Requirement change

A requirement change normally derives from the needs of the customer. In this type of change, the customer would identify a consideration or specification related to the service or product that is being supplied. Perhaps experience or use of previous products and services has brought certain issues or deficiencies to light that will need to be addressed by the supplier. In many cases neither the customer or the supplier has noticed that the product or service needs this modification and the supplier will be expected to react quickly and efficiently to rectify the situation. In this instance, a 'take no action' or 'hedging' approach to the contingency would not be appropriate.

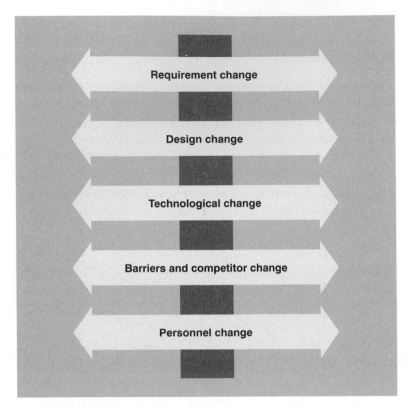

Fig 11.2 The five recurring changes

Design change

A design change normally originates from the developers of the product or the service, although in some cases design changes occur at production stage. The identification of a better way to design or configure the product or service would be as a result of the normal flow of ideas and innovations that derive from pre-testing or pre-production test runs. The organisation would have the opportunity to fully incorporate the proposed changes to the product or the service, to take no action and produce the product as it is, or perhaps to try to produce some of the products or services in the original form and some in the new way. In the latter case, the organisation would then have the opportunity to be able to judge objectively the relative merits and demerits of both approaches.

Whether the organisation chooses to take on board the proposed design changes or not will very much depend on the relative importance that can be attached to the change and source of the suggestion. If the change proposer has a position of power and authority within the organisation, then there may be no other choice but to incorporate these changes.

Technological change

A technological change will affect the product or service. This may be critical in the sense of timing the identification of the relevant change in technology. If the change is apparent at a relatively early stage in the development of the product or service, then the organisation will be able to make subtle changes that may not affect long-term plans. However, when the organisation discovers that a technological change will occur at precisely the wrong moment (perhaps just as the product is about to be launched or repackaged), then the choices will be very different. At this point, the organisation will be able to consider either the 'take no action' approach, which could have long-term effects on the viability of the product, or 'hedging' which could mean that the product or service is delayed while the technological changes are investigated. In all cases, technological changes need to be considered in terms of the organisation's ability and willingness to incorporate them into their overall decision making.

Business or competitor change

A business or competitor change brings about a series of events affecting the business environment or the conditions under which the organisation operates, which could result in the need to develop and implement contingency plans and can come from a variety of different sources and influences in the external environment. The organisation would have to be able to take a proactive approach if it encounters the launch of a new product or service from a competitor or a considerable fluctuation in interest rates or currency values. Obviously, some products and services will be more or less affected by these considerations and changes, but the organisation would not be able to adopt either a take no action approach or, for that matter, a hedging stance. If the organisation does not decide to take immediate action, then it could find itself in a very difficult position which would require more drastic action once the full impact of the change in the business environment has been appreciated.

Personnel change

A personnel change is either related to the organisation itself or, as importantly, the change in personnel at a major customer. If the organisation had enjoyed a close, ongoing relationship with a particular individual within a customer's organisation, it would have to rethink the way in which it does business with that customer. The organisation would be advised to take some form of immediate action to ensure that it can re-establish the relationship with the customer.

One of the most dangerous periods for a supplier in these cases is the point immediately after the replacement of a key buyer or contact in a major customer's organisation. The possibility of the new buyer or contact having an ongoing relationship with another supplier is a very real one. The existing supplier would need to act promptly and try to arrange to see the new employee at the earliest opportunity.

The problems that could be associated with new personnel coming on to the scene within the organisation itself can again present a series of decision-making choices. Given the fact that the original post-holder was fully involved and appraised of the current status and progress of the activities, the new post-holder will have to be incorporated and fully briefed at the earliest possible point. This assumption is based on the fact that the organisation intends to replace the individual precisely in line with the roles and responsibilities of the previous post-holder. Adjustments may be necessary in terms of the roles and responsibilities allotted to those involved in a particular project, product or service if the balance of the team is changed as a result. For the most part, this personnel consideration would involve the possibility of customers no longer dealing with the supplier or additional duties needing to be allocated to team members (in respect of design, technology etc.).

Reappraising the situation

Any of these changes will involve a degree of repositioning and reappraisal of the situation. The actual options open to the organisation would not normally include either 'taking no action' or hedging, but the degree of the change may mean that the organisation can 'sit back' and wait for the full ramifications of the change to become clear before it does anything about the situation. The point of no return, when the organisation has to do something about the change, is when the product, service or project is slipping in terms of performance, schedule or progress. Unless the organisation has reappraised the particular activity and decided that the slippage is not relevant, then it will be forced to take some kind of action and bring one of the contingency plans into operation.

 # Obtaining more information

It is vitally important that the decision maker is in receipt of all necessary and relevant information in order to ensure that rational decisions can be made. Given the fact that the decision maker will often have to operate without perfect knowledge or perfect information, it is inevitable that, at some point, a reassessment of the situation will be necessary. The search for a more complete set of data to assist the framing of the new contingencies can be a very frustrating procedure. We should not assume that the decision maker will ever be in a position that suggests to them that they have completed this task. Having said this, the decision maker will have to try to redouble the efforts to obtain this information if they ever expect to be able to make a fully rational decision that is based on all of the facts.

Although the decision maker may already have identified the probable sources of information and be aware of the comparative difficulties of obtaining the data, this aspect needs to be revisited. After all, given that the decision maker is now having to consider the alternative courses of action that are now available, the nature of the task at hand and the associated problems will have created a new set of information needs. Before we consider the ways in which the additional information can be gathered, it would be prudent to consider the factors that will affect the complexity of the information-gathering process.

Task uncertainty factors

Task uncertainty factors relate to 'newness' or the fact that the situation requiring the information is unknown to the decision maker. Obviously, the more unique or unknown the problem is, the greater the need for the decision maker to have a more comprehensive range of information on which to draw. Decision makers who have to operate in conditions where the tasks are non-routine, or perhaps where every problem that they face is a 'one-off', will need to develop a comprehensive network of information-gathering sources in order to ensure that they are appraised of all of the factors that are relevant to that decision.

For the contingency planner, this is a very real state of affairs: the tortuous route of consequences that has brought about the need to frame or implement a contingency will have many of the same features as a non-routine decision-making process. On the other hand, if the contingency has many of the features of a previously encountered set of problems, then the information gathering may not be as complex as we have suggested. In all cases, however, the establishment of a process that allows the decision maker to gather information from a variety of different internal and external sources would greatly improve the prospects of the decision maker's ability to make a considered appraisal of all of the factors that need to be taken into account.

Complexity

The complexity of the elements that make up the decision will refer to the range of different tasks and activities that form a part of the decision as a whole. In this respect, the decision maker will need to consider all of the independent parts of the contingency, taking them as a whole and also trying to establish a clear progression in terms of the order in which they need to be addressed. In this way, the information needs will be phased, requiring the decision maker to obtain the basic 'underpinning' data before expanding the data search to include to more detailed aspects of the situation.

It is important to see the information needs as being an expanding flow of information gathering: the deeper the decision maker looks into the problem the greater the demand for more information. In order to manage this aspect of the data-collection exercise, the decision maker must be able to order the information gathering by gradually unravelling the layers of information rather than trying to collect a mass of data that would confuse and make the process all that more complex to handle.

Interdependence

The degree of interdependence of the decisions associated with the contingency plan will need to take account of the potential implications of an initial decision and how it will affect the other factors involved. In other words, the decision maker's early decisions related to the contingency will be important, as this will have a net effect on the rest of the decision-making process. Not only will the decision maker need to have a clear knowledge of the situation before new decisions are made, but they will also need to be aware of the information needs at that time.

As the decisions are made, the information needs will change too. This will bring about a constant change in the information-gathering process in order to address the new situations and the decisions related to them. The more decisions are made, the greater the changes in the underlying situation and consequently the greater the changes in the nature and the sources of the information.

Information needs

Nearly every information-gathering exercise associated with a decision, regardless of whether this is a contingency or not, will be a unique process. We will develop this point and the process of identifying the contingencies in the last chapter.

Let us develop the argument in terms of the information needs that can be identified in three different states.

Regular information needs

Regular monitoring of the external environment may have a bearing on the current situation and that of the contingencies. In addition to this, the organisation should also monitor the way in which a particular solution to a problem has been put into effect, coupled with the measurement of efficiency criteria that can be related directly to the problem and its solution. Finally, the solution needs to be measured in terms of its performance against the particular strategies and objectives that it was designed to meet.

Information needs in stable conditions

These information needs primarily relate to organisations that have either an established market or product/service. The probable changes can be monitored in terms of very slight (although not necessarily insignificant) concerns. Typically, there will be a need to collect information relating to the internal workings of the organisation in order to assess the production considerations, the implementation of the contingency and the general effectiveness of the solution.

One of the main points of concern here is that organisations which have enjoyed the relative stability of an established product, service or market will neglect the information-gathering processes. This will lead to a reactive set of responses (requiring *ad hoc* contingency planning in the main) rather than being proactive (the planned approach to contingency planning). If the organisation does not keep up a regular watch and data-collection exercise then it will tend to lose the initiative and may allow competitors to 'sneak' into the marketplace without realising this until it is too late.

All information gathering needs to revolve around the concept of *stability distur-bance*. In other words, the data collection needs to be able to recognise the changes in the environment as they happen so that contingency plans can be employed to attempt to re-establish the equilibrium state that the organisation formerly enjoyed.

Given that the majority of organisations cannot rely on a stable environment, their information needs and gathering exercises probably need to be adapted to the *uncertainty* state, as outlined below. To be precise, in the stable environment the information needs would tend to be concerned with the following:

◆ the effectiveness of implementing decisions;

◆ the performance evaluation of solutions against predetermined objectives;

◆ not, necessarily, the actual changes in the input conditions.

Information needs in conditions of uncertainty

The more uncertain the state in which the organisation finds itself, the greater the need to invest considerable time and resources in information gathering. Indeed, the complexity and scope of the information need to be far more detailed and con-sidered than is the case for an organisation that has a relatively stable environment in which to operate. Given the fact that these organisations often operate in condi-tions that preclude routine methods of doing things, the information-gathering systems need to be far more flexible. This will enable the organisation to collect data on single issue or one-off problems as they occur.

In this respect the data sources need to be varied and under constant review. Clearly, the relevance and age of the data will play a large role in the organisation's ability to cope with the situation and prepare contingency plans capable of han-dling the problem. Since these organisations are often involved in one-off decision making, the methods of implementation and measurement need to be tailor-made to each situation. Given that the objectives and the related strategies are constantly changing, the benchmarks against which the efficiency can be measured are diffi-cult to quantify and be precise about.

It is a fair assumption that these organisations are also involved in areas of business activity that have a strong technology background. In this respect, the complexity of each of the decisions, or contingencies, is such that only specialist staff can be employed to investigate or examine the exact nature of the situation. There will be a tendency to rely on the specialist knowledge of particular groups of employees or consultants, which leads to another pertinent problem. If the situation is too com-plex, then how can the general decision makers hope to appreciate all of the subtle nuances of the problem? Their information needs will be very different from those of the specialists. There is only one real solution to this apparently insurmountable problem: the network of information and communications needs to be very sophis-ticated and flexible. The key decision makers need to know the facts in order to make an informed decision.

Selection between different courses of action

Selection between diverse courses of action necessarily entails evaluation of the options. In order to be able to carry out this evaluation, the decision maker must be in a position to understand and describe the probable outcomes related to each of the options. In our assessment of the evaluation factors or criteria, we need to assume that the decision maker is aware of the objectives and that the organisation has an established means of setting the decision-making criteria to aid the evaluation process. These can be best identified by considering the three major areas of critical evaluation.

Effectively, the organisation can evaluate diverse courses of action in the following ways:

i) the feasibility of each of the potential courses of action;

ii) the acceptability of each of the potential courses of action;

iii) the vulnerability of each of the potential courses of action.

Feasibility

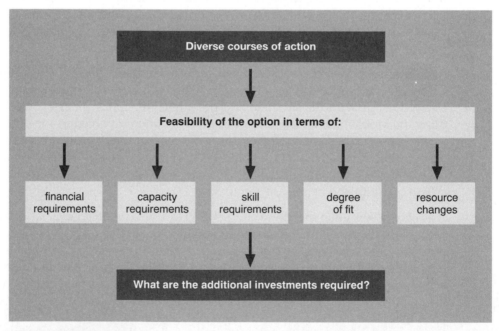

Fig 11.3 Feasibility

Financial requirements

As with the majority of decisions, the primary question will be related to the financial implications of the course of action. Essentially, this will almost certainly come down to the basic questions of 'How much will this course of action cost the company?' and 'Can we afford it?'. For the most part, the question of financial commitment is far more complex than it might appear. Some of the costs associated with the course of action may be 'one-off' payments that do not have a long-term implication in terms of either relative cost or the movement of financial resources from another area of the business's activities.

The higher the cost of the course of action, the more likely it is to take on a strategic dimension. If it will have a net impact on the rest of the organisation, the decision maker will have to refer to cash flow and the fact that other activities may have to subsidise the additional expenditure. At this point, the decision maker will certainly have to refer the matter to more senior decision makers, as well as informing other decision makers who will have to make changes to their plans and expenditure.

Capacity requirements

The capacity requirements will demand that the decision maker determines the quantity of resources, materials and other aspects that are required for each of the different courses of action. Estimations will have to be made of the time required for each of the subtasks and activities that are an integral part of the overall decision. In this way, the decision maker will be able to assess the relative expenditure in terms of the organisation's ability to cater for the additional capacity requirements. Some of the estimates can be based on the number of 'person hours' or 'person weeks' that can be directly identified as being a consequence of each of the alternative courses of action.

If the decision maker knows the start and finish dates for each of the courses of action, then it is possible to estimate the workload involved during that period. In this way, the aggregate workload can be combined and compared to the existing workloads. The next step would allow the decision maker to see what the differences are in terms of extra capacity needed to carry out the different courses of action.

Skill requirements

Any decision option, whether it is a contingency or an alternative course of action, will require the organisation to identify the necessary human skills. For alternative courses of action which are very similar to those already being carried out by the organisation, there may not be a overriding requirement for new skills and aptitudes. In this respect, those courses of action which more closely mirror the present skill requirements may appear to be more attractive to the decision maker.

However, many alternative courses of action come into existence as a result of a lack of particular skills within the organisation, so identification of new skills that will be required would probably be necessary even if the organisation chose to retain the present course of action.

This may appear to be an easier set of decisions than is actually the case. The problem is not necessarily related to being able to obtain or identify individuals (internally or externally) who are capable of doing the jobs required, it is the initial identification of the skills that will be required. If the decision maker is unaware of the skills that will be needed to carry out particular tasks associated with the alternative courses of action, it will be impossible to be able to take on the individuals to do them. The first step must be related to being able to classify the skills and expertise that will be needed, followed by the decisions regarding the strategies to be used in filling this 'skills gap'.

Degree of fit

The 'degree of fit' consideration requires the decision maker to take the existing operations and activities into account when the alternative courses of action are investigated and assessed. The decision maker is looking for alternative courses of action which sit more happily with the existing activities, as they may otherwise have too great an impact on what is already being done.

The basic question of 'Do we have the resources and the skills to carry out this alternative plan?' needs to be upgraded to 'Do we have the resources and the skills to carry out this alternative plan without disadvantaging or detracting from the other things that we have to do?'. The answer to the question lies in two areas: whether the alternative course of action is complementary to the other activities, and whether it can exploit skills and abilities that are not being fully utilised. If the alternative course of action cannot be seen to be doing either of these, then the degree of fit is not good and the decision maker may discount this option. On the other hand, if the decision maker can see positive advantages in terms of complementing or exploiting existing activities and skills, then the course of action may be far more attractive.

Typical ways of measuring the degree of fit may be related to specific areas of the organisation's operations or activities. In this way, a product or a service that seems to fit in well with the existing product lines could be described as having a good 'marketing fit'. Other courses of action may complement the existing production or operational activities, in which case the organisation will have found a course of action that has a good 'operations fit'.

Resource changes

The resource changes which we have already considered in terms of skills, capacity and costs could mean that the alternative course of action is not viable. However, these considerations assume the worst case when individually these changes will be too acute to consider the option as viable.

There are other situations when it is not the individual impact on one of these that is the determining factor, it is the combined effect on them that may be too complex or drastic. Individually, the organisation may be able to compensate for the effect of the course of action on its operations and resources but, taking the whole effect on the different aspects of operations, the strain and reorganisation may not be acceptable.

Acceptability

Turning to the next phase of consideration of alternative courses of action, there are two main points of interest here, the impact on the operations of the organisation and the financial impacts (*see* Fig 11.4). Both of these considerations will have to be investigated and evaluated by the decision maker.

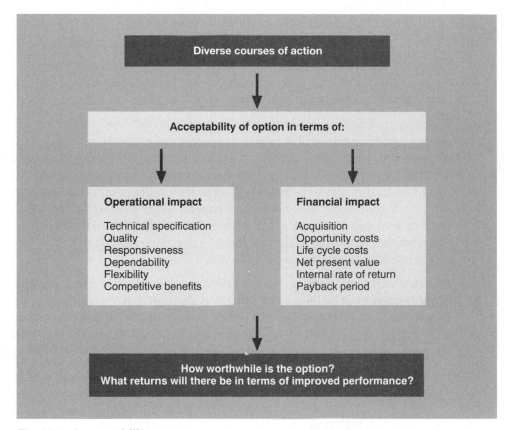

Fig 11.4 Acceptability

Many of the financial criteria have already been dealt with earlier in this book, so we will concentrate on the impact on the operational factors.

Operational impact

The technical specifications of the option may allow the decision maker to argue for its implementation on the basis that it more closely matches the requirements of the customer and that it will, consequently, have longer-term benefits to the organisation as a whole (lower levels of complaints and higher sales). The quality issues will relate to the decision maker identifying the fact that the option will offer the opportunity for the organisation to reduce the failure rate of a finished product or a general improvement in the quality of a service. Again, this might mean that the organisation will be able to enjoy certain savings, particularly if the number of faults and mistakes are minimised.

The responsiveness consideration refers to the organisation's ability to react to customers' needs and requirements as quickly as possible. If the alternative course of action will allow the organisation to shorten waiting times for individual customer attention, delivery and service, this will again be of general benefit to the organisation in terms of reputation and profitability.

Dependability refers to possible improvements to the reliability and timing of services, deliveries and other aspects (such as scheduling).

The alternative courses of action can be compared to the current ways of doing things. Will each increase the chances of something happening when it is supposed to? Will they facilitate the completion of the project or activity within the predefined deadlines and timing sequences?

The final consideration or factor is the relative flexibility of alternative courses of action. Just how easy will it be to incorporate the necessary changes to services, allocation of resources and other criteria in relation to the current operational procedures and activities? Will the alternative courses of action offer benefits to the organisation in terms of being able to provide a more comprehensive or efficient service to both internal and external customers? There may well be benefits that the decision maker can identify in this respect that will form the basis of a good selling proposition to senior management and other decision makers who may be affected by the use of the preferred course of action.

Probably the most significant measure of acceptability and overall assessment of the operational impact is the way in which the alternative courses of action will influence the organisation's competitive ability. In this respect, a number of key questions will have to be answered by the decision maker. Broadly this will mean that some degree of assessment (quantifiable) will be imposed on the following criteria:

1 In using our present contingency plans or strategic plans, is the organisation considerably better, clearly better or marginally better than our nearest competitor?

2 In using our present contingency plans or strategic plans, is the organisation's performance about the same or fairly close to the nearest competitor?

3 In using our present contingency plans or strategic plans, is the organisation's performance marginally worse, usually worse or consistently worse than the majority of the nearest competitors?

Clearly, the identification of a situation when the organisation is usually better will call the alternative courses of action into question, unless they can offer even better levels of performance. However, when we consider that the organisation may view itself as only as good as or worse than the competition, the decision maker may be in a better position to argue the case of the alternative courses of action. Obviously, there would have to be some definable benefits to the organisation and senior management would not accept a worsening of the situation. Typically, the measurement of performance could relate to some of the factors below, which are often measured on a nine-point scale. Table 11.1 attempts to illustrate how the alternative course of action could improve the situation.

Table 11.1 Measurement of performance

Comparison criteria	1	2	3	4	5	6	7	8	9
Estimated cost					O		C		
Product quality		O	C						
Manufacturing quality	C	O							
Enquiry leadtime				C					
Manufacturing leadtime							C		
Design flexibility			C	O					
Delivery flexibility			C		O				
Volume flexibility								C	O

C refers to the present situation and O refers to the estimated impact on the relevant variable after the implementation of the alternative course of action.

Source: Adapted from Slack, N. *Achieving a Manufacturing Advantage*, Mercury Books, 1991.

Making a choice

We have investigated the ways in which the decision maker can attempt to quantify the alternative choices, but we have to appreciate that at some stage the decision maker will have to make a choice. This allows us to investigate the options open to the decision maker, bearing in mind that even once the decision has been made, the options are not always as straightforward as we might expect.

Although evaluation is a complex procedure in itself, it is further complicated by the fact that this stage of investigation and analysis will also strongly influence the ultimate choice of the course of action. In other words, consciously or unconsciously, the decision maker will be choosing while the evaluation process is underway. Each of the aspects of the different courses of action will have been (hopefully) minutely examined and the decision maker will already have some idea about not only the relative merits of each of the options, but also the one that gives the most satisfaction (personally) and the one that meets the majority of the objectives required (the one that is likely to be more acceptable on a corporate level). This process will probably bring about a tendency to be rather biased when it comes to making the final decision about the course of action, but this bias should be avoided if possible and the options should only be measured in terms of the broader and objective criteria that we have outlined above.

Decidophobia

Actually making the choice at the end of the day may be one of the most difficult things to do, particularly if there is not much to choose between each of the alternatives on offer. This may be compounded by the fact that the decision maker is now forced to discount options that *could* work for those that it is felt *will* work. The dividing line between these two factors may be a very thin one. This could lead to a state of *decidophobia* (as outlined by Albrecht (1980)), when the decision maker is unwilling to make any choice at all as they all have a degree of risk attached to them. The probable solutions to this state of mind are:

a) Remembering that the choice is not the end of the process, it is the implementation of the choice that is important.

b) Given a 'level playing field' all of the options could work if sufficient care and attention is paid to them, but who really knows what the true outcome of the discarded choices will be if they are never followed through?

c) If one or more of the choices are not that different in either risk or impact, the final choice may be all that more simple, since it will not be that important which one is chosen at the end of the day.

d) The decision maker should always try to be consistent in the way that the different courses of action are evaluated and analysed. In this way, there is more chance that the correct one has been chosen.

e) If the correct level of effort, resourcing and other factors is applied to any of the choices, there is a good chance that it will be as successful as any of the others.

Evaluation

Many decision makers try to apply the notion that the alternative course of action should be *better* in some way than current practices and operations. This approach means that the decision maker needs to apply some kind of measurement or value to each of the courses of action. This is a necessary process so that the different courses of action can be compared with one another and with the current policies or strategies.

There is no real blueprint for this kind of analysis, but the decision maker could employ one of the following methodologies:

i) Compare the likely outcomes of the alternatives to that of the historical performance of similar strategies and contingencies (or those that are being replaced).

ii) Compare in a similar way to the above, but base the comparisons on an external standard (perhaps taken from the performance or experience of a similar organisation).

iii) Attempt to make the comparisons based on the 'ideal' or *absolute* standards, in other words what the decision maker or organisation would hope the performance would be like in an ideal world.

iv) Make comparisons based on the baseline of what would happen if the decision maker decided to do nothing. This is known as a *do-nothing standard*. At the very least, this would give the decision maker the opportunity to measure the estimated performance in terms of a finite standard.

The decision maker may well still be skirting around the issue and will not yet have the confidence to make the final decision. Questions will still loom very large regarding the feasibility and acceptability of the proposed course of action. Let us try to analyse the thoughts that may be going through the mind of the indecisive decision maker:

1 Acceptability rests on the extent to which the course of action will lead to a satisfactory outcome for all concerned. Some courses of action may be at one extreme, when they will satisfy the needs and the aspirations of everyone, and others will be at the other end of the spectrum and satisfy no one. Most will lie in the middle and it is these that will cause the maximum amount of indecision.

2 Somewhere on the continuum between total satisfaction and absolute dissatisfaction there will be a point that can be identified as being more acceptable than unacceptable to the majority. The decision maker may be well advised to look here for the solution to the quandary that is being faced.

3 Just how feasible an option will ultimately be must depend on the organisation's ability and willingness to apply the correct level of resources, time and effort to it. Once again, there is a continuum that can be examined. At one extreme the option may be too complex or expensive to be 'in the running' at all. At the other end of the continuum, the organisation may feel that the option will underutilise the resources available to them. Again, somewhere there is a happy medium that is just about feasible without adversely affecting the overall prosperity or health of the organisation.

Confidence

The decision maker and, for that matter, the senior management to whom the individual will be ultimately answerable need to have confidence in the course of action. Whether this confidence can be derived from the examination and assessment of the feasibility and acceptability of the option is open to question. What is more important, in the majority of cases, is whether the decision maker is relatively certain about the possible outcomes and consequences of the chosen option. After all, once the course of action or new contingency is implemented, the control of it begins to slip out of the hands of the decision maker.

There is a way in which this apparent paradox can be quantified and assessed in terms of the degree of control that the decision maker needs to retain (in order to feel confident about actually implementing the plan) and the degree of impact that the decision is likely to have on the area of activity or the organisation more generally. The two sets of criteria can be described in the following ways:

i) Degrees of control over the option:
    – largely under the control of the decision maker;
    – partially under the control of the decision maker;
    – little or no control in the hands of the decision maker.

ii) Impact on the benefits or objectives:
    – a low impact with little benefit;
    – an average impact with a reasonable benefit;
    – a high impact with major benefits.

By cross-referencing these two criteria the decision maker can identify the fact that control will still be high when the impact on the objectives is low, but, on the other hand, the decision maker may lose control over the situation when the impact on the objectives is high.

Consensus

As an alternative to this form of decision making, which still relies on the individual decision maker taking the decision on their own, the decision could be based on some form of consensus. Any decision-making process which relies on a number of individuals agreeing on a particular course of action will be fraught with difficulties. Not only will the individuals which make up the decision-making group (whether this is a board meeting, interdepartmental meeting or a meeting which involves the participation of stakeholders such as shareholders or other investors) have differing objectives and vested interests, but they will often express one option privately and a completely different one publicly.

Obtaining a true consensus of opinion may not be necessary provided that the decision-making group can at least commit themselves to a particular course of action. Are we actually looking for a decision-making group that is prepared to agree to almost anything that the proposers of particular options put forward for them to 'rubber stamp'? The answer must be no. This approach would, in effect, mean that the advantages of multiple decision makers, that there are opportunities for options to be fully and frankly discussed and chosen on merit, have been reduced to the same level as if there was only one decision maker. If, however, the decision-making group is too distant in terms of differing goals, objectives and viewpoints, then the decision-making process may be a long and tortuous one.

Managing the choice process

So far we have looked at the various pitfalls of the different decision-making processes in terms of being able to assess, evaluate, check acceptability and feasibility, and test for the degree of fit. Is there a scientific and proven way of arriving at the right decision for the right sets of circumstances? In short, no; but there are some ways in which the choice process can be managed in such a way as to limit the possible mistakes relating to the uncertainty and lack of confidence in the possible options.

Decision trees, as we have seen, are one method that can be employed to explore the possible consequences of implementing certain choices. Equally, the decision maker could make use of various computer programs that have been developed to aid decision making. On the other hand, there are more traditional forms of decision making that could allow the decision maker to arrive at the right choice for the situation. These more traditional approaches include the following (*see* Fig 11.5):

◆ choices based on the outcomes of negotiation;
◆ choices based on the judgement of one or more individuals;
◆ choices based on the creative inspiration of one or more individuals.

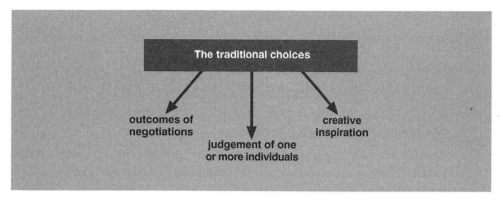

Fig 11.5 The traditional choices

How can these choice options fit into the overall decision-making process in a practical and usable fashion? Broadly speaking, we can categorise the choice options and ally them to the following sets of circumstances:

1 If there is a degree of consensus regarding the probable outcomes of the options and the decision makers are happy that the range of options will all fit into the parameters of the declared objectives, then the choice should be made by computation.

2 If there is a consensus of opinion that the options will fit within the parameters of the objectives, but there is disagreement regarding the probable consequences of the options to be chosen, then the choice should be made on the basis of judgement.

3 If the decision makers can agree over the outcomes of the options, but they are unsure about the impact and fit in relation to the objectives, then the choice should be made after there has been a period of negotiation.

4 If the decision makers cannot agree about the outcomes or the degree of fit to the objectives, then the choices are obviously the wrong ones. The only real option open is to search for new courses of action that will find support from some or all of the decision makers. Alternatively, one of the decision makers should take the lead and make the decision for everyone.

Detailed contingency planning

In creating any form of contingency plan the key is to ensure that there is a high degree of co-ordination between the following aspects:

i) the schedules involved (including milestones and deadlines);

ii) the costs and budgets that have been predetermined and accounted for;

iii) the human resources that will be employed;

iv) the capital assets that will be involved;

v) the achievement of all of the subtasks and plans that form integral parts of the overall contingency plan.

Communication is also a key factor. Not only must the primary decision maker or the individual responsible for the development of the plan be accessible and available, but the senior management, the team members and any other personnel must also have clear communication channels to one another.

Despite the fact that there is no real blueprint for the successful creation of a detailed contingency plan, there are a number of key steps or considerations that must be borne in mind:

1 The contingency plan creator must ensure that all of the key personnel or team members are involved in the planning of the contingency at the earliest possible opportunity.

2 These team members must be involved with the contingency plan throughout the whole of the process, right up to the point when the contingency plan is completed, submitted and then approved.

3 Any cost or budgeting estimates must be realistic, likewise the timescales and milestones should be based on at least a 50 per cent chance of achievement.

4 The contingency plan creator also needs to ensure that the team members make clear work commitments to the contingency plan and if they work for other managers that this has been agreed through negotiation. In this way, everyone knows what is expected and there can be no arguments about the 'sharing' of team members.

5 The contingency plan creator must know that the assets, resources and other commitments made by the organisation are reliable, agreed and forthcoming when they are needed.

6 These commitments must take the form of written agreements so that no one can go back on their word.

7 The team members must realise that the creation of a contingency plan involves a series of clear steps or phases. In this respect, the planning process which identifies the steps to be taken is not changed without good cause. If the steps or sequence of activities are changed then there is a danger that the whole of the planning process will be thrown into confusion.

8 The contingency planning leader must appreciate the fact that there are many other criteria that could affect the outcome of the work. These would include the following:

– the clarity of the project, its scope, its realism, its objectives and size;

– the team members' ability to cope with the pressures, their experience, their willingness to co-operate and their sustained commitment;

– the willingness of the organisation to support the planning process throughout the duration of its life and that this support is apparent to all those concerned.

These considerations can be broken down into a series of key questions which underpin the whole of the process:

a) What are the objectives of the contingency plan?

b) How will we know that the contingency plan addresses the factors that are necessary?

c) Are we sure that the commitments made in terms of resourcing will be honoured by the organisation?

d) Are we aware that the degree of information and co-operation required from other areas of the organisation will be forthcoming?

e) Do we know how long the planning process will take?

f) Are we sure about the timing of the contingency plan in terms of when it is proposed to be implemented (assuming that it is approved)?

g) Do we have a reasonable idea of the costs involved?

In our definition of the 'ideal' contingency plan, it is possible to go one stage further, breaking down the whole of the planning process into a series of stages and taking us as far as the approval and implementation stage. Again, we do not offer this as a 'foolproof' way of ensuring that the contingency planning process works in every eventuality, but the steps outlined below are essential to have any prospect of being able to create and implement a workable strategy that can attempt to achieve the declared objectives and win the support of the organisation.

Define the scope and objectives of the contingency plan

◆ Review the objectives.

◆ Identify any concerns about the viability of the planning process, particularly in terms of the budget and the schedule.

◆ Renegotiate the parameters or scope of the planning process if necessary and make alterations as required.

◆ Personally review the adequacy of any specifications or standards that will be applied.

◆ Evaluate the external influences on the contingency plan.

◆ Be prepared to operate as the sole individual who has a full understanding of all of the activities and tasks that will be involved throughout the planning process.

◆ Make sure that you have created a filing system that is capable of holding all of the relevant documentation that will be generated, including all drafts, reports and other correspondence (dispose of what is irrelevant).

Create a model for the contingency plan

◆ Develop a simulation of the efforts that will be required to see the planning through.

◆ Identify the sequence of tasks that will be required, arising out of the model that you have created.

◆ Identify the major categories (phases) of work, break them down into tasks and describe them.

◆ Encourage the team members to contribute to this process and get them to brainstorm and discuss their own ideas about how the planning will work in reality.

◆ With the team's assistance, create a network which shows the dependencies and interrelationships of the tasks.

◆ Identify the key tasks that underpin all of the other tasks and those that will have an important effect on the overall work effort.

Estimate costs and resource needs and schedule the contingency planning

◆ Develop task estimates which incorporate the time, effort and resources required for each task.

◆ Prepare a preliminary schedule based on the dependencies already identified and the task estimates.

◆ Compare the preliminary schedule to the original objectives of the contingency plan in terms of timing, costs and budgets.

◆ If necessary, negotiate any amendments or revisions to the estimates that have been made.

◆ In extreme circumstances, now negotiate changes to the contingency plan's objectives.

◆ Now decide whether the contingency planning process, in its current or renegotiated form, is workable.

◆ Prepare the true schedules and budgets that will be applied to the contingency plan from now on.

Balance the contingency plan against other current planning processes and similar activities

◆ Remember that different projects and planning processes are competing with one another for resources.

◆ Remember that there are limited resources, so be assured that the allocation of resources to your contingency planning is both fair and practicable.

◆ Balancing the competing projects may well depend on your willingness to call on resources in a phased manner. Only ask for what you need when you actually need it. The attendant dangers of having visibly unused resources at times when other projects need these will be very difficult to explain to senior management.

◆ Try to acquire some understanding of the anticipated supply and demand of resources. This will help you manage to obtain what you need when it is needed.

Seek approval and publish the contingency plan

◆ Detail the contingency plan's targets.

◆ State the preferred dates for implementation of the plan.

◆ Detail the costs associated with the plan.

◆ Clearly state the resource utilisation.

◆ Obtain agreement to the plan from your line manager.

◆ Obtain agreement to the plan from the functional managers that will be affected by the plan.

◆ Negotiate with the above, if necessary, and be prepared to make some minor adjustments (which remain in the spirit of the plan but do not risk ruining the plan itself).

◆ Obtain commitments from the above to take to the senior management.

◆ Present the plan in its final form and hope that the arguments are strong enough to gain the support of senior management.

◆ Since they will have already seen initial drafts and reports regarding the plan, this should be a 'rubber-stamping' exercise, but be prepared for the worst by considering the nature of the criticisms that may be made.

◆ Agree to make any necessary changes that senior management may insist on.

◆ Distribute your contingency plan to all interested and involved parties and be prepared to offer advice and assistance on its implementation, implications and control.

Review questions

1 What are the potential dangers in not ensuring that there is a workable alternative plan available?

2 Clearly distinguish between the terms *take no action* and *hedging* in the decision-making context.

3 There are five common recurring changes, describe them and give an example of each.

4 What do you understand by the terms *repositioning* and *reappraisal*?

5 What are task uncertainty factors?

6 'The degree of interdependence of the decisions associated with the contingency plan will need to take account of the potential implications of an initial decision and how it will affect the other factors involved.' What is meant by this statement?

7 How might an organisation evaluate the courses of action open to it?

8 Any decision option, whether it is a contingency or an alternative course of action requires that the organisation identifies the necessary human skills needed. What are the human resource implications of this statement?

9 What do you understand by the terms *degree of fit* and *skills gap*?

10 Suggest some ways in which a decision maker could quantify the potential impact of alternative courses of action on the organisation.

11 'Although evaluation is a complex procedure in itself, it is further complicated by the fact that this stage of investigation and analysis will also strongly influence the ultimate choice of the course of action that the decision settles upon.' What do you understand by this statement?

12 What is a state of *decidophobia* as outlined by K.G. Albrecht (1980)?

13 Many decision makers try to apply the notion that the alternative course of action should be *better* in some way than the current practices and operations. How could a decision maker analyse and quantify these different courses of action?

14 Outline at least three traditional forms of arriving at the correct choice of alternative.

15 In creating a contingency plan it is important to ensure a high degree of co-ordination between which criteria?

Contingency plans

In this final chapter, we revisit some of the ways in which contingencies can be identified and evaluated in terms of their likelihood and impact on the organisation. The principal focus revolves around the identification and management of the risk factors that may be involved when considering the alternative strategies open to the organisation and the decision makers. The scheduling of the contingency activities, also outlined in the previous chapter, will need to be reinvestigated as well as the monitoring arrangements necessary to ensure that implementation of the contingencies is proceeding in the correct and presumed direction.

We also take the opportunity to look at some contingency plans in context, allowing us to evaluate their effectiveness and applicability in the circumstances in which they were used. Ultimately, you will need to be able to carry out this evaluation exercise, and some of the methods already considered elsewhere in this book will assist you in doing this.

Above all, we will need to consider the main ways in which the decision maker approaches the problems associated with change and how change control can be used to develop and implement the relevant contingency plans. In effect, we need to begin with identification of the key objectives of change control so that we can see how they refer to the development of contingencies. The three most important considerations are:

1 What exactly are the options open to the decision maker when a change occurs that will need the establishment, development or implementation of a contingency plan? In other words, what are the limits or parameters of the decision maker's power and authority in any given situation? Above all, this consideration will determine the scope of the options that are available and either limit the choice of contingencies that can be used, or mean that the decision maker will have to refer the matter to a more senior decision maker in order to get authorisation to deal with the problem.

2 What are the agreed procedures and regulations that relate to the use of contingency plans? This aspect will determine the length of time and the complexity of the decision-making processes prior to the actual use of a contingency plan. This is a very important consideration in itself, since it can mean that the organisation or the decision is tied to a particular series of actions before any real

attempt to deal with the problem can be made. Naturally, at the earliest possible point the decision maker will have to make an assessment of the problem as well as of the likely implications of using the contingency plan. At the very least, this information will have to be made available to other interested parties within the organisation before the contingency plan can be approved.

3 There also needs to be a mechanism which allows the decision maker and other relevant parties to make informed judgements based on the additional resources and effort related to the use of the contingency plan. In this respect, the decision maker needs to be able to quantify some of the criteria that would ultimately assist in the decision of whether to approve or discount the contingency plan as either being viable or non-viable. The decision whether to use a contingency plan will, inevitably, be based on clear criteria related to the overall strategies and objectives of the organisation.

 ## Identifying contingencies and evaluating their likelihood and impacts

It is important to appreciate the significance of workable change-control systems that facilitate the necessary processes required to establish the nature and implications of any change. Although, in the majority of cases, organisations would not use as formal a set of procedures as the one outlined below, this does represent the kind of considerations that are necessary in order to ensure that the changes and the contingencies are handled in the most effective manner.

Change-control form

The identification of a possible change that could influence the scope or the nature of a strategy could be detailed on a change-control form (*see* Fig 12.1). This would describe the nature of the change and how the individual perceives its impact on the strategies currently being used. Having identified that a change is in operation, the individual may be in the best position to judge the initial effects that are likely to occur in the short term. On receipt of this initial warning, the decision maker responsible for the project, product or service in question (or perhaps the decision maker who has overall responsibility for attempting to meet particular objectives or targets) will be able to put the rest of the formal process into action.

Change-control log

The responsible decision maker will need to keep a change-control log (*see* Fig 12.2) which facilitates recording of the identified changes and the source of the information. An initial reaction would be expected at this stage and the decision maker would need to 'set the wheels in motion' in terms of calling a meeting of the relevant parties or consulting with a more senior decision maker regarding the implications of the change.

CHANGE-CONTROL SHEET

Part one – change request

Name ....   Department...
Extension ....   Date ....

Description of change

Benefits and considerations

Part two – project/area controller

Date received...
Recommendations

Part three – committee

Date received...
Comments

Part four – investigation team (if applicable)

Date undertaken ....
Summary of findings

Part five – approval of change incorporation

Date decision taken ....
Priority rating   high/medium/low
Summary of comments

Signature of approval manager

Fig 12.1 Change-control form

Change originator and number and date received	Project/area controller and date	Committee stage and date	Investigation team start and finish dates	Approval/ rejection and date

Fig 12.2 Change-control log

Management group

Most products, services and projects will have an associated group of individuals who are responsible for the management aspects. If the change requires the implementation of a contingency, then this group will need to meet and decide whether the change warrants the use of one of the contingencies that may have been previously developed for this very set of circumstances. In certain cases, the decision may be either to wait, to do nothing (as the change does not warrant the implementation of a contingency) or to seek further information before any irreversible decision is made. In the majority of instances, a particular member of the group responsible for the product, service or project will be assigned the task of investigating the change and the net effects of any use of contingencies.

Assessing the impact

The team responsible, either individually or collectively, will need to investigate the impact of the change and the contingencies that are under review for implementation. Clearly, time may be of the essence and this process will either be able to be carried out in considerable detail or will have to be short-circuited in order to meet predetermined deadlines. In addition to this, the change and the use of contingencies may be so complex that the investigating team will have to make some educated guesses about the likely impacts and, indeed, the likelihood of the change having a drastic (or significant) impact at all.

At this point, the investigating team may discover that the alarm caused by the identification of the change is not as critical or pertinent as was first assumed or feared. If the likelihood of the change is high, the impact may not necessarily be a negative one. In many cases the changes that are identified will actually open more doors and opportunities than present awkward problems that need to be solved. Consideration also needs to be given to the fact that the product or service may be entering its twilight years or months.

Consider the contingencies that could be employed if the organisation has a range of products that are linked to British interest in a major sporting event. What could it do, in terms of contingencies, if the British interest ended? Perhaps it would consider that the natural lifespan of the products has already been 'played out' and the need to consider contingencies as a result of changes is irrelevant. On the other hand, changes which trigger the need to consider contingencies at the pre-launch or development stage will tend to have a far greater effect on the team's responsiveness to contingencies. In this case, the whole of the project may be put into question by even the most innocuous of changes. A prudent organisation would have identified the possibilities of the changes and established a range of contingencies that could tackle this situation.

Making a decision

The final decision regarding the change and the implications related to the use of the contingency plan will be made by either the key decision maker, an appropriate senior manager or the team as a whole. Careful evaluation of the potential impacts will be made after having considered the reports compiled by the investigators.

It is important to realise that the impact of the contingency (and the change that caused the implementation of that contingency) may well be felt in other areas of the organisation other than the product/service or project that has been directly involved. In this respect, the implementation of the contingency may have to be referred to more senior management, or other decision makers at the same level of responsibility, in order to gauge their reactions and obtain their opinions on the matter. In this way, approval or disapproval of the contingency plan should be seen as a more integrated process, particularly if its apparent impacts are likely to be felt across the whole of the organisation.

Impacts of contingency plans

How can the decision maker responsible for the ultimate implementation of a contingency plan judge its likely impact in a broader sense? Clearly, the use of a contingency may well have an impact on one or more of the following:

i) the specifications of the project, product or service;

ii) the standard operating procedures that underpin most of the routine decision-making responsibilities;

iii) the schedules related to the product, service or project in terms of launch, fulfilment of customer needs, or other considerations such as availability of stocks and support services;

iv) the costs associated with the particular product, service or project, particularly if the budget will be exceeded or will need to be changed radically in order to compensate for the implementation of the contingency;

v) the allocation of resources that had been agreed to cover ongoing or developmental needs. This is of great significance if the relative allocation of resources needs to be seriously changed, as it will have an impact on the availability of resources for other projects elsewhere in the organisation;

vi) the utilisation of assets such as the production facilities or the workforce. The contingency may cause a delay, meaning that the organisation will need to find another period that the production department can devote to the manufacture of the product. In other cases, the organisation will have scheduled the time required for the product and this will entail the rescheduling of other products and services to replace the delayed product.

All of these considerations can be classed as *baseline changes* since they will fundamentally change the nature of the project. Once we have looked at the various risk strategies that can be employed, we will return to the process of investigating the primary sources of the changes and the subsequent need to implement some form of contingency. Some, as we will see, will be internally driven and other will be as a result of external considerations. The monitoring of these potential baseline changes is crucial to the effective and efficient management of the organisation and will, ultimately, determine whether the organisation has the ability to achieve the objectives that it has set itself.

Selection of risk strategies

As we have seen, the decision maker and the organisation need to have a series of different strategies in place in order to cope with potential changes in the different 'states' or environments in which it operates. On the one hand, the organisation has to be aware of the different opportunities that may present themselves at various times and have some idea about how it would seek to exploit them. At the same time, the organisation has to have a series of strategies prepared to deal with the variety of threats which could harm the organisation in some way. Obviously, these threats will include those that can be dealt with using standard operating procedures, but others may require far more in-depth thought before they can be implemented.

The organisation needs to engage itself in a constant balancing act that can provide viable alternatives to deal with certain situations as they arise, as well as being as innovative as possible. This innovation serves a number of useful purposes, not least the fact that the organisation can react in ways that cannot be predicted by the competition, offering the organisation the opportunity to out-manoeuvre others despite the fact that the situation or problem may appear to be a difficult one.

As we have also seen, successful management means that the organisation has to develop a range of strategies that are based on the management of opportunities and risks. For the most part, organisations will consider that it is vital to try to base as much of their strategy on the maximisation of opportunities, while at the same time attempting to reduce the number of risks that they feel they must take in order to take advantage of the opportunities.

Opportunities

Although we have already considered the nature of opportunities and the possible responses of organisations to them, it is worth restating some of the main opportunities that could lead to a certain amount of risk taking:

Additive opportunities

From time to time, the organisation may be presented with an ideal opportunity to make better use of the resources to hand. These *additive* opportunities often only involve very little actual change to the way in which the organisation operates. The identification of a new market for an existing product could be cited as an example of an additive opportunity and, as such, the organisation would not face a great deal of risk in trying to exploit this new market opportunity. In seeking to develop this new market, the organisation is not really making any great changes to the way in which it serves its existing markets.

The only point of risk that could be attached to this opportunity is when the organisation attempts to divert too much of its time, attention and resources to the new market, to the detriment of the existing markets. In reality, this would only tend to happen once the new market has proved itself to be a more profitable area of business than that in which the organisation currently operates.

Complementary opportunities

Creating synergies within the organisation is something that most organisations would cite as being ultimately desirable. If the organisation can identify allied areas of operations that are *complementary* to the existing nature of the business, the organisation need only make a relatively small investment to exploit the possibilities. The synergistic effect means that the addition of some extra expertise or machinery in the organisation can lead to greater economies, a better service to the existing customer base, better use of resources or the opportunity to develop new markets that could be potentially attractive to the organisation.

Again, the risk level is quite low, although the organisation has to be aware of the fact that the new products or activities that have been added to its portfolio will need careful and close management for the initial period in order to assess the impact that it is having on the organisation as a whole. At the same time, the organisation will need to be careful about the level of funding and the relative allocation of other resources to this new area of activity in order to ensure that existing operations are not compromised or neglected.

Breakthrough opportunities

Opportunities will occasionally present themselves when the organisation finds itself having to make fundamental changes to the ways it operates in order to exploit them. These *breakthrough* opportunities will make much greater demands on the organisation than the first two types of opportunities already discussed. They will demand that the organisation allocates considerable resources, human and physical, in order to develop the opportunity.

Since these opportunities demand a much greater level of attention and detail, they will also be far more risky. At this point the organisation will need to consider very carefully the relative advantages and disadvantages of the situation and try to come up with a viable strategy that seems to be capable of coping with the opportunity without seriously undermining existing activities.

Typically, we have seen organisations trying to struggle with these breakthrough opportunities in the fields of new technology, specifically the introduction of information technology and all of its attendant problems.

Risks

Overlaying the nature and degree of the risks that can be associated with these opportunities is problematic in itself. The categorisations, although broad and generalised, do give an overall impression of what might be at stake when the decision makers attempt either to cope with the opportunities that are thrust on them or to exploit them through their own initiative. The risk categories are as follows:

Risks that must be accepted in order to survive

Depending on the nature of the organisation and the business environment in which it operates, there may be occasions when there is no other alternative but to take risks. If this is not done, the organisation may be seriously damaged in terms of its market share and ability to compete. Although the majority of organisations will be at pains to pre-test and check the products and services that they launch on to the market, there may not be the time or the resources immediately available to investigate fully the long-term effects of the product or service, or, for that matter, to consider how the introduction of new products may affect the consumer or the market itself. In these cases, the organisation will have to react and take the risk of launching the product or service before all of the normal and sensible checks have been made.

This is not to say that the organisation will not have the opportunity to do some test marketing of the product or service, but it may not have the chance to 'roll out' the product or service fully into test markets and gauge the general reactions and consequences of the launch.

Risks that can be afforded

Risks that can be afforded by the organisation would include those that would not adversely affect the business even if they failed. In this respect, organisations will tend to be more likely to risk a relatively small investment in a project or in the development of a new market that might seem to offer the opportunity for some longer-term benefits.

A typical example of this is exploratory drilling and other studies in the oil, gas and other natural resource areas of business. Following geological studies, extraction companies will be prepared to spend not inconsiderable sums of money in trying to assess the viability of a field or area. This is very much taken as part and parcel of the normal activities of the organisation. In this respect the speculative nature of the exploratory work will be based on very real scientific knowledge and understanding of the potential returns that a successful investigation might provide.

For other organisations, the speculative nature of certain exercises and projects may not appear to be based on anything more than a hunch or a feeling (perhaps from some initial market research) that a particular product, service or market is worth the investment necessary. In all respects, the organisation needs to feel that it can afford to take on the possible losses, even if investigations prove that the project is not viable.

Risks that cannot be afforded

Risks that the organisation cannot afford to take would include situations when it would like to take advantage of a particular opportunity but does not have the capital or other resources to follow it through. Perhaps the organisation has identified an opportunity that lies outside its normal area of expertise. The acquisition of technical assistance and other help from consultants or experts may not be possible given the present state of the organisation. In these cases, the organisation will have to make sure that it restricts its activities to the present level of operations and remains within its area of expertise until a point arrives when it can afford the additional expenses of attempting to exploit the new opportunity.

Many organisations will, from time to time, identify potential opportunities in allied areas of business activity, but the lack of true understanding about that market and the implications of involvement may not be obvious to them. Although some organisations would seek to try to exploit the opportunity all the same, they will almost certainly be operating with less than perfect information and a distinct lack of expertise. This would make any level of involvement in the new area of interest a very risky proposition indeed.

Risks that the organisation cannot afford not to take

This category of risk is very closely allied to breakthrough opportunities which we have already discussed. There are certain situations when the organisation may find itself unable to ignore the fact that there is an opportunity out there waiting to be exploited. If it ignores this opportunity, it may face the prospect of not being able to keep apace with its competitors. New developments in different markets are presenting themselves all the time, and no organisation will be able to spread itself wide enough to be able to cover all of the potential opportunities as they arise.

This aspect of the risk-taking situation needs to be tempered with a certain degree of caution. While it infers that the organisation cannot afford to miss the opportunity, it may not be possible to cover all of the eventualities. Often these risks are accompanied by the promise of extremely large returns for the investment in time, money and resources; however, the risks are very real. If the organisation neglects its core business in the pursuit of an 'unmissable' opportunity, there may be dire consequences in the long term.

Balancing opportunities and risks

How, then, can the organisation hope to juggle the potential opportunities and risks? Even if it is aware enough to identify the opportunities in the first place, how can it be assured that the opportunity is a good one and is not accompanied by an unacceptable level of risk that could adversely affect its health and future? Although this is not an exhaustive list, organisations would take some of the following into consideration.

Maximising opportunities or minimising risks?

If the organisation focuses too strongly on the maximisation of opportunities rather than the minimisation of risks, then it may place itself in potentially difficult situations. While the identification and possible exploitation of opportunities is a good idea in business terms, the organisation may end up taking too many risks. In the same way, the proposed exploitation of opportunities as and when they arise may be desirable, but this might place too a great a strain on the organisation in terms of its finite supply of resources and manpower.

Comparing opportunities

If the organisation is unable to consider opportunities in the context of its overall objectives, rather than on their merits as individual opportunities, there may be the risk that they cannot 'see the wood for the trees'. In other words, the identification of opportunities may be one thing, but if the organisation cannot divorce each from the other opportunities, it may never make a decision about what to pursue or have the ability to consider the potential benefits of one opportunity over another. Each opportunity needs to be given sufficient detailed attention in order to be able to see its short-, medium- and long-term implications.

Appropriateness

The opportunities, and their attendant risks, must be considered in terms of their application and appropriateness to the organisation itself. It is not sufficient to consider the implications of an opportunity and how it may have affected another organisation or another market and then try to apply or overlay these conclusions on to our organisation. Each organisation has its own distinctive characteristics, incorporating the various strengths and weaknesses that are inherent in its structure and operations. In this respect, the organisation needs to think about how the opportunities and the risks will affect it, precisely and individually.

Running alongside this is the fact that opportunities that have been exploited by one organisation may not be appropriate to any other organisation. Basing decisions on a 'copy-cat' series of responses is not a very reliable way of ensuring that the organisation makes the most of the opportunities. By blindly following the activities and exploitation procedures of another organisation, there will be no opportunity to look at all of the possible implications in terms of risk assessment.

Above all, the opportunity, whatever it may be, must be capable of fitting into the operations and activities of the organisation. Ideally, the new opportunity should build on the strengths of the organisation using, wherever possible, its services, facilities and manpower in a complementary manner, rather than simply being 'shoehorned' into the operations just because it sounds like a good profitable idea.

Incorporation into existing operations

Organisations should also consider opportunities in terms of their ability to incorporate them easily (or otherwise) into existing operations. Some opportunities, for the minimum investment of resources, will offer good returns with very little impact on the organisation's other activities. Some opportunities will offer the organisation the chance to streamline and improve the whole way in which it approaches problems and operations.

Immediate and straightforward opportunities will be relatively easy to implement and will not carry a considerable degree of risk. However, longer-term and more difficult opportunities may well affect the actual nature and operations of the organisation in the long term. It is these opportunities that need to be very carefully considered and analysed to ensure that they do not become threats to the organisation, despite their apparent attractiveness at the time. Innovation and development, while useful and desirable for the most part, do bring with them a series of risks and threats that can be avoided if the organisation thinks ahead.

Scheduling contingency activities and monitoring arrangements

As we have said earlier, identification of the sources of baseline changes will influence the way in which the organisation decides to approach the possibility of implementing a contingency plan. Clearly, monitoring arrangements are a very important consideration here. Let us consider the major sources of change (*see* Fig 12.3) before we embark on an examination of how to deal with them.

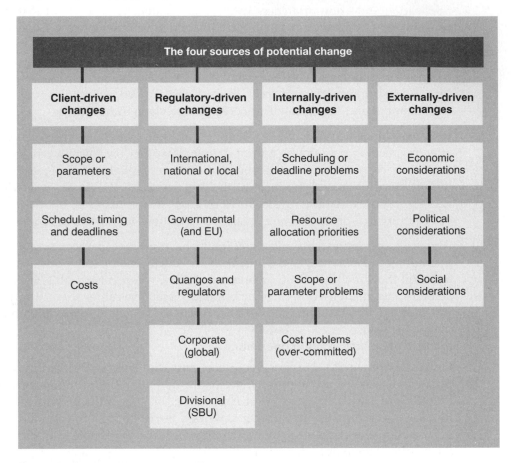

Fig 12.3 Changes to the baseline

Client-driven baseline changes

Scope

The scope or the parameters of the product, service or project will have originally been determined through close co-operation with the intended customer or client. Regardless of the closeness of this relationship with the customer or client, the organisation needs to be acutely aware of the fact that customers may change their minds about what they think or want the product to do. Clearly, it is better for the customer to identify the potential differences between what they want and what they think that they are getting at the earlier stages of the development of the product. If the supplier has carried out all of the necessary development work and has actually gone into production and the customer changes their mind, then this could be disastrous.

The way in which customers perceive the product or service being provided to them by the supplier is all important. To a large extent, this may be more of a communications problem than an actual mismatch between the specifications and the scope of the product or project. In any case, the supplier needs to address this quickly and efficiently, allaying the fears of the customer and reassuring them that the differences are not as critical as they might appear to be from first impressions.

Costs

The customer may express concerns about ongoing or eventual costs that are related to the work being carried out. Assuming that a budget or total cost was agreed at the outset of the relationship between the supplier and the customer, we would be fair in suggesting that this aspect has been dealt with, but this is often not the case. Initial agreements may have been made in radically different sets of circumstances when customer priorities were very different. The emergence of new considerations in respect of the customer's perceptions of the importance of the deal may adversely affect the way in which they view the relationship and the agreements already made with the supplier.

On the other hand, if the project or service is obviously going over budget, then the customer has every right to consider reappraising the situation and putting pressure on the supplier to reduce the costs and remain within the agreed budget. Budget reductions are by far the most common occurrence, but the customer may be prepared to increase the budget in order to force the supplier to place greater importance or emphasis on their project. In some cases, the customer may be in a position where they wish to dispose of a cash surplus that would otherwise be subject to taxation or other reductions.

Schedule

The scheduling, timing and associated deadlines are often a cause of conflict and concern for both the customer and the supplier of the service or product. The alteration of dates, perhaps through no fault of either side, will have an impact on both the supplier and the customer.

Gearing up to complete a particular project will involve the establishment of various milestones that can give a good indication of whether the project is on schedule or not. In the final analysis, changes in milestones, deadlines, timings and completion are cost related. On the one hand, the customer may not be able to afford the costs related to late deliveries or completion, or perhaps the implications of not obtaining the product earlier than they had agreed. On the other hand, the supplier may not be able to stand the costs of the additional manpower and resource needs either to better the intended completion date or to catch up sufficiently to meet the deadline agreed. In both cases, the supplier faces the dual concerns of switching resources from other projects and failing to meet those deadlines, or, as seriously, losing the work with the customer who is insisting on additional effort.

Internally-driven baseline changes

Conditions will often be altered within the operations of the organisation that will force the decision maker to consider implementing contingency plans.

Scope

The first main consideration relates to the scope, parameters or the very nature of the product, service or project involved. In these instances, the organisation may find itself having extreme difficulties producing a final outcome that meets with the approval of the customer, or, more particularly, the quality assurance controls used by the organisation. In extreme cases, the customer will have to be informed that the supplier is unable to meet the technical specifications agreed for the product or project.

Schedule

Meeting the schedules and milestones is just as critical to the supplier as it is to the customer. This is further complicated by the fact that the supplier may be relying on other businesses to provide support, components or other materials in order to complete the work. Renegotiation of the deadlines needs to be carried out with due reference to all of the parties concerned and they all need to know what the other pressures or considerations are that might affect the timetable of the joint project.

Costs

Cost problems can be a very real concern for the supplier. In this respect the organisation will have worked out all of its costings on the basis of a particular deadline or completion date. Coupled with this is the fact that the organisation will have also allocated specific levels of resources to meet the needs of the project. The costing problems will have a twofold effect: first, the supplying organisation may not have the financial ability to meet the amended costs of the project; and second, the customer may not be prepared to allow the supplier to pass on these extra costs.

Resources

Particularly if the period of the project extends over a number of months or even years, the allocation and the demand on the resources of both the supplier and the customer will change. If the project makes high resource demands over an extended period, there is no guarantee that the supplier will be able to meet these needs. Again, this brings us to the question of whether the customer is prepared to renegotiate the terms of the agreement.

Regulatory-driven changes

Regulatory-driven changes relate to those in the following categories, but this is by no means an attempt to give comprehensive coverage of the subject. Each different organisation will be faced with a variety of different regulatory concerns:

i) Governmental changes, either at national or local level, could cause new regulations or controls to come into effect which would require the development of contingency plans. This is particularly true of cases involving environmental issues.

ii) Institutional changes include the potential switching of responsibilities from local to national government, or national government to quango, and could mean that the organisation will have to adapt to a series of new rules and regulations as well as having to deal with a radically different set of individuals in the new organisation.

iii) The organisation as a whole may be operating in a number of different countries. Clearly, it does not have to comply with the rules and regulations of one country in the other countries in which it operates. However, most of the more socially responsible organisations will adopt the strategies and contingencies that have been applied in the country with the most stringent rules and regulations. Normally, this does not mean that the organisation is simply following the line that is dictated in the 'home' country. Certainly, the overlaying of the EU regulations has had an impact on both organisations based in Europe and those which have significant markets there.

Externally-driven changes

Externally-driven changes relate to those broader economic, political and social considerations that we have considered in-depth at various stages of this book. They would naturally demand that the organisation carries out some regular form of SWOT or SLEPT analysis in order to keep abreast of the current state of affairs.

 Monitoring and evaluation

Having considered the scope and nature of the majority of changes and problems that might beset the decision maker, we can now turn our attention to the ways in which the project or area of responsibility can be controlled through a careful and systematic monitoring process.

The monitoring and evaluation process consists of five distinct phases, each of which can be further subdivided into specific areas for investigation and monitoring. Above all, this process offers the decision maker the ultimate ability to control the project or area of responsibility with the least chance of actually missing a key aspect that could adversely affect the outcomes.

Phase 1: Updating the status and progress of the work in order to judge the current performance and efficiency of all factors involved

Trying to assess the performance in terms of the progress and effectiveness of a particular aspect of work, or the impact of a contingency plan, will demand a great deal of data from a variety of different sources. Clearly, there are some data sources that are more easily identified or controlled: these would include the exact proposed schedule, the costs involved, quality assurance tests, human resources employed, fixed costs associated with the project and materials/components, and other consumables used. Actually deciding how progress or performance can be measured, given that the area of responsibility is likely to be complex, can involve the examination of tasks that have been carried out already, tasks that are in the stages of being tackled and the probability that the next stage of tasks will be started at the agreed time (according to the schedule).

The actual mechanisms that are in place to capture the data need to be as simple as possible. This will facilitate and encourage individuals to make clear indications of the nature and scope of the information that they have collected. Naturally, this data gathering should be a continuous process derived from sources such as:

◆ team meetings designed to assess the status of the tasks that have been allocated to individuals;

◆ review sessions for the decision maker to update the status and progress of the project as well as taking into account necessary changes in line with the implementation of contingency plans and other factors;

◆ full review meetings that allow all of the individuals involved to make a contribution in terms of their assessment of the data and the impact/effectiveness of the contingency plans in use;

◆ regular reviews of all of the reports, logs and other indications of time and effort spent on the project, both as a result of the introduction of the contingency plan and the normal procedures.

In order to ensure that the decision makers and the relevant team members have access to the right kind of information that matches their particular needs, it is vital that the monitoring systems address three main considerations:

i) the level of information detail;

ii) the timing or frequency of the information flow;

iii) the content of the information.

Senior decision makers require simplified and summarised information that is well presented (preferably in a graphical format). The frequency of the data supply should cover a minimum of a fortnight or a month and they only require an overview which indicates the problems that have been encountered together with recommendations to solve them.

Supervisors of the monitoring process have slightly different information needs. They require some additional operational detail, perhaps supplied on a weekly basis, but they do require that all of the monitoring data is included in their information packages.

The monitoring team members require a considerably higher level of detail, probably in the form of lists with attached action points and allocation of responsibilities. In addition, they would have to be updated at least on a weekly basis, but the data that is passed on to them need only relate to the areas of responsibility with which they are directly involved.

Any monitoring or status report should address a certain set of issues, particularly if it is designed to be used as a decision tool by the key decision makers. Equally, these reports can also be passed on to senior management so that they can have a clearer idea of the status and progress of the contingency plans. Ideally, the reports should include the following:

a) the exact progress of the contingency plan, particularly the progress made from the last reporting period;

b) an assessment of the actual position in relation to the position that was anticipated or predicted for this period (in other words, is the contingency plan ahead of schedule or behind?);

c) what the next logical stages of the contingency plan will be (in other words, what will happen soon?);

d) how the team members and the key decision maker intends to ensure that they are going to achieve the objectives identified above;

e) what the level of resourcing and allocation of resources will be for the next stage of the contingency plan;

f) whether anything since the last reporting period has indicated that the overall timing and progress of the contingency plan will have to be amended or reconsidered.

Phase 2: Analysing the impact of changes to the contingency plan and attempting to identify causes and impact

Any change to the predicted outcomes of a contingency plan, either during its implementation or after it has been employed, will have to be monitored and evaluated in a logical manner.

Clearly, the starting point is the comparison between the actual results or status of the contingency plan and the planned or predicted outcomes. This will enable the decision maker to identify the variances and judge the impact against a number of different criteria. The main considerations will be schedules, budgets, resources and results.

Having identified that there is a variance between the actual and planned results (outcomes), the next problem is to determine the cause(s). This process may well result in the identification of some of the more common reasons for contingency plan failure, which include the following:

◆ the objectives that were assigned to the contingency plan were not reasonable or feasible;

◆ the contingency plan itself was incomplete, flawed or ineffective given the circumstances in which it had been designed to be used;

◆ the organisation does not have adequate communication systems to ensure that all of the relevant parties that needed to know about the contingency plan were consulted at each stage of development and implementation;

◆ estimates made in relation to the allocation of resources required were not carried out correctly and had flaws;

◆ the situation or external environment either moved too fast for the contingency plan to work or developed in a different way to that which had been anticipated;

◆ the staff delegated to control the contingency plan were inadequate in terms of experience, knowledge or numbers.

Phase 3: Deciding on the next course of action arising out of the identification of variances

As we have seen in the previous chapter, the decision makers have a number of options open to them after having identified the variances. We can add the following to the list of possible actions:

1 Decide to do nothing about the variances as it is felt that the overall impact is not significant, or the impact on the contingency plan is not clear as yet, or the decision maker judges that the situation is only temporary and will be reversed soon.

2 Decide to make some minor modifications to the contingency plan, perhaps with reference to one or more of the underpinning criteria, such as scheduling or resource allocation.

3 Decide to 'hedge' in the sense of making some temporary changes to the contingency plan, but with a view to re-examining the situation in a few days to see if there has been any significant impact.

4 Decide to attempt to renegotiate the terms of the project or area of activity relating to the contingency plan. This would probably involve some form of tradeoff, such as downsizing the scope of the contingency plan in return for an assurance that the schedules will now be met.

Phase 4: Producing a new set of objectives for the contingency plan and reassigning resources and responsibilities

Although the decision maker may not want to have to go to the trouble of redefining the parameters and objectives of the contingency plan, there may be no other alternative. The production of a new contingency plan (as this is what it really means) will be just as difficult as coming up with the original contingency plan in the first place. This will mean that the decision maker has to reallocate all the manpower, resources and budgets to match the new demands of the revised plan.

As an alternative to the production of a full contingency plan, the decision maker may decide to produce an *exception report*. In essence, this means that the decision maker only has to describe the key aspects of the revised plan and therefore does not have to produce the entire contingency plan review. In all cases, however, the decision maker will be forced to consider the following areas of the plan and how they have changed. This is very important as it will not only highlight the differences, but will also identify the relationships between the new criteria and what is already in place.

Scheduling changes

◆ Identification of all the aspects of the contingency plan that have failed or have not been carried out on time, why this has happened and what steps will have to be taken to get them back on track.

◆ Identification of the higher-risk aspects of the contingency and how they have affected the overall plan, also how this can be avoided or remedied.

◆ Identification of aspects of the contingency plan that are under-resourced or have used up more resources than was anticipated as a result of being behind schedule.

◆ Identification of all of the subtasks that make up the overall contingency plan and why they have not been completed, along with the implications.

Resourcing changes

◆ Identification of the resources that are not being effective.

◆ Identification of the resources that do not have the correct specifications in order to do the job required (this would include the human ones).

◆ Identification of the resources that are being employed to get the contingency plan back on schedule rather than being used for the purpose for which they were originally allocated.

◆ Identification of the resources that had been allocated to working on ways of dealing with the problems associated with the contingency plan prior to the reporting stage and the revision activities now underway.

◆ Identification of, and the reasoning behind, the resources which are not compatible with one another and the project in general.

Costing and budgeting changes

◆ The overall impact on the organisation as a result of the ineffective use of the resources on the contingency plan.

◆ The costs and implications regarding the budget of the contingency plan being revised and how this will affect the overall viability of the project.

◆ Identification of the costing methods used for both the original and the revised contingency plan and how these could be improved.

Phase 5: Informing senior management about the outcomes of the monitoring process and requesting responses to the proposed changes

At some point, if senior management is not already aware of it, the decision makers will have to 'come clean' about the progress and effectiveness of the contingency plan. Not all of the news will be negative, of course, but the decision makers will expect senior management to want to pass a critical eye over the progress and effectiveness of the decisions that have been made.

The communication process will take a number of different forms, very much dependent on the structure of the organisation and the seniority of the main decision maker responsible for the project or the area of activity. Typically, these communication methods would include the following:

a) regular informal discussions focusing on the problems and experiences related to the contingency plan;

b) infrequent formal presentations to senior management so that they can obtain a clearer picture of the overall progress, problems and proposed solutions;

c) monthly reports which outline the progress and other aspects of the contingency plan;

d) contributions to regular multi-project review meetings or assessment boards that are concerned with the overall integration of the various projects, contingency plans and strategies being employed in the organisation.

Preparing and evaluating contingency plans

We have devised a scenario which you can use to apply all of the contingency planning stages outlined in this chapter. The scenario is fictitious, but incorporates many aspects that are familiar to organisations.

Example

Levy & Sons Ltd

To the inexperienced eye, the success of the Levy family is a rags to riches story. When the father and mother fled Europe in the late 1930s, they arrived at Southampton with two small suitcases and the clothes they were wearing. Abraham Levy was a master craftsman, constructing simple but elegant furniture in Hamburg from a small workshop. Although he was not a physically strong man, he more than made up for this with his ability to work with wood. Consequently, he quickly obtained a position as a master craftsman in the East End of London within a few weeks of arriving in the country.

During the war years, despite the fact that the factory was demolished during the blitz, Abraham gradually became the real decision maker in the company. Two years after the war, the owner Benjamin Pietri died and, since he had no sons or daughters, left the company to Abraham. In due course, Abraham's three sons joined the company and took over many of the responsibilities previously handled by their father. By the early 1960s, the new company, Levy & Sons Ltd, had gained a wide reputation for building basic veneered furniture of a consistent and high quality. Throughout the rest of the decade and into the 1970s, the company experienced a general growth pattern, only slowed by fluctuations in the popularity of this type of product.

By 1976, after a few years of gentle persuasion from his wife and his sons, Abraham retired, passing on 90 per cent of the shares to his sons, Joshua, Isaac and Benjamin. He retained the remaining 10 per cent of the shares so that he would still have a reason to keep going to the factory even though he was now retired.

At first, the brothers were happy with the new arrangements. Broadly, they split the responsibilities of production, sales and accounts between them. However, by the beginning of the 1980s the three brothers had agreed that they should initiate a programme of expansion. They were restrained from this until the death of their father, but still determined to carve out a name for the company in other, allied areas of sales and production.

Their first acquisition was the veneer manufacturer next door to the factory. This company, Commercial Road Veneers Ltd, had been experiencing a number of cash-flow problems arising out of a very rapid expansion scheme. Although the acquisition of this company was to prove to be very beneficial to the brothers, it should have been a warning to them as well.

The next acquisition had to wait until the early 1990s, when the opportunity came from a very unlikely source. Abraham had arrived in England with another family who had lived in Berlin. They too had been involved in the furniture business, but had concentrated on retailing. The Davidsons (they had changed their name to an English one as they had felt that the previous one was unpronounceable) had been more lucky. They had been able to sell their chain of five furniture stores and managed to get the cash out of Germany. As a consequence, the family had built up another retail empire based in the North of England. From time to time they had bought stock from the Levy's, but the families had not seen one another for several years. At the sons' insistence, their mother accompanied them to visit the Davidsons and proposed that they merge. To the sons' delight, the offer of shares in Levy & Sons Ltd and some cash bought a 51 per cent shareholding in the Davidsons Furniture Ltd chain of stores (of which there were eight).

The sons were confident that they now had a dependable market for the products made in the factory and the only thing that was missing was the ability to deliver the stock at a reasonable cost. This led to the purchase of a small haulage company based in Halifax that seemed to fit the brothers' requirements. The company, Norman Green Transport & Haulage (Halifax) Ltd, had relied on the house removals market for the past few years. Given the slump in house prices and the reluctance of home buyers to take on bigger mortgages, the business was almost on its knees when the brothers appeared on the scene. The deal was struck and Norman Green gratefully accepted shares in both Levy & Sons Ltd and Davidsons Furniture Ltd (together with an undisclosed cash figure to help pay off his personal debts).

This new addition to the growing family of companies meant that the brothers could now manage one of the companies each:

◆ Joshua – Levy & Sons Ltd
◆ Isaac – Davidson Furniture Ltd
◆ Benjamin – Norman Green Transport & Haulage (Halifax) Ltd

This vertical integration brought with it a number of economies of scale, and allowed them to be much more competitive in the marketplace. The operations of the companies were not limited to the support of the others and each of the brothers was actively engaging in takeover and merger plans of their own. It was at this point that the problems of co-ordination, direction and identification of objectives began to loom large in the minds of the brothers, their bankers and the other shareholders.

At first it seemed that the brothers would be prepared to compromise and prioritise the objectives and needs of the group of companies as an integrated unit. That was until a meeting last week when each of the brothers presented the combined shareholders' meeting with a list of separate demands and requirements.

Joshua – Levy & Sons Ltd

There is no reason why the furniture factory should not be moved to the north. This would mean a number of savings for the group as a whole. Key staff would be prepared to make the move and this could also mean that the brothers could sell Norman Green Transport & Haulage (Halifax) Ltd, after having transferred four or five of the lorries over to Levy & Sons Ltd for a reasonable price.

Isaac – Davidson Furniture Ltd

The time for expansion is right and there is a similar chain of retail outlets in the Newcastle area that could be obtained for no more than £1.75 million. The funding should be allocated across the three companies (meaning a 25 pr cent investment from the other two companies and 50 per cent from Isaac's company).

Benjamin – Norman Green Transport & Haulage (Halifax) Ltd

Half of the fleet of 12 lorries should be replaced and the funding for this renewal be provided on the basis of 30 per cent from each of the other companies and 40 per cent from his own. The costs for the renewals would be in the region of £140 000 per lorry.

Understandably, the three proposals were met with varying degrees of alarm by the shareholders. There had been a long-standing agreement that joint ventures were the way in which the companies did business. Indeed, each of the companies had borrowed money from the others at various times and had always been given a preferential rate of interest. Some of the assets of each of the companies did, on paper, belong to one of the others, but these proposals seemed to go much further than all of this.

After considerable debate and disagreement, the brothers decided that they would work together and try to reach a compromise. They also recognised the fact that they needed to identify all of the alternative courses of action in order to make an informed decision about the way forward. The brothers could not agree about which one of them should have the responsibility, authority and power to investigate the options. It was at this point that someone suggested that they call in the services of a consultant. They would abide by the recommendations made by a neutral third party.

Review questions

1 What are the three key objectives of change control?

2 Outline the kinds of information and data likely to be written on a change control form.

3 What is the purpose of a change control log?

4 The decision maker responsible for the ultimate implementation of a contingency plan must be able to judge the likely impact in what broader sense? The use of a contingency may well have an impact on which aspects of the nature of the plan?

5 What are *baseline changes*?

6 What are *additive opportunities*?

7 Synergies relate to complementary activities undertaken by the organisation. How can the organisation seek to achieve these synergies?

8 Define the term *break-through opportunity*.

9 'Risks are those factors that must be accepted in order to ensure survival.' How true is this statement?

10 An alternative to the above statement is that risks are those options that can be afforded by the organisation. How does this statement differ from the previous one and what are the implications in terms of the reduction in alternatives?

11 To what extent do you agree with the notion that risks are the options that the organisation cannot afford to take?

12 How can an organisation be assured that an opportunity is a good one and is not accompanied by an unacceptable level of risk that could adversely affect the health and the future of the organisation?

13 Distinguish between client-driven and internally-driven baseline changes.

14 Outline the major legislative controls and influences that may affect an organisation's ability to cope with change.

15 Distinguish between SWOT and SLEPT analyses.

16 Outline the five main stages of the monitoring and evaluation process related to contingency planning.

17 What is an exception report?

18 How might an organisation determine the resourcing changes required by a contingency plan?

19 Outline the possible contingency planning in the case study.

20 To what extent would the organisations in the case study have benefited from an objective look at the alternatives at each stage of their development?

Further Reading

Adams, J.L., *The Care and Feeding of Ideas*, Penguin, 1988.

Albrecht, K.G., *Brain Power*, Prentice Hall, 1980.

Baird, B.F., *Managerial Decisions Under Uncertainty*, Wiley, 1989.

Bennis, W.G. and Nanus, B., *Leaders: The Strategies for Taking Charge*, Harper & Row, 1985.

Bryant, J.W., *Financial Modelling in Corporate Management*, Wiley, 1982.

Burns, T. and Stalker, G.M., *The Management of Innovation*, Tavistock Publications, 1996.

Butler, G.V., *Organisation and Management*, Prentice Hall, 1986.

Child, J., *Organisation: A Guide to Problems and Practice*, Chapman, 1988.

Cooke, S. and Slack, N., *Making Management Decisions*, Prentice Hall, 1991.

Cummings, T.G. and Huse, E.F., *Organization Development and Change*, West Publishing, 1985.

Deal, T.E. and Kennedy, A.A., *Corporate Cultures: The Rights and Rituals of Corporate Life*, Addison-Wesley, 1982.

Drucker, P.F., *The New Society: The Anatomy of the Industrial Order*, Heinemann, 1951.

Drucker, P.F., *The Practice of Management*, Heinemann, 1979.

Fayol, H., *General and Industrial Management*, Pitman Publishing, 1949.

Fiedler, F.E., *Theory of Leadership Effectiveness*, McGraw-Hill, 1967.

Gregory, G., *Decision Analysis*, Pitman Publishing, 1988.

Handy, C.B., *Understanding Organisations*, Penguin, 1985.

Harrison, E.F., *The Managerial Decision Making Process*, Houghton Mifflin, 1981.

Harrison, R., 'How to describe your organisation', *Harvard Business Review*, Vol 50, 1972.

Hellriegel, D. and Slocum, J.W. Jr, *Management* (6th edition), Addison-Wesley, 1992.

Hellriegel, D., Slocum, J.W. Jr and Woodman, R.W., *Organizational Behaviour*, West Publishing, 1986.

Holloway, C.A., *Decision Making Under Uncertainty: Models and Choices*, Prentice Hall, 1979.

Hunt, J.W., *Managing People at Work: A Manager's Guide to Behaviour in Organisations*, 1986.

Johnson, J. and Scholes, H.K., *Exploring Corporate Strategy* (2nd edition), Prentice Hall, 1989.

Knutson, J. and Bitz, I., *Project Management*, Amacom, 1991.

Kuhn, J.W. and Shriver, D.W., *Beyond Success; Corporations and their Critics in the 1990s*, Oxford University Press, 1991.

Likert, R., *New Patterns of Management*, McGraw-Hill, 1961.

Likert, R., *The Human Organisation*, McGraw-Hill, 1967.

Likert, R. and Likert, J.G., *New Ways of Managing Conflict*, McGraw-Hill, 1976.

Little, J.D., in *Management Science*, Vol 16, No 8, 1970.

McGregor, D., *The Human Side of Enterprise*, McGraw-Hill, 1960.

Mack, R., *Planning on Uncertainty*, Wiley, 1971.

Maslow, A., *Motivation and Personality*, Harper & Row, 1954.

Mayo, E., *The Social Problems of an Industrial Civilisation*, Routledge, 1949.

Megginson, L.C., Mosley, D.C. and Pietri, P.H. Jr, *Management: Concepts and Applications*, Harper & Row, 1986.

Mills, G., *Controlling Companies*, Unwin Hyman, 1988.

Mintzberg, H., *The Structuring of Organisations*, Prentice-Hall, 1975.

Moodie, P.E., *Decision Making: Proven Methods for Better Decisions*, McGraw-Hill, 1983.

Morgan, G., *Creative Organisation Theory*, Sage, 1989.

Mullins, L.J., *Management and Organisational Behaviour*, Pitman Publishing, 1993.

Napuk, K., *The Strategy Led Business*, McGraw-Hill, 1993.

Perrow, C., *Organisational Analysis*, Tavistock Publications, 1970.

Rivett, P., *Model Building for Decision Analysis*, Wiley, 1980.

Schein, E.H., *Organisational Pyschology*, Prentice-Hall, 1988.

Slack, N., *Achieving a Manufacturing Advantage*, Mercury Books, 1991.

Stacey, R., *Dynamic Strategic Management for the 1990s*, Kogan Page, 1990.

Stacey, R., *The Chaos Frontier: Creative Strategic Control for Business*, Butterworth-Heinemann, 1991.

Stacey, R., *Managing Chaos*, Kogan Page, 1992.

Stevens, M., *Practical Problem Solving for Managers*, Kogan Page, 1988.

Stewart, R., *Choices for the Manager: A Guide to Managerial Work and Behaviour*, McGraw-Hill, 1982.

Sutherland, J. and Canwell, D., *Advanced Business* (2nd edition), Hodder & Stoughton, 1995.

Taylor, F.W., *Scientific Management*, Harper & Row, 1947.

Thompson, J.D. and Tuden, A., *Strategy, Structures and Processes of Organisational Decision in Comparative Studies in Administration*, University of Pittsburg Press, 1959.

Vroom, V.H. and Yetton, P.W., *Leadership and Decision Making*, University of Pittsburg Press, 1973.

Weber, M., *The Theory of Social and Economic Organisation*, Macmillan, 1964.

Woodward, J., *Industrial Organisation: Theory and Practice*, Oxford University Press, 1980.

Index